UNGOVERNED SPACES

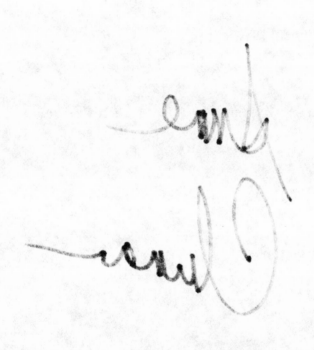

# UNGOVERNED SPACES

*Alternatives to State Authority in
an Era of Softened Sovereignty*

Edited by Anne L. Clunan
and Harold A. Trinkunas

STANFORD SECURITY STUDIES
An Imprint of Stanford University Press
Stanford, California

Stanford University Press
Stanford, California

Special discounts for bulk quantities of Stanford Security Studies are available to
corporations, professional associations, and other organizations. For details and
discount information, contact the special sales department of Stanford University
Press. Tel: (650) 736-1782, Fax: (650) 736-1784

Printed in the United States of America on acid-free, archival-quality paper

Library of Congress Cataloging-in-Publication Data

Ungoverned spaces : alternatives to state authority in an era of softened sovereignty /
edited by Anne L. Clunan and Harold A. Trinkunas.
     p. cm.
  Includes bibliographical references and index.
  ISBN 978-0-8047-7012-5 (cloth : alk. paper) — ISBN 978-0-8047-7013-2 (pbk. : alk.
paper)
   1. Failed states. 2. Nation-state. 3. Sovereignty. 4. Security, International. I. Clunan,
Anne L., 1968– II. Trinkunas, Harold A.
   JC328.7.U54 2010
   320.1—dc22

                                        2009049645

Typeset by Bruce Lundquist in 10/14 Minion

To our families.

# Contents

# Acknowledgments

This book would not have been possible without the valuable contributions of numerous individuals and organizations. We especially are grateful to Daniel Ziblatt and John C. Leslie for their insightful comments and suggestions regarding the concept and causes of ungoverned spaces and to Deborah Avant for making us think harder about the question of security and violence. David Hamon and others at the Advanced Systems and Concepts Office of the Defense Threat Reduction Agency and Richard Hoffman of the Center for Civil-Military Relations at the Naval Postgraduate School were instrumental in providing intellectual guidance and arranging financial support for the initial conference that led to the book. Colin Lober and Gwendolyne Sanders of the National Security Affairs Department of the Naval Postgraduate School provided the organizational support required for a successful conference, and Elizabeth Skinner provided valuable copyediting advice during the production of this volume. The authors, of course, did all the heavy lifting required to produce a book based on the findings of the conference. Any value this book might have is due to their thoughtful, professional, and collegial contributions.

# UNGOVERNED SPACES

# INTRODUCTION

# Ungoverned Spaces?

## The Need for Reevaluation

### Anne L. Clunan

"Ungoverned spaces" are increasingly cited as a key threat to the U.S. government and its interests throughout the world.[1] Often these spaces are seen as synonymous with failed states, or states that are unable to effectively exercise sovereignty. A primary goal of U.S. defense strategy now is to improve "effective sovereignty" in such areas in order to deny sanctuary to terrorists, proliferators of weapons of mass destruction (WMD), narco-traffickers, and gangsters. According to the World Bank, in 2006 the number of states lacking effective sovereignty rose to twenty-six, from eleven in 1996.[2] The term is often extended to virtual realms, such as cyberspace and global finance, to connote the ease with which non-state actors can avoid state surveillance and undermine state sovereignty.[3]

This volume is a response to the increased concern in policy circles over ungoverned spaces. It seeks to unpack the implicit and explicit assumptions and the state-centric bias that infuse the term as it is commonly understood both through analysis of the concept of ungoverned spaces and through empirical investigations of whether and how ungoverned spaces come into existence and generate security threats. This is done with an eye to pointing out the deficiencies in common usage of the term and in prescriptions of what should be done about ungoverned spaces. In place of a focus on ungoverned spaces, we suggest that understanding threats from non-state actors today is best accomplished through examining the origins and nature of alternative authority and governance structures in contested spaces. This examination, moreover, must take into account the broader global trend of softening sovereignty. The chapters that follow highlight that the sources of ungoverned spaces—of alternative authority structures—are far more complex than "state failure," "lack of state capacity," or "lack of political will." Although these factors play a role, in many cases, these spaces emerge precisely because of states' deliberate policy choices or with the witting collaboration of state authorities, usually in combination with the forces of globalization and local socioeconomic dynamics.

## Why Reevaluate Ungoverned Spaces?

We care about the appearance of ungoverned spaces in the language of diplomacy and statecraft for both policy and theoretical reasons. Politically, the term "ungoverned spaces" connotes a novel and inherently dangerous threat to the security of states and the international state system. This threat is most commonly associated with state failure or with, in somewhat more polite terms, the growing number of "fragile states."[4] National governments in the developed world and international organizations have focused on the lack of effective sovereignty and the development of ungoverned spaces in these states as reasons for external interventions of all sorts into the affairs and territories of states. From a policy perspective, ungoverned spaces have attracted a great deal of attention from the U.S. government because of the perception that these areas, most recently conceptualized to include both physical territory and cyberspace, may shelter terrorist organizations and other criminal networks that pose a threat to national security. Government understandings of threat have evolved since the end of the Cold War, distinguishing areas that are differently governed, such as those under tribal rule, from those that pose a national security problem by providing safe havens for terrorists or insurgents because of an absence of governance.[5] Some, recognizing "the destruction launched from broken lands," call for interventions that meld economic development with security.[6] Clearly, this approach has some merit, since we can observe the activities of some terrorist organizations in quasi-sovereign and sovereignty-free zones such as South Lebanon, southern Colombia, and Somalia. International organizations, particularly the United Nations, have come to share some of these concerns because they are often called on to lead the international response to civil conflicts in ungoverned and contested spaces.

We should also be cautious, however, when considering the implications of this policy trend, as some analysts are prone to produce extreme scenarios that visualize the intersection of WMD proliferators, criminal organizations, and terrorists—or other similar catastrophic networks—to justify labeling all ungoverned spaces as potential threats. Indeed, the growing prominence of this issue in developed world policy circles, needless to say, provokes concerns in developing countries that the concept of ungoverned spaces is merely the latest window dressing for neoimperialism. Conversely, policy elites in developing states may also invoke the presence of ungoverned spaces to solicit Western aid and sanction armed intervention, with an eye to marginalizing and suppressing their political opponents out of a desire for personal political survival, rather than for genuine security concerns.

The official definitions of ungoverned spaces, moreover, are often breathtakingly broad and extend, wittingly or not, across physical and virtual domains and from stable and strong states lacking the "political will" to govern to prototypical failing and failed states. A recent U.S. Defense Department report highlights that threats to the United States arise in "ungoverned, under-governed, misgoverned, or contested physical areas (remote, urban, maritime) or exploitable non-physical areas (virtual) where illicit actors can organize, plan, raise funds, communicate, recruit, train, and operate in relative security."[7] The security issue then is not simply one of lack of governance, but a normative judgment on the type of governance in a particular space.[8] Governance by non-state actors—whether of territorial spaces, cyberspace, or financial systems—is implicitly equated with risks to state security. The scope for intervention is consequently vast, and the focus too often is on the security of states, rather than of human beings.

What is troubling from a policy and analytic perspective is the failure of scholars and policymakers to recognize that prescriptions for managing ungoverned spaces are too often state-centric and outmoded; many assume that alternative governance structures inherently undermine state power. They assume that increased state capacity, state building, and in some cases, state creation are the cure to the security problems stemming from ungoverned spaces. Yet more often than not, prescriptions are based on an anachronistic image of the state as the mid-twentieth-century welfare state, or on the privatizing, outsourcing state of the late twentieth century. In both cases, the state is assumed to be the critical actor in providing governance and generating authority. Prescriptions are frequently for top-down strengthening of state institutions and state regulations, with little recognition of the impact of bottom-up aspirations in generating alternative authority and governance structures that may complement or outperform state efforts.

In the world as it is in the early twenty-first century, however, state sovereignty has softened, and the paradigm of the state system is therefore misleading for policymakers and theorists; the state is joined by a number of other actors, benign and malign, who sometimes compete and sometimes collaborate in providing governance and security through bottom-up and horizontal forms of organization. In many places, states are themselves a main contributor to insecurity at the human and global levels. As such, what in Chapter 2 are described as "dangerous spaces" may arise as much from state actions as from state failures. In lieu of the term "ungoverned spaces," with its assumption of the state's absence—the lack of state authority and governance—we prefer the concepts of alternative authority and governance structures, as these, in some places and some times, may incorporate or coexist with state authority and governance.

The concern over ungoverned spaces as areas lacking effective state sovereignty is fundamentally a product of the reluctance of policy practitioners and scholars to fully grapple with the world of the twenty-first century. As the next chapter argues, the global diffusion of multiple waves of Western liberal ideology and its technologies has made this a world of softened sovereignty, where competitions over authority are commonplace and the state does not corner the governance market. In some areas, such as in many global cities, the Internet, and global finance, ungoverned spaces have arisen as a result of the deliberate removal of state regulation in response to the spread of neoliberal policy prescriptions in the late twentieth century. In other areas, such as the tribal areas of Pakistan and Afghanistan and much of Africa, states simply never exercised authority while other authority structures persisted, so talk of "state failure" and "ungoverned spaces" is misleading.

The concern over putatively ungoverned spaces is a reflection of the decline in the effectiveness of states as political and social constructs. Preoccupation with this phenomenon is broadly mirrored in the recent literature on states, globalization, and governance, and it includes not only the disorder that attends failing states or civil wars, but also the withering of party systems as vehicles for organizing public demands and the progressive shrinking of the welfare state across the world as a mechanism for satisfying these demands.[9] The decline of these institutions has important implications for the legitimacy of states as the predominant producers of governance and security. It also leads us to examine more closely the implications of phenomena such as the liberalization of the international economic order. Such liberalization is seen by Western liberal democracies as largely good in the economic realm, but its attendant softening of sovereignty has made liberalization more questionable in the political and security arenas. In the world today, the traditional notions of security have been expanded well beyond the Cold War confines of interstate conflict, strategic power balances, and national security.

Today, a multitude of factors have forced the broadening of security to include human and global levels, not just the national.[10] These factors include the persistence of intrastate violence and decline of interstate violence; the uneven distribution of state-provided public goods; the transboundary effects of environmental degradation, economic development, population movement, and disease diffusion; the rising interdependence in global finance and manufacturing; and the explosion in cross-border and intrastate societal interconnectedness through information and communications technology. Levels of economic development and access to policing and social services—issues once far removed from security studies—are now seen as central factors in producing security, not just for individual human beings but nationally, regionally, and globally, as Chapters 6, 7, 9, and 10 in this volume suggest.

## Plan of the Book

In seeking to explain when and how ungoverned spaces contribute to human, national, and global insecurity, this volume deliberately casts a broad net to incorporate the many physical and nonphysical spaces where authority is contested and space is said to be "ungoverned" and dangerous. The chapters empirically cover urban and rural sites of alternative authority structures, economically developed and underdeveloped countries, territorial spaces, and nonphysical or virtual spaces. They cover a variety of traditional and nontraditional security concerns, ranging from flows of WMD, narcotics, migrants, dirty money, and cyberdata to terrorists, drug lords, warlords, insurgents, and radical Islamist groups to human privacy and security. The method of analysis is also diverse, ranging from accounts that emphasize material foundations to those that highlight ideational and discursive bases of alternative authority and governance structures. This substantive and analytic diversity gives us greater purchase in understanding the world "as it is":

the conditions that give rise to alternative authority structures and modes of governance and that make such alternatives to the state harmful to human, national, and global security.

Part I of the book is concerned with how we best should conceptualize the phenomena of ungoverned spaces and the threats they may pose. Chapter 1, by Anne Clunan and Harold Trinkunas, lays out the theoretical underpinning and rationale for the book's focus on alternative forms of authority and governance, given the context of the softening of state sovereignty. In Chapter 2, Phil Williams offers a first cut at categorizing areas of alternative governance that pose harm to security at the human, national, and international levels—what Williams terms "dangerous spaces." This categorization emphasizes that in the current era of global connectedness, "ungoverned" or "dangerous spaces" may appear as readily in well-governed, "strong," and "stable" states as in poorly governed, "weak," and "failing" ones.

In Part II, the authors highlight how and why preexisting social structures in remote areas of failed and failing states exert authority over the control of violence. Such alternative social structures can frustrate state efforts to assert centralized control regardless of the strength or weakness of the state, as in Ty Groh's discussion in Chapter 5 of the resistance of Pashtun tribes along the Pakistan-Afghanistan border to British, Soviet, and Pakistani rule. More surprisingly, William Reno, in Chapter 3, demonstrates that even in failed states, such extant social authority structures can generate controls over violence that promote community-level human security rather than predation when such structures incorporate warlords who are marginalized by state power and authority. Also contrary to conventional wisdom, Ken Menkhaus and Jacob Shapiro find in Chapter 4 that tribal structures and norms, together with territorial remoteness, make failed states undesirable havens for terrorists. Contrary to the assumptions of Western policymakers, these factors impeded Al-Qa'ida's early recruiting efforts among Muslim tribes in Somalia and ironically made this exemplar of a failed state a less desirable base for operations than its more stable neighbor, Kenya.

In Part III, the authors analyze urban and densely populated regions and find that exclusion—the lack of political, economic, or social incorporation—from official or licit spaces creates room for alternative forms of governance to emerge, particularly over the provision of the goods of policing and conflict resolution. Non-state actors wielding violence have become authoritative governors along with police forces, as Enrique Desmond Arias notes in Chapter 6, which examines the densely populated urban areas of some of Latin America's medium-to-strong states. Here, we see hybrid systems of urban governance, which Arias labels "violent pluralism," that extend their reach beyond the cities. Anne Marie Baylouny highlights in Chapter 7 how violent non-state actors, including Islamist groups such as Hizbullah, gained authority through the provision of basic security services to those living or working in densely populated "unofficial" spaces and economies in the Middle East. In Chapter 8, Loren Landau and Tamlyn Monson demonstrate how in Johannesburg alternative, "subterranean" forms of authority over the freedom of movement and the rights of work and residency have evolved among migrants, locals, and the police in ways that undermine the South African state's sovereignty over its population.

Part IV focuses on the phenomenon of alternative economies that appear in the shadow of the state. The contributions by Vanda Felbab-Brown (Chapter 9) and Lyudmila Zaitseva (Chapter 10) underscore how both the presence and absence of the state is the crucial force behind alternative economies. Felbab-Brown emphasizes how the demand for illicit goods and access to illicit resources have generated trafficking economies in Afghanistan and Latin America. Similarly, Zaitseva notes how the demand for and supply of nuclear and radiological materials in neighboring countries have made the former Soviet Union, and particularly the Caucasus, a WMD trafficking "hot spot." Both chapters point out that the absence of state control in these regions has made alternative trafficking economies possible. Ironically, however, the presence of the state itself is the genesis for illicit and informal economies, whether they be markets for illegal drugs and WMD (the subject of the two chapters in this part) or for the protective services, dispute resolution, work and residency permits, or tax shelters that appear in earlier and subsequent chapters. As Williams notes in Chapter 2, and as Felbab-Brown ably demonstrates in Chapter 9, it is the asymmetries in states' taxation and regulation in a world of globalized demand that create the incentives for engaging in "jurisdictional arbitrage" in the form of smuggling or trafficking. Instead of state failure and strength, the incentive comes from the very existence of sovereign prerogatives regarding regulation and export control. It is thus the longstanding desultory control of a relatively strong and capable state, the Soviet Union and later Russia, over its nuclear and radiological material that is arguably the chief cause of WMD trafficking, rather than state failure in the newly independent states.

Part V shifts the focus from territorial places to nonphysical ones: the virtual spaces of financial and data flows that many have argued augur the end of state sovereignty.[11] Here, the contributors focus on the governance structures that have arisen out of the contest of authorities among corporations, civil society actors, and international organizations as well as states. In Chapter 11 Bill Maurer takes up the issue of global capital flows. The global financial crisis that began in 2007 heightened concerns raised after the terrorist attacks of September 11, 2001, and the 1997–1999 Asian financial crisis that non-state actors—in the form of terrorist financiers, money launderers, and, more recently, hedge funds, offshore banks, and wealthy individuals—are able to take advantage of the "offshore" world of finance. These fears arise over both these actors' efforts to evade state surveillance over their funds and the activities they underwrite, and their ability thereby to erode state capacity to levy revenues to pay for public services.[12] Maurer demonstrates how once again states are as much to blame as non-state actors for the creation of offshore banks and tax havens that place terrorists, money launderers, corporations, and wealthy individuals beyond the reach of states. Financial actors, who manipulated liberalism's discourse to their neofeudal ends, prodded states—caught in the sway of neoliberalism's penchant for reduced scrutiny and regulation of private and corporate wealth—to actually weaken the piecemeal anti-money-laundering and counterterrorist-financing regime that was developing before and immediately after the September 11 attacks.[13]

The Internet is typically viewed as a prototypical ungoverned space, one designed deliberately to prevent centralized control and surveillance by states, or any other actor. Yet, the two chapters dealing with Internet governance suggest that the Internet is far from ungoverned; indeed, governance consists of unofficial quasi-partnerships between states and corporations. Despite well-publicized fears about cyberwarfare and President Barack Obama's decision to create a cyber-security tsar, both chapters highlight how states and corporations have created governance structures for the Internet and private data flows. J. P. Singh, in Chapter 12, demonstrates how states, initially having succumbed to the discursive power of neoliberalism, created a governance structure for the Internet that places control in the hands of a private U.S. company, the Internet Corporation for Assigned Names and Numbers (ICANN). This governance structure survived the efforts of developing countries and the European Union to give authority over the Internet back to states through an intergovernmental organization, the United Nations. As Ronald

Deibert and Rafal Rohozinksi point out in Chapter 13, ICANN in turn is part of a hierarchical and physical governance structure that places governance over the Internet in the hands of states and a handful of corporations. State control over market access also plays a role in dictating control over private data flows. Singh shows how U.S. government authority over access to the U.S. air passenger market forced corporations to disobey their own national laws regulating the use of private data. Deibert and Rohozinksi detail the efforts of states to compel Internet companies to provide personal information about their users in return for market access. Corporations are seizing on states' concerns over Internet data to sell software that enables states to maintain the upper hand in blocking unwanted information exchanges and surveilling Internet communication within their borders. All three chapters of Part V highlight that states and corporations benefit from the coexistence of ungoverned and governed spaces in finance and cyberspace.

The book concludes with an assessment of what is new about ungoverned spaces—the alternative authority and governance structures that the empirical chapters so amply demonstrate—and the global and local conditions that produce them. It ends by comparing the implications of ungoverned spaces for national and human security and providing some thoughts on what policies may better manage the fact of softened sovereignty and alternative authority structures.

## Conclusion

We seek in this volume to highlight the conditions—those of a contemporary world characterized by a softening of sovereignty and growing interconnectedness across all countries and at all levels of human interaction—in which the concern over ungoverned spaces has emerged and the new conceptions of authority and security that these conditions demand. These conditions shape the effectiveness of different policy responses.

The very real concern about lack of sovereign authority over many functional and geographic regions reflects the reluctant recognition of and broader angst regarding the erosion of the territorial state as the sole arbiter of global, national, and local politics, economics, and security. As a result of the empirical realities revealed in this book's chapters, we suggest that in some areas the concern is overblown; in others it is valid, but responses premised on top-down state-centric approaches—ranging from training and equipping militaries to building the capacity of state bureaucracies—are unlikely to prove sufficient to supplant what James Rosenau terms the multiple spheres of authority that provide governance in today's multicentric world.[14] This perspective reflects our assessment as scholars of the world as it is, not necessarily a normative preference for such a turn of events. Rather, borrowing from Richard Falk, we find that "the globalized world taking shape makes [us] . . . nostalgic for the realities and potentialities for a moral evolution of a society of states."[15] Ungoverned spaces and the alternative authority structures they represent, in other words, are here to stay whether we like them or not, and states should focus on how best to manage, exploit, and coexist with them to provide human and national security to their populations.

## Notes

The views expressed here do not reflect the views of the U.S. Navy or the U.S. Department of Defense but are solely those of the author.

1. See, for example, Vice Admiral Lowell E. Jacoby, U.S. Navy, Director, Defense Intelligence Agency, "Statement for the Record: Senate Select Committee on Intelligence," 24 February 2004, http://www.au.af.mil/au/awc/awcgate/dia/jacoby24feb04 .pdf.

2. Karen DeYoung, "World Bank Lists Failing Nations That Can Breed Global Terrorism," Washington Post, 15 September 2006, A13.

3. Ronen Palan, *The Offshore World: Sovereign Markets, Virtual Places, and Nomad Millionaires* (Ithaca, NY: Cornell University Press, 2003); Jorg Raab and H. Brinton Milward, "Dark Networks as Problems," *Journal of Public Administration Research Theory* 13, 4 (2003): 413–39; and John Arquilla and David Ronfeldt, eds. Networks and Netwars: The Future of Terror, Crime, and Militancy (Santa Monica, CA: RAND, 2001).

4. As indicators of this growing concern, fragile states are the subject of the 2010 United Nations World Development Report, and the Fund for Peace has been publishing a "Failed States Index" in collaboration with Foreign Policy Magazine since 2004. In 2009, this index listed 60 states as failing or failed out of the 193 states in the international system. Accessed at http://www.foreignpolicy.com/articles/2009/06/22 /the_2009_failed_states_index, 3 August 2009.

5. Robert D. Lamb, "Ungoverned Areas and Threats from Safe Havens," final report of the Ungoverned Areas Project prepared for the Under Secretary of Defense for Policy, Department of Defense, Washington D.C., January 2008, 15–20. The report is the product of a U.S interagency working group devoted to defining ungoverned spaces and outlining responses to them. The report's definition of an ungoverned area is "a place where the state or the central government is unable or unwilling to extend control, effectively govern, or influence the local population, and where a provincial,

local, tribal, or autonomous government does not fully or effectively govern, due to inadequate governance capacity, insufficient political will, gaps in legitimacy, the presence of conflict, or restrictive norms of behavior. For the purposes of this report, the term 'ungoverned areas' encompasses under-governed, misgoverned, contested, and exploitable areas as well as ungoverned areas. In this sense, ungoverned areas are considered potential safe havens" (p. 6).

6. Robert B. Zoellick, "Securing Development," speech at the United States Institute of Peace, Washington, D.C., 8 January 2009. Accessed at http://siteresources .worldbank.org/NEWS/Resources/RBZUSIPSpeech010809.pdf, 3 August 2009.

7. Lamb, "Ungoverned Areas," 6.

8. Ibid., 4.

9. See Stephen D. Krasner, *Sovereignty: Organized Hypocrisy* (Princeton, NJ: Princeton University Press, 1999); Thomas Risse, "Governance in Areas of Limited Statehood: How Far Do Concepts Travel?," paper presented at the International Studies Association Annual Convention, San Francisco, CA, March 26–30, 2008; Thomas Risse and Ursula Lehmkuhl, "Governance in Areas of Limited Statehood—New Modes of Governance?" SFB-Governance Working Paper Series (Berlin: Freie Universität SFB 700, 2006); and Michael Zürn and Stephan Leibfried, "Reconfiguring the National Constellation," in *Transformations of the State?* ed. Stephan Leibfried and Michal Zürn (Cambridge: Cambridge University Press, 2005).

10. For such a broadening, see Thomas Homer-Dixon, *Environment, Scarcity, and Violence* (Princeton, NJ: Princeton University Press, 1999).

11. Susan Strange, *Retreat of the State: The Diffusion of Power in the World Economy* (Cambridge: Cambridge University Press, 1996); Manuel Castells, *The Internet Galaxy* (New York: Oxford University Press, 2001); Stephen Kobrin, "Back to the Future: Neomedievealism and the Postmodern Digital World Economy," *Journal of International Affairs* 51, 2 (Spring 1998): 361–86.

12. Palan, *Offshore World.*

13. On that nascent regime, see Anne L. Clunan, "The Fight against Terrorist Financing," *Political Science Quarterly* 121, 4 (Winter 2006): 569–96.

14. James Rosenau, "The Disorder in the Prevailing International Order," paper presented at the Conference on Ungoverned Spaces, Monterey, CA, 2007; and James Rosenau, *Turbulence in World Politics: A Theory of Change and Continuity* (Princeton, NJ: Princeton University Press, 1990).

15. Richard Falk, "State of Siege: Will Globalization Win Out?" *International Affairs* 73, 1 (1997): 123–36, at 125.

# PART I
## CONCEPTUALIZING UNGOVERNED SPACES AND ALTERNATIVE AUTHORITY

# 1  Conceptualizing Ungoverned Spaces

*Territorial Statehood, Contested Authority,*
*and Softened Sovereignty*

## Anne L. Clunan and Harold A. Trinkunas

## What Are Ungoverned Spaces?

The term "ungoverned spaces" is a misnomer. It originally arose from the state-centered conceptualization developed by many governments and international organizations confronting the apparent emergence following the Cold War of politically disordered territories in which state provision of governance goods had collapsed. Ungoverned spaces are viewed as social, political, and economic arenas where states do not exercise "effective sovereignty" or where state control is absent, weak, or contested.[1] In reality, many so-called ungoverned spaces are simply "differently" governed. These can range from tribal or clan-based governments in Somalia or Pakistani Waziristan, to areas ruled by persistent insurgencies such as the Revolutionary Armed Forces of Colombia (Fuerzas Armadas Revolucionarias de Colombia, FARC), to major swathes of the Internet controlled by corporate entities such as the Internet Corporation for Assigned Names and Numbers (ICANN), or the creation of corporate transnational governance structures such as the *lex mercatoria*.[2] It is not so much ungoverned spaces that should concern us, since these are effectively quite rare, but rather the contested spaces within and between states where other types of actors rule.[3] Here, we move from definitions of ungoverned spaces based on the absence of state governance to a focus on the idea of "softened sovereignty." Ungoverned spaces therefore exist where territorial state control has been voluntarily or involuntarily ceded in whole or part to actors other than the relevant legally recognized sovereign authorities.

This conception of ungoverned spaces also serves to differentiate the focus of this project from the debate over fragile, failing, and failed states found in the academic and policy literature.[4] While the weakening of the state clearly contributes to the phenomenon we seek to explain, whether it becomes a threat to the security of other states depends on what alternative actors arise to take the place of the state, and whether they produce an environment that threatens others. The attention to failed states is really the product of a 1990s concern with the consequences of the end of the Cold War and the twenty-first-century fear that transnational terrorists may be using failed states as safe havens or staging areas.

We argue that this focus is too narrow because it misses the ungoverned spaces that exist in the international system, within otherwise consolidated states, and in new virtual domains. A broader definition of ungoverned spaces allows us to examine challenges to sovereignty posed by phenomena such as transnational actors. These include political entities such as intergovernmental organizations and nongovernmental organizations (NGOs) or terrorist networks, and economic ones such as major corporations or transnational criminal enterprises. It also allows us to examine the implications of lack of effective sovereignty within otherwise organized states, such as in border areas and inner cities of the United States and the suburban *banlieus* in France. In addition, it highlights the growing importance of virtual realms: politically as channels for terrorists, social movements, and political parties to mobilize, but also economically for new forms of corporate and international governance.

More fundamentally, the current policy approach to ungoverned spaces rests on an underspecified conceptualization of "good governance" and "effective sovereignty" that appears to take the Western welfare state of the twentieth century as its model and as the basis for global order in the twenty-first century.[5] We maintain that such a view of sovereignty must be revised to place it within a broad historical evolutionary context that recognizes the Western welfare state as a form of political organization that arose out of specific political, ideological, and economic conditions. The revision should take into account the effects of globalization (broadly construed) that pose fundamental challenges to well-established states in the West, let alone less-developed states elsewhere, as well as to the concept of statehood and state sovereignty.[6] Moreover, the issue of governance and sovereignty must be viewed in a context of transnational relations that has altered the mix of actors that affect them. This context illuminates the limits of what states can (and cannot) do to manage potential threats that emerge from such spaces, as well as the extent to which such spaces are in fact threatening.

This chapter analyzes the concept of ungoverned spaces to determine whether these areas are truly ungoverned. The essential issue, we find, is not lack of governance per se, but rather who governs these spaces. Governance de facto exists in areas frequently claimed as ungoverned spaces, such as feral cities, failed states, offshore financial markets, marginally regulated reaches of the Internet, and tribal areas such as those found on the Afghanistan-Pakistan border, yet it is mostly exercised by non-state actors ranging from insurgents to warlords to clans to private corporations. The notion of ungoverned spaces can be more broadly applied to legal, functional, virtual, and social arenas that either are not regulated by states or are contested by non-state actors and spoilers. We suggest that the terms "alternative authority" and "softened sovereignty" better capture the reality of governance of territorial and virtual spaces by a mix of non-state and state actors rather than the term "ungoverned spaces." In this volume, we seek to explain when areas of softened sovereignty emerge, as well as when quasi-sovereign entities provide the goods normally associated with states, including security. It is not just the decline of effective sovereignty that should interest us, but also how human beings construct alternative forms of governance in the absence of states.

We also aim to develop a more accurate framework for understanding contemporary security threats in a world of softened sovereignty. In other words, when does the fact of softened sovereignty combine with contests over authority to give rise to *dangerous* spaces, as Phil Williams calls them in Chapter 2? In that sense, one of the outcomes of this volume is to determine the conditions in which governance or its lack poses a threat to security at three levels: human, national, and global. States often view ungoverned spaces as threats because of their potential to provide havens for organized crime, terrorist movements and insurgencies, money laundering, illicit trafficking, and proliferation networks. An improved understanding of when and how alternative forms of governance impede or encourage hostile non-state actors has important policy implications for how states, particularly the United States, prioritize their responses to emerging threats.

This chapter discusses some of the key concepts underpinning the current interest in ungoverned spaces, as well as the overarching context in which the questions of governance and security responses have emerged. This context is characterized by "complex interdependence" or a "multicentric world," aided by the global diffusion of neoliberalism and subnational and transnational organizations, as well as the unspoken and contradictory assumption that territorial Western states of the mid-twentieth century are the benchmarks for sovereignty and world order in the twenty-first century. This context prevents states from "solving" the problems posed by ungoverned spaces, and at best allows for the management of ungoverned spaces through a variety of traditional and nontraditional mechanisms that engage subnational, regional, transnational, and international actors.

## Challenging Traditional Understandings of Territorial Sovereignty and Statehood

The concerns expressed about ungoverned spaces stem largely from the premise that territorial state sovereignty is the natural and right form of political organization that delineates and produces world order. Historically, however, territorial state sovereignty and territorial statehood are relatively recent phenomena. Territorial statehood and sovereignty originated in Western Europe in the seventeenth century but only reached their apex in the early to mid-twentieth century with the development of territorial states that were not only "effectively sovereign," in the nineteenth-century legal sense of being able to police their own societies and repel attack, but also in the twentieth-century socioeconomic sense of providing public goods and services beyond security to their populations.

Other statelike forms of political organization had long existed outside of the West, whether in the form of suzerainty in China or the Mongol Khanate, but these were less focused on the hardened and contiguous frontiers that distinguished the European states and represented a more dispersed form of governance, with a core of central control that gradually diminished in the periphery.[7] The European territorial state became "globalized" during the era of European imperialism and the creation of a global economy, when European governments imposed territorial state formations on their colonies around the world. As Christopher Clapham notes, "this resulted in the creation of a kind of state radically different from any that had existed before: a state whose territory, boundaries, and structure of government, and to a large extent economy and sometimes even population, were imposed and organized from outside. . . . It also meant a hardening of the state—in terms of fixed frontiers, citizenship rules, and hierarchical structures of government—in ways that could create damaging tensions between the old form of state and the new." He goes on to suggest that "the 'problem' of 'failed states' is most basically about whether the grafting of such states . . . onto unpromising rootstock can be made to take—even with the various kinds of fertilizer provided by the international system in the form of universalist ideologies, incorporation into the global economy, and the provision of diplomatic and military support."[8]

Recognition of the problems potentially posed by ungoverned spaces has led states to focus on "effective sovereignty" and "good governance" as remedies. For example, the U.S. government has identified increased governmental legitimacy, and legal, judicial, regulatory, security, law enforcement, intelligence, and public service capacity and economic opportunity, as important means to combat threats from ungoverned spaces.[9] These requirements reflect the classic territorial, rule of law, legitimacy, and interventionist dimensions of the Western state of the mid-twentieth century.[10] The territorial dimension encompasses control over the use of force, revenues, and resources—in other words, the nineteenth-century European conception of "effective sovereignty," in which states were sovereign only when they could levy the resources to protect themselves effectively from external or internal threats to their rule.[11] The rule of law generally embraces the notion of "good governance," or the institutions of law, courts, oversight, and transparency that make up a *Rechtsstaat* or "constitutional state." The legitimacy dimension reflects the notion that states are responsible to their publics and requires a political community of citizens loyal to both the state and its laws. The interventionist dimension denotes the twentieth-century requirement for state provision of public welfare through the promotion of economic growth and social equality.[12] The slew of existing programs to build state institutions and capacities—funded by government and intergovernmental organizations—attests to the common assumption that strengthening states is the primary solution for a range of global and local ills, such as insurgencies, ideological militancy, human trafficking, nuclear and narcotics smuggling, corruption, and underdevelopment. There is less recognition, however, that such efforts today are complicated by constraints that globalization has imposed on the states doing the "grafting."

## How Do Ungoverned Spaces Come About?

Ungoverned spaces are most commonly thought to result from entropy and civil conflict. The wars that have occurred since the end of the Cold War in the republics of the former Yugoslavia, the Horn of Africa, and Afghanistan all illustrate the phenomenon of failed and failing states and its production of contested and uncontrolled spaces. In particular, the reordering of the international system following the Cold War clearly disrupted governing coalitions in certain conflict-prone regions and altered the cost-benefit calculation made by local political leaders regarding the use of force. This in turn led to increased contestation for power in some already weak states.[13] Neglect, carelessness, and errors committed by major powers during the transition in the international system also have contributed to conflicts. The consequences of such behavior drove major powers and leading intergovernmental organizations to consider mechanisms for ameliorating or suppressing civil conflict during the 1990s. The result was a major expansion of the United Nations' peacekeeping role, significant changes in the attitude of the North Atlantic Treaty Organization (NATO) toward out-of-area missions, and the mobilization of transnational civil society to address emerging and festering crises. The terrorist attacks of September 11, 2001, and afterward have only reinforced this attitude within the global policy community, fostering a more tolerant attitude toward external intervention in conflict zones. Ungoverned spaces, however, are also the unintended consequences of recent transnational phenomena such as globalization.

### Post-Statist Governance?: Globalization and Contested Authority
The questions of whether globalization has fatally weakened states and the international states system and whether we already have entered a post-statist world order continue to spark debate among scholars. If we wish to understand how and when ungoverned spaces may pose threats to states, this debate raises the issue of whether the context of globalization has fundamentally altered states' willingness and ability to effectively govern along the four dimensions outlined above, even in the most developed states, including the United States.[14] Leading states have sought to promote economic liberalization and democratization as global goods, but ironically, these very efforts have helped open spaces for non-state actors to contest state authority. In fact, the governance goods traditionally provided by states, such as security, laws, and welfare, may now be provided by local or transnational actors. Powerful domestic constituencies within the leading powers support the

expansion of this new liberal democratic international order and are hostile to sovereignty-strengthening measures, such as greater oversight of transnational trade and finance or greater restrictions on the activities of civil society. Has the group of forces lumped under the rubric of globalization changed the sources and modes of governance to such an extent that the premise of governance by territorial states—even within the Organization for Economic Cooperation and Development—is neither realistic nor achievable?[15] If so, then ungoverned spaces—in the sense that primacy of territorial state control is lacking—become ubiquitous and territorial sovereignty anomalous. In such circumstances, efforts to establish or reestablish territorial sovereignty will likely have considerable second- and third-order consequences.

Much of the answer hinges on whether one believes that territorial states—at least the most powerful ones—are the managers of globalization, who use transnational and subnational forces to further their interests in an open global economy and neoliberal world order, or that transnational and subnational actors and forces have enmeshed territorial states in a complex web of interdependencies that they neither wish to nor can fully disrupt or control.[16] From the perspective of realists and Marxists, globalization is business as usual: powerful states pursuing their national interests and capitalistic ends.[17] While there is little dispute that powerful states have had a major hand in creating globalization, many suggest that these states no longer can control the forces they helped unleash.[18] Powerful states created "virtual" ungoverned spaces in the areas of offshore finance and information communications. These areas now have powerful non-state actors, in addition to states themselves, committed to ensuring a continued lack of regulation and may well be beyond the ability of their creators to assert full control.[19] For James Rosenau, globalization has meant that authority is increasingly disaggregating into a rapidly growing number of centers at every level of community and across a wide range of non-state actors, creating a "multicentric world" alongside the state-centric world of traditional international politics.[20] In such a view, efforts to protect national security through unilateral interventions in "ungoverned" spaces are likely to prove counterproductive and the instrumental use of international organizations and NGOs to be considerably more difficult.

## Softened Sovereignty and Governance

The current era of what we call "softened sovereignty" arises from several historical waves of ideological globalization pushed by powerful Western states that revolutionized the forms of political-economic organization around the world. Each impelled a contest of authorities between new and old. As noted above, the territorial state system created in Europe over the seventeenth to the nineteenth centuries was exported during the first wave of European colonization, culminating in the creation of de jure sovereign territorial states throughout the world with the onset of decolonization from World War II to 1974. The period of decolonization was informed by the liberal ideology of sovereign equality, establishing territorial states that were equal in law, regardless of their size, power, ethnic coherence, or effectiveness in governing their populace, thus setting up the conditions for many of the contested territorial spaces we see today in Palestine, Pakistan, and Africa.[21] After World War II, facing an encroaching communist ideology, the United States led the way in establishing the political foundations for a liberal economic order, premised on the right of all populaces to state-provided social welfare, while at the same time promoting an open international economic system. By the 1990s, a more reflexively capitalistic neoliberal economic ideology largely replaced this "embedded" or social democratic liberalism.[22] In so doing, it created a contest of authorities among territorial states, their polities, and economic actors, in which the territorial state retreated in the face of economic pressure from multinational entities, shrinking its social welfare functions and loosening its control of national resources.[23] The global diffusion of neoliberalism also altered the international trading and financial orders to produce a form of political economy in which states gave private actors, particularly in finance, tremendous power to govern themselves.[24] During the second half of the twentieth century and accelerating in the 1990s, a wave of liberal humanism challenged the theory of liberal equality that had enshrined territorial states, regardless of regime type, as the proper vessels of sovereignty. Instead, powerful Western states and human rights organizations advocated the universal superiority of their construct of human rights over local cultures and territorial sovereignty, prompting a contest of authorities between a liberal pluralism that accepted the de jure equality of sovereign states, non-Western ideologies of rights, and this newly powerful anti-pluralist liberal humanism.[25]

In short, these waves of liberalism have first imposed the concept of territorial statehood and sovereignty and then undermined it, producing the softened sovereignty of today in which even the most capable states must contend with the interests of private actors in their efforts to govern. Western liberal imperialism created contested territorial spaces. Western embedded liberal, and then neoliberal, ideology brought about contested authorities—contested control of the economy, polity, and society—and retreat of the territorial state. Western liberal humanism created the contending authorities over universal liberal values (anti-pluralist liberalism, liberal pluralism, and non-Western ideologies of rights). Western liberalism created the criteria for "good governance" that states are expected to adhere to today, while at the same time undermining the ideological legitimacy and institutional capacity of state authority. In Richard Falk's words, "territorial sovereignty is being diminished on a spectrum of issues in such a serious manner as to subvert the capacity of states to control and protect the internal life of society, and non-state actors hold an increasing proportion of power and influence in the shaping of world order."[26] The result is a world in which state authority is not absolute, exclusive, or necessarily primary. These waves of globalization have brought about contending authorities not just territorially, as in the case of Hizbullah and the Lebanese state, but among national and local governments, local and transnational corporations, and NGOs and international organizations.

We should also keep in mind that states have deliberately created ungoverned spaces or accepted softened sovereignty when it suits their purposes. Sometimes this is done for diplomatic reasons, such as the ungoverned spaces that have existed until 2002 along Saudi Arabia's borders with Yemen and Iraq, where none of the parties exercised effective sovereignty as a means to avoid diplomatic tensions over contested boundaries. Similarly, disputed territories along the Salvadoran-Honduran border were allowed to remain ungoverned during the 1980s (even though they formed convenient rear areas for insurgents) because the government of El Salvador wanted to avoid a resurgence of the tensions that had led to the 1969 Soccer War with its neighbor. States also deliberately foster ungoverned virtual spaces, such as "offshore" financial institutions, the largest of which, ironically, are in New York City and London.[27] By strictly enforcing banking secrecy laws, many small states have been able to attract a lucrative financial services sector that provides high-paying jobs where few alternatives are available. Competition among these states to provide such spaces has in turn led to the development of an extensive offshore banking network that is used for all manner of legal and nefarious purposes. Major powers (and their courts) have traditionally tolerated such spaces because they allow intelligence agencies to move money invisibly, corrupt politicians and businesspeople to hide questionable gains, and even legitimate enterprises to structure their financial transactions to minimize taxes and improve international competitiveness. Moreover, the hegemony of neoliberal ideology made the very premise of state regulation of private wealth suspect, as shown in Chapter 11. The meager progress made by the global financial community in regulating these centers since 9/11, despite the official concern given to terrorist financing networks, suggests that such ungoverned spaces can generate powerful constituencies that will lobby for their continued existence.[28]

## When Are Ungoverned Spaces a Threat? and to Whom?

Most of the interest in the U.S. policy community regarding ungoverned spaces is driven by the perception that they are a threat to national security because they are the rear areas in which hostile non-state actors, principally terrorists and insurgents, can organize, recruit, train, and recuperate. Military operations in Afghanistan, Waziristan, Yemen, and Somalia have clearly been justified with this threat perception in mind. The potential threats emanating from ungoverned or contested spaces, however, pose threats at two other levels: that of the international system and that of human beings and human security.

The focus on ungoverned spaces as a danger first emerged during the 1990s when they were seen as a threat to global governance and the emerging liberal international economic order. The great human toll of conflicts in contested spaces in states such as the Congo, Cambodia, Colombia, Sierra Leone, Liberia, and Lebanon prompted many states and international governmental organizations to focus on the threat posed by ungoverned spaces. Disorder, particularly from civil war or failed states, was seen as dangerous for global good governance. Contested spaces thus threatened the stability of neighboring states by subjecting them to refugee flows and criminal networks allied with warring parties in the conflict, but they were also perceived as threats to the norms that were supposed to underpin good governance in the international system, such as respect for human rights, transparency, and the rule of law.[29]

Many states have had to contend with internal dissent, persistent insurgencies, and organized crime, yet in this volume we argue that these phenomena should be considered part of a continuum of potential threats posed by ungoverned spaces, in this case threats to human security. In extreme cases, the state's inability or unwillingness to provide personal and economic security may lead citizens to turn to non-state actors to provide such security, as a number of the chapters that follow suggest. Ironically, while the emergence of a vibrant civil society is seen as a hallmark of modern developed democracies, the withering away of states due to globalization or liberalization has in some cases empowered non-state actors to the extent that they exercise quasi-sovereign authority over the people within their domain. In addition, the weakening of the state and its legitimacy and ability to provide security and welfare has led citizens to accept alternatives to the Western liberal international order, for example, populist governments in Latin America, the Hizbullah insurgency in Lebanon, and the increasingly authoritarian regime in Russia.

We should also be clear that alternative forms of government and alternative governing actors may be perceived as threats to states even in cases where there is no threat to global governance, national security, or public safety. Hundreds of millions of people across the globe depend on states for their livelihoods. If alternative forms of governance are able to provide state-like goods such as security and well-being to those within their domain more effectively than governments, then it is only natural to assume that loyalty will follow. States have traditionally been able to command loyalty not only for normative or aspirational reasons, but also because the security, regulatory, and judicial bureaucracies have been the most effective protection racket available.[30] If only from an evolutionary perspective, it is normal to expect that all states will perceive ungoverned spaces as threatening, even if they contain no threats. Their very existence represents the potential for the emergence of competitive forces and thus threatens the livelihoods of the millions of bureaucrats who make up the state. Nevertheless, it is not clear that ungoverned spaces always produce a threat to states, and we will attempt a more nuanced assessment of when ungoverned spaces become threats at the conclusion to this volume.

The concern over ungoverned spaces has also led to a shift in attitudes toward sovereignty across governments and international organizations. This may have potentially wide-reaching consequences for the state system. The international community's experiences in rebuilding states after civil conflicts and humanitarian and human rights disasters have helped further weaken the norm of juridical sovereignty and made it easier to justify intervention in states that lack effective sovereignty over their national territories.[31] International debate over intervention in the Darfur conflict in Sudan is only the most recent example of how this attitude has spread to include not only governments, but transnational civil society. Calls for a norm of "contingent sovereignty" at the United Nations that would differentiate among nations according to the nature of their regimes emphasize the direction of this shift, with all its implications for international security.

## Conclusions: State and International Responses to Ungoverned Spaces

Although academic and policy interest in ungoverned spaces, whether they are territorial, liminal, or virtual, has grown since the end of the Cold War, these spaces have existed since the inception of the modern nation-state.[32] In fact, much of the early process of state formation in Europe was concerned with bringing small statelike entities under the control and authority of sovereign modern states. Similar arguments can be made about the colonial projects of European nations to reorder spaces around the globe that were not governed by states (at least as they were known in Europe) into entities under the sovereignty of those nations. The decolonization and anti-imperialist projects of leaders in the developing world after World War II also took state building as a paradigm for the new postcolonial entities. Lamentations of the weakness of states in the developing world, their lack of control over national territory, and their inability to exercise authority are common among scholars of comparative and international politics, but few of these observers take seriously non-state alternatives to governance.[33]

Even though the success of the modern state-building project around the world has come into question with the seeming proliferation of ungoverned spaces, the fact remains that states and international governmental organizations remain distinctly reluctant to conceive of or sanction alternatives to states for the provision of governance. All departures from such modes of territorial authority have been temporary or involuntary, as occurred in Kosovo or Cambodia or Timor Leste or Lebanon, and were designed to eventually produce renewed, stronger states. International assistance to ungoverned spaces has typically been designed to rebuild state authority. The United States alone spends hundreds of millions of dollars to strengthen the capacity of states around the world to provide governance, including international military education and training, counterterrorism assistance, antinarcotics assistance, programs designed to strengthen the rule of law, and even traditional economic and military aid.[34] Similar programs are supported by other major powers such as Japan and the European Union. Even China, in its pursuit of greater access to raw materials in Southeast Asia, Africa, and Latin America, has stepped up its offers of assistance, almost exclusively to states. In policy terms, this reluctance to countenance alternatives to states has led to questionable policies of unchecked support for particular state leaders, such as Mikhail Gorbachev during the last years of the Soviet Union, or General Pervez Musharaff of Pakistan more recently. Leading powers will go to almost any lengths to keep particular allied leaders in power over their states, even if these are failing or weak, for fear of the alternatives that may arise if they are deposed.

This push to keep states at the center of the provision of governance is, however, in tension with much of liberal globalization. The extension of neoliberalism during the 1990s brought a new approach to governance that was designed to downsize and privatize much of the state. This goes beyond the decline of the welfare state but in many ways includes a critique of other aspects of state spending on development and security. This conceptualization still concedes that states are the fundaments of the international order but accepts only a limited scope for them. Taken to its logical conclusion, the effect of the extension of civil society, democratization, globalization, and liberalization is progressively to limit the state to a "night watchman" function in which almost all governance falls outside the state. Instead of a strong central government, domestic and transnational civil society and corporations are to step into this gap, empowered to provide governance-like functions.[35] It should be no surprise that by doing so, some civil society and corporate entities are able to capture the loyalty of the populations they serve.

Certain recent trends suggest that state resistance to non-state provision of governance may be eroding further. Certainly in virtual ungoverned spaces, such as the Internet, there has been much greater creativity in constructing non-state alternatives to governance. In certain regions of the world, non-state actors have provided statelike functions for extended periods of time, either because states cannot or will not or because the threat is too minor to seriously engage the full attention of the great powers. Hizbullah in Lebanon, FARC in Colombia, and the operations of the Mara Salvatrucha in the urban spaces of El Salvador and Honduras all serve to confirm this trend. Transnational civil society often plays a key role in building governance structures in contested areas, including participating in the administration of refugee camps or providing health and development assistance directly to target populations, rather than through the states that nominally have sovereignty over them. This extends even to traditionally core state functions, such as defense. The privatization of security and the growth of private military corporations suggest that non-state alternatives to the provision of force at a level traditionally reserved to states will become more common.[36] Certainly, the boast by the Blackwater USA corporation that it could assemble a peacekeeping brigade for operations in the Darfur region of Sudan is one example of the growth of private military power.[37] The use of private entities by states and international governmental organizations to provide governance-like functions in contested and uncontrolled areas, whether it is mercenary forces operating as peacekeepers or NGOs administering healthcare in refugee camps, may in fact be the wave of the future.

## Notes

The views expressed here do not reflect the views of the U.S. Navy or the U.S. Department of Defense but are solely the views of the authors.

1.  Robert D. Lamb, "Ungoverned Areas and Threats from Safe Havens," draft 0.61, draft working paper/predecisional paper developed by the Under Secretary of Defense for Policy through the Ungoverned Areas Project, an interagency project managed by the Deputy Assistant Secretary of Defense for Policy Planning, Department of Defense, Washington D.C., May 2007: 1 (copy on file with authors).

2.  A. Claire Cutler, *Private Power and Global Authority: Transnational Merchant Law in the Global Political Economy* (New York: Cambridge University Press, 2003), 180–236.

3.  See Phil Williams, Chapter 2 of this volume, for further discussion of these issues.

4.  Tobias Debiel and Axel Klein, *Fragile Peace: State Failure, Violence and Development in Crisis Regions* (London: Zed Books, 2002); George Klay Kieh Jr. and George Klay Kieh, *Beyond State Failure and Collapse: Making the State Relevant in Africa* (Lanham, MD: Lexington Books, 2007); Kees Koonings and Dirk Kruijt, *Armed Actors: Organised Violence and State Failure in Latin America* (London: Zed Books, 2004); Gerard Kreijen, *State Failure, Sovereignty and Effectiveness: Legal Lessons from the Decolonization of Sub-Saharan Africa* (Leiden: Martinus Nijhoff, 2004); Jennifer Milliken, ed., *State Failure, Collapse and Reconstruction* (Malden, MA: Blackwell, 2003); Robert I. Rotberg, *State Failure and State Weakness in a Time of Terror* (Cambridge, MA: World Peace Foundation/Brookings Institution Press, 2003); Robert I. Rotberg, *When States Fail: Causes and Consequences* (Princeton, NJ: Princeton University Press, 2004); Daniel Thürer, Matthias Herdegen, and Gerhard Hohloch, *Der Wegfall Effektiver Staatsgewalt* (Heidelberg: C. F. Müller, 1996); James Stevenson Wunsch and Dele Olowu, eds., *The Failure of the Centralized State: Institutions and Self-Governance in Africa* (Boulder, CO: Westview, 1990).

5. Lamb, "Ungoverned Areas," draft 0.61: 5–8, 12–15; and Robert D. Lamb, "Ungoverned Areas and Threats from Safe Havens," final report of the Ungoverned Areas Project prepared for the Under Secretary of Defense for Policy, Department of Defense, Washington D.C., January 2008 (copy of both on file with authors), 17, 26–30. Robert Lamb participated in the conference the authors organized on Ungoverned Spaces in 2007 at the Naval Postgraduate School; the final report reflects this. We thank him for providing the draft and final report to us and his good humor in the face of our critique.

6. Christopher K. Ansell and Giuseppe Di Palma, eds., *Restructuring Territoriality: Europe and the United States Compared* (Cambridge: Cambridge University Press, 2004).

7. On suzerain states, see Hedley Bull, *The Anarchical Society* (New York: Columbia University Press, 1977). On the distinction between European and other states, see Christopher Clapham, "The Global-Local Politics of State Decay," in *When States Fail: Causes and Consequences*, ed. Robert I. Rotberg (Princeton, NJ: Princeton University Press, 2004), 78–79.

8. Clapham, "Global-Local Politics," 79.

9. Lamb, "Ungoverned Areas," final report, 13–17.

10. Michael Zürn and Stephan Leibfried, "Reconfiguring the National Constellation," in *Transformations of the State?* ed. Stephan Leibfried and Michal Zürn (Cambridge: Cambridge University Press, 2005), 2–7.

11. Jackson terms this "de facto sovereignty," as opposed to the de jure sovereignty enjoyed by many developing countries today. Robert H. Jackson, *Quasi-States: Sovereignty, International Relations, and the Third World* (Cambridge and New York: Cambridge University Press, 1990).

12. Zürn and Leibfried, "Reconfiguring the National Constellation," 2–7.

13. Alex Gourevitch, "The Myth of the Failed State: Intervention and Third World Sovereignty," paper presented at the annual meeting of the International Studies Association, Hilton Hawaiian Village, Honolulu, Hawaii, 5 March 2005, http://www.allacademic.com/meta/p71075_index.html.

14. Ansell and Di Palma, *Restructuring Territoriality*.

15. We understand globalization to refer to the speed, quantity, and especially cheapness of global flows of labor, capital, production, knowledge, and ideas, for which the politically critical corollary is the diffusion of authority over people, ideas, knowledge and technologies, capital, productive processes (whether of services or goods), and their respective transportation networks.

16. Gilpin argues for the former and Rosenau for the latter in Robert Gilpin, *Global Political Economy* (Princeton, NJ: Princeton University Press, 2001); James Rosenau, *Turbulence in World Politics: A Theory of Change and Continuity* (Princeton, NJ: Princeton University Press, 1990); and James N. Rosenau, *Distant Proximities: Dynamics beyond Globalization* (Princeton, NJ: Princeton University Press, 2003). See also Robert O. Keohane and Joseph S. Nye, *Power and Interdependence*, 2nd ed. (New York: Harper Collins, 1989). For an overview of the debate between realists skeptical

of globalization and their critics, see David Held and Anthony McGrew, "The Great Globalization Debate," in *The Global Transformations Reader*, ed. David Held and Anthony McGrew (Cambridge: Polity Press, 2003).

17. Stephen D. Krasner, *Defending the National Interest: Raw Materials Investments and U.S. Foreign Policy* (Princeton, NJ: Princeton University Press, 1978).

18. Richard Falk, "State of Siege: Will Globalization Win Out?" *International Affairs* 73, 1 (1997): 123–36; Saskia Sassen, *Territory, Authority, Rights: From Medieval to Global Assemblages* (Princeton, NJ: Princeton University Press, 2006); and Susan Strange, *Retreat of the State: The Diffusion of Power in the World Economy* (Cambridge: Cambridge University Press, 1996).

19. Milton L. Mueller, *Ruling the Root: Internet Governance and the Taming of Cyberspace* (Cambridge, MA: MIT Press, 2004); and Ronen Palan, *The Offshore World: Sovereign Markets, Virtual Places, and Nomad Millionaires* (Ithaca, NY: Cornell University Press, 2003).

20. Rosenau, *Distant Proximities*, 11–16.

21. Jackson, *Quasi-States*; Robert H. Jackson and Mark W. Zacher, "The Territorial Covenant: International Society and the Legitimization of Boundaries," paper presented at the annual meeting of the American Political Science Association, San Francisco Hilton and Towers, 29 August–1 September 1996; Daniel Philpott, *Revolutions in Sovereignty: How Ideas Shaped Modern International Relations* (Princeton, NJ: Princeton University Press, 2001); and Gerry Simpson, "Two Liberalisms," *European Journal of International Law* 12, 3 (2001): 537–72.

22. John Gerard Ruggie, "International Regimes, Transactions, and Change: Embedded Liberalism in the Postwar Economic Order," *International Organization* 36, 2 (1982): 379–415.

23. Mark Blyth, *Great Transformations: Economic Ideas and Institutional Change in the Twentieth Century* (Cambridge: Cambridge University Press, 2002).

24. Cutler, *Private Power and Global Authority*; Rodney Bruce Hall and Thomas Biersteker, "The Emergence of Private Authority in the International System," in *The Emergence of Private Authority in Global Governance*, ed. Rodney Bruce Hall and Thomas Biersteker (Cambridge: Cambridge University Press, 2002); and Palan, *Offshore World*.

25. Simpson, "Two Liberalisms."

26. Falk, "State of Siege," 125.

27. Palan, *Offshore World*.

28. Anne L. Clunan, "The Fight against Terrorist Financing," *Political Science Quarterly* 121, 4 (2006): 569–96; and Jeanne Giraldo and Harold Trinkunas, eds., *Terrorism Financing and State Responses: A Comparative Perspective* (Palo Alto, CA: Stanford University Press, 2007).

29. Marina Ottaway and Stephan Mair, "States at Risk and Failed States: Putting Security First," *Policy Outlook* (September 2004), Carnegie Endowment for International Peace, Washington D.C., http://www.carnegieendowment.org/files/Ottaway_outlook3.pdf.

30. Charles Tilly, "War Making and State Making as Organized Crime," in *Bringing the State Back In*, ed. Peter Evans, Dietrich Rueschemeyer, and Theda Skocpol (Cambridge: Cambridge University Press, 1985).

31. An academic defense of effective in lieu of juridical sovereignty can be found in Jackson, *Quasi-States*.

32. Stephen D. Krasner, *Sovereignty: Organized Hypocrisy* (Princeton, NJ: Princeton University Press, 1999).

33. Jackson, *Quasi-States*.

34. See "The National Security Strategy of the United States of America," 17 September 2002, for an overview of U.S. international assistance strategies, http://www.globalsecurity.org/military/library/policy/national/nss-020920.pdf.

35. Rosenau, *Distant Proximities*.

36. Deborah Avant, *The Market for Force: The Consequences of Privatizing Security* (Cambridge: Cambridge University Press, 2005).

37. Rebecca Ulam Weiner, "Peace Corp: As the international community dithers over Darfur, private military companies say they've got what it takes to 'stop the carnage, if only someone would hire them,'" *Boston Globe*, 23 April 2006.

# 2 Here Be Dragons

*Dangerous Spaces and International Security*

Phil Williams

Although it turns out to be myth rather than reality, the notion that medieval cartographers marked unknown territories with the phrase *hic sunt dracones* (here be dragons) captures some of the dynamics of the Middle Ages. The phrase, in legend at least, was meant to demarcate unknown and unsafe areas or "terra incognito" where the laws, rules, and norms of "civilized society" did not apply. Wales in the thirteenth century was regarded by the Plantagenet kings as such an area, one that King Edward I ultimately brought under his control. The key to this assertion of control and the subjugation of Welsh aspirations for self-government was an alliance between the king and the marcher lords whose territories bordered Wales, an ability to manipulate the inherent rivalry and distrust among the Welsh lords themselves, and finally the creation of a permanent military presence with the construction of a series of strategically located and virtually impregnable castles, many of which remain standing today. Even though the Welsh had charismatic leaders such as Llewellyn the Great, as well as a remarkable capacity to fight guerilla campaigns based on the superiority of the Welsh longbow over the English crossbow, they lacked a resource base adequate for sustained and successful resistance against English power. The conventional wisdom, therefore, is that King Edward imposed law on a lawless region and began the process that led to a unified Britain dominated by the English crown. In fact, Wales was not lawless; it already had a set of laws and norms that were ahead of England in many respects, including acknowledgement of the rights of women and tolerance for illegitimacy. Edward's military success did not create governance out of disorder; it merely replaced one form of governance with another that was more centralized, distant, and based on domination by an alien culture and the suppression of nationalist aspirations.

This story of medieval Wales is a cautionary tale for any attempt to analyze ungoverned spaces or lawless areas. Although some of these spaces are truly lawless and ungoverned, many of them simply have different, alternative, and sometimes even hybrid forms of governance. The terms most analysts use are inherently state-centric and implicitly assume that the state, based as it is on centralized, top-down control and direction, better meets peoples' needs than any other form of governance. The twenty-first century, however, might be one in which the state undergoes a long recessional and other forms of governance come to the fore. James Rosenau's "two worlds of world politics," the state-centric and the multicentric, are on an increasingly uncomfortable collision course between top-down control and bottom-up aspirations.[1]

This is not to deny that many security challenges in the twenty-first century stem from a mix of subnational and transnational forces and that these challenges can be encapsulated in terms of spaces. International relations theorists obsessed with realism, liberalism, constructivism, and their neovariants have typically paid little attention to spaces. Some observers, however, have captured important facets of these challenges, often stemming from what they see as the long-term decline of the Westphalian state. This was perhaps most forcefully articulated in the 1990s by Robert Kaplan, although the hyperbole inherent in his vision of the coming anarchy enabled critics to dismiss the alarming trends that he identified. Ironically, most of these trends have subsequently intensified rather than abated.[2] Some of them are captured in the notion variously characterized as the New Middle Ages, new medievalism, or neomedievalism.

Initially developed by Hedley Bull, the concept of the New Middle Ages has been best articulated by Gregory O'Hayon, Philip Cerny, and Mark Duffield.[3] As Duffield's succinct summary of Cerny's analysis noted, global politics has become neomedieval in that it is characterized by "competing institutions and overlapping jurisdictions of state, non-governmental and private interest groups . . . more fluid territorial boundaries; the increasing inequality and isolation of underclass and marginalized groups . . . the growing importance of identity politics, ethnicity, and multiple and fragmented loyalties . . . contested property rights, legal statutes, and conventions . . . the spread of geographical and social 'no go areas' where the rule of law is absent . . . and a growing disarticulation between the technologically innovative north and the south."[4] Cerny himself argues that these elements constitute a long-term "durable disorder," in which the system as a whole stumbles along with problems managed and contained rather than solved.[5]

Cerny's encapsulation of global politics is compelling—especially as he emphasizes the linkages between this durable disorder on the one hand and globalization and connectivity on the other. When combined with technology that has become much more diffused and easily acquired, the result is not only an empowerment of "sovereignty-free actors," but a turbo-charging of global politics.[6] The speed of travel and communications, the ease and low cost of business transactions, the volume and velocity of financial flows, the pervasiveness of television, the ubiquity of cellular phones, and the growing reach of the Internet have created a world that would be unintelligible not only to citizens in the Middle Ages, but also to many of those who lived in the first half of the twentieth century. We live in an era when political conditions and the dispersion of authority increasingly resemble the Middle Ages, but the forces of modernity, technology, and globalization add new considerations that make security challenges even more daunting and complex.

Against this background, this chapter argues that the major security challenges of the twenty-first century can be understood in terms of spaces and gaps: geographical, functional, social, economic, legal, and regulatory. It is difficult, though, to find an appropriate term for describing these spaces. The notion of ungoverned spaces, for example, fails to capture the possibility of alternative forms of governance to that provided by the state. The same problem exists with the term "lawless areas." Although the term "disorderly spaces" is somewhat better, even this ignores the reality that what initially appears as disorder often exhibits its own form of order. Accordingly, this analysis uses the term "dangerous spaces." Although this is not ideal, it helps to provide a viewpoint for understanding the variety of ways in which security challenges emanate within and from different kinds of spaces. This chapter initially examines the concept of space and then identifies some of the dangerous spaces that have become an integral part of the global security challenge.

## The Concept of Space

The concept of space is more varied than often thought. Deriving from the Latin word *spatium*, which referred to area, room, and an interval in time or space, according to Merriam-Webster's dictionary the word space has at least ten different meanings. Even leaving aside space in music, mathematics, and writing, as well as the region beyond the earth's atmosphere, the concept of space encompasses (1) a period of time or duration; (2) "a limited extent in one, two, or three dimensions" that can be "an extent set apart or available"; (3) "a boundless three-dimensional extent in which objects and events occur and have relative position and direction"; (4) "accommodations on a public vehicle"; (5) opportunities for advertisers in broadcasting; and (6) an opportunity to assert identity or enjoy privacy. These different meanings of space have important implications for security in the twenty-first century, as do the following characteristics of spaces.

- Space can be controlled. The Westphalian state system is based on the notion of sole authority and exclusive jurisdiction over a defined territorial space. This notion of control also applies to legal and regulatory spaces, where again the state has traditionally sought a monopoly.
- Space can be filled, by things or people. In this connection, one way of thinking about space is as a repository for people; thus it is obvious that the distribution of people (or things) in geographic spaces can vary enormously. This is evident in the distinction typically made between urban and rural areas. Urban areas are characterized above all by a high concentration of people in a limited space, whereas rural areas are characterized by sparse population. Yet geography is not the only form of space that can be filled. Legal, regulatory, and functional spaces are also filled, to one degree or another. This is particularly important in the present discussion, as key security problems revolve around spaces in which governance does not exist and spaces in which governance is contested from within. When considering spaces that are ungoverned or unregulated, it is necessary to examine legal and regulatory spaces in which governance is nonexistent or weak.
- The corollary of space being controlled or filled is that this process is often incomplete and leaves gaps. These can be gaps in authority or in control over territory, or legal, regulatory, or functional gaps. The old adage that nature abhors a vacuum can be modified to suggest that nature abhors gaps of

whatever kind. Consequently, when the state does not fill these gaps, other entities will attempt to do so. In some cases, competing forms of governance emerge as non-state entities seek to become surrogates for the state. The other response is simply to exploit the room for maneuver and the opportunities the gaps provide. Where there are gaps in social control mechanisms, for example, organized crime will act with a degree of impunity that would otherwise not be possible.

- Space can be contested. Historically, the contestation has often been over territorial demarcations about where one authority ended and another began. These continue to exist, for example in violently contested spaces in the Middle East and Kashmir. Yet, in many cases, the issue is not territorial control but who provides effective governance. In this context, it is important to note that when top-down governance is inadequate, we often witness the emergence of nascent or bottom-up forms that grow out of local communities and, for all their shortcomings, often fulfill the needs of these communities. In some cases, such as the Brazilian *favelas* (ghetto-ized urban squatter settlements), there are what might be termed hybrid forms of governance. Enrique Desmond Arias has shown, for example, that governance in the *favelas* of Rio de Janeiro is provided by a mixture of drug traffickers, the police (representing the state), and community organizations.[7]

- Another dimension of space is what is often described as the "space of flows," through which people, money, commodities, information, messages, digital signals, and services move.[8] Such flows have become truly global; the space of flows is now a global space. Most of the flows are lawful and largely beneficial in their effects. Some flows, though, are illicit in nature and can pose major security threats, exacerbating disorder and spreading both violence and the capacity for violence.

- Spaces can also be understood to provide economic and social opportunities. In some cases, these opportunities are extensive; in others, they are very limited. Indeed, the traditional distinction between the developed and the developing world is based largely on the economic and social opportunities afforded by different spaces. This is not to suggest, however, that there is uniformity in either world. The developed world has what can be termed zones of economic exclusion,[9] while the developing world has zones of opportunity and wealth. In some cases, the contrasting opportunities are sharply juxtaposed.

• Space can also be understood in terms of time. This temporal dimension of space is perhaps the hardest component to digest. One way of thinking about it, however, might be in relation to physical spaces that are contested by governments and insurgents: during the day, the forces associated with the formal authority structure are often dominant; during the night, the constellation of forces is very different. Who controls the night is one of the best single indicators of the progress of the struggle.

In short, spaces can be physical or nonphysical, can be subject to governance that is strong or weak, can be wholly ungoverned, or can be the focus of contested governance. Although attention has to be given to ungoverned or poorly governed spaces, which often become spaces of contested governance, it is also necessary to consider contiguous spaces of divergent governance (borderlands, frontiers); spaces of partially regulated, unregulated, and illegal flows; and sharply juxtaposed spaces—whether in cities, states, or regions—between zones of opportunity and zones of exclusion.

## Dangerous Spaces

Dangerous spaces are difficult to contain or insulate. High levels of connectivity in a globalized world bring enormous benefits but also significant costs. Part of the problem is the incentive structures that are created both by state policies and by the asymmetries or inequalities among them. Rich, powerful, and relatively stable states generally promulgate the rules for the international system and determine what activities and products are legal or illegal. When this is combined with large economies and lucrative markets, incentives are inadvertently created for the supply of goods that are prohibited, regulated, restricted, or stolen. "Dark networks," which often operate from dangerous spaces, exploit these opportunities.[10] Indeed, "the state-smuggler relationship" is "a paradoxical one, defined by irony and contradiction. The smuggler is pursued by the state but at the same time is kept in business by the state. . . . State laws provide the very opening for (and high profitability of) smuggling in the first place."[11] Similarly, differences of legal, administrative, economic, or financial systems have been described by Nikos Passas as *criminogenic* asymmetries, which offer both incentives and opportunities for criminal and terrorist organizations.[12] In effect, jurisdictional asymmetries encourage jurisdictional arbitrage, provide market incentives, and offer safe havens for dark networks.

Given asymmetries and connectivity, quarantines are difficult to impose and maintain. It is impossible to stop flows into dangerous spaces, and it is impossible to stop flows out of them. Emerging or reemerging diseases incubated in a dangerous space (whether a city lacking clean water, hygienic conditions, or good health care or a jungle being encroached by illegal logging that brings human beings into contact with previously unknown pathogens) can result in an epidemic or even pandemic. Similarly, organized crime or terrorist networks that develop in these spaces can subsequently use them as safe havens while targeting other areas. There are also connections between such spaces, connections that involve illegal transactions and flows from one dangerous space to other dangerous spaces or to well-governed spaces, the transmission of knowledge and expertise from one dark network to another, and the creation of support structures for actors and organizations that thrive on ineffective state governance.

In thinking about spaces and security, therefore, it is essential to consider vectors of transmission. In effect, the danger flows out from its origin or locus in zones characterized by turbulence, through various forms of connectivity, to zones of order and stability. Interconnectivity is central to security in the twenty-first century. In effect, we face a combination of disorder similar to that of the Middle Ages, with modern technologies that allow the dangers to spread and even to mutate in complex and unpredictable ways. Now, we turn to developing a rudimentary typology of dangerous spaces.

### Strong, Stable States with Governance Gaps

In the modern state system, geographic spaces are still organized according to principles of national sovereignty, which emphasize exclusive jurisdiction, clear lines of demarcation, comprehensive and pervasive authority through laws and regulations, and the monopoly of the use of force within the space controlled by the state. In this Westphalian state system, war-making and state-making, as Charles Tilly noted, were mutually reinforcing.[13] Not surprisingly, therefore, there is a natural tendency in advanced postindustrial states and societies to see the problem of dangerous spaces as external. This is a mistake: even in sovereign spaces under the jurisdiction of strong states with high levels of legitimacy, space is not uniformly controlled. No-go zones such as inner cities, where law enforcement is absent, or rural areas under the control of insurgents are becoming increasingly common. In some countries, this is enough to challenge the idea of comprehensive and pervasive authority; in others, it is dismissed as little more than a nuisance. Yet it appears that more and more spaces are contested rather than controlled. The riots and widespread burning of cars in the suburbs of Paris and other French cities in the fall of 2005 revealed that, whatever the French authorities did during the day, they could not control the night. Alienated and marginalized communities of Muslim immigrants from North Africa have become common through much of Western Europe and could increasingly pose similar challenges to state authority in other European countries. Such communities often receive low levels of provision and support from the state and do not readily submit to its social-control mechanisms. Moreover, the radicalization of second- and third-generation immigrants has led to the emergence, especially in Britain, of what has been termed "home-grown" terrorism. The irony there is that some of those who engaged in the fertilizer bomb plot, which was disrupted in March 2004, had consistently received benefits from the British welfare system. Scrutiny of the dangerous spaces within the state, therefore, is as important as looking outward for threats.

## Weak and Failed States with Capacity Gaps and Functional Holes

While states remain the dominant form of political organization, there are some indications that the state is in long-term secular decline. Some contemporary wars, for example, especially civil wars in Africa, have been more about state disruption and collapse than state consolidation. Moreover, the number of weak states has increased significantly since the end of the Cold War. This was inevitable: many of the states that emerged out of decolonization were "quasi-states" that shared few attributes of the modern legitimate democratic state apart from a common concept of sovereignty.[14] Yet the increase also reflects the dynamics of transition in the former Soviet bloc, as well as a more pervasive crisis of authority from which relatively few states are completely immune.

The term "weak states" is typically used to describe states with characteristics such as a low level of state legitimacy, weak border controls, poorly articulated and/or ineffective norms and rules, untrammeled competition among rival factions, the lack of economic or social services for the citizenry, the absence of legal regulation of and protection for business, the lack of social control mechanisms embodied in a fair and efficient criminal justice system, and the inability to carry out typical and traditional state functions with either efficiency or effectiveness. One way of thinking about this is in terms of capacity gaps that create functional holes. Indeed, the state has to be understood not only as a territorial space, but also as a functional space. The state fulfills certain functions on behalf of its citizens, including the provision of security, law and order, and economic opportunities and safeguards. Many states fail miserably in terms of economic management and social welfare. Functional holes of this kind create pressures and incentives for citizens to engage in criminal activities—a notion consistent with what Joel Migdal termed "survival strategies."[15] Amidst conditions of economic hardship, extralegal means of obtaining basic needs often become critical to survival. For countries in which there is no social safety net, resort to the informal economy and illicit activities is a natural response to the economic and social gaps created by the failure of the state. From this perspective, organized crime and drug trafficking, along with prostitution, are rational responses to dire economic conditions. Such activities are coping mechanisms in countries characterized by poverty, poor governance, and ineffective markets. Illicit means of advancement offer opportunities that are simply not available in the licit economy. The difficulty, of course, is that the filling of functional spaces by organized crime not only perpetuates the weakness of the state, but can spill over to other societies, bringing with it violence and corruption.

Finally, states are legal or regulatory spaces. When the state fills these spaces with appropriate laws and regulations, society functions effectively. Sometimes, however, the state can overregulate and create perverse incentives for criminality, as the United States did during Prohibition. Problems also arise when the state fails to fill these spaces with appropriate, adequate, and accepted legal and regulatory measures. In some cases, non-state actors step in to fill the gap. Sometimes this is benign, but it can have unfortunate consequences. In Russia during the 1990s, for example, the failure to provide a regulatory framework for business that offered legal protection, contract enforcement, recourse for debt collection, and peaceful arbitration encouraged organized crime to become a surrogate for government.[16] Debt collection and business disputes were settled not by the courts, but by intimidation and contract killings. What could have been an ordered space within a smooth transition became a disordered space that at times seemed to jeopardize the move to a market economy.

A variant on this theme of gaps in regulatory space can be found in several African states, where the absence of regulations for key economic sectors, especially the extraction of minerals and other natural resources, fuels criminal activity—by political leaders, by domestic and transnational criminal organizations, and by rebel armies and warlords. While a well-defined regulatory space might not be a sufficient condition for stopping the criminal looting of state resources, it is almost certainly a necessary condition. Moreover, the absence of such a framework gives the problem a self-perpetuating quality: political or territorial control of certain regions not only yields rich rewards to criminals (or rebel groups), but also deprives governments of resources that could help to fuel growth and create better infrastructure.

In some instances, weak states gradually move into the category of failing states. This occurs when they are unable to stem the deterioration of public and economic life resulting from weakness. Unless this process is halted, they can become failed states, which are "tense, deeply conflicted, dangerous, and contested bitterly by warring factions" and "typified by deteriorating or destroyed infrastructures." In extreme and rare cases, failure can even turn into collapse.[17] Somalia tends to be the poster child for this syndrome. Although the distinctions between some of the categories are fuzzy, it is clear that various degrees of weakness are closely bound up with the emergence of dangerous spaces.[18]

## Alternatively Governed Spaces

In some states, the forces of tradition remain stronger than those of modernity, and the key power brokers are warlords, who are often also tribal or clan leaders (another reason that the idea of the New Middle Ages has such resonance). As Richard Shultz and Andrea Dew have noted, tribes and the clans that are their subdivisions are some of the most important units of analysis in conflict situations ranging from Somalia to Afghanistan.[19] One of the characteristics of societies in which tribes, clans, and warlords play central roles is that such entities typically put their own interests above any notion of collective or public interest as symbolized in state structures and institutions.[20] Yet, the non-state actors can have more legitimacy among the general population than the state, a legitimacy that stems from tradition, cultural norms, and informal political processes that work.[21] In addition, they often have connections outside the state. Indeed, "one of the more disturbing trends of non-state armed groups is the extent to which such groups . . . are cooperating and collaborating with each other in networks that span national borders and include fellow tribal groups, criminal groups, and corrupt political elements."[22] In effect, state authority is subject to challenge both from within by non-state armed groups and from without by transnational movements, organizations, and forces. In other instances, the problem is not clans but insurgent movements that are also closely connected with transnational dark networks. The Revolutionary Armed Forces of Colombia (FARC), for example, developed cooperative links with the Irish Republican Army and with Mexican and Brazilian drug-trafficking organizations.

### Confrontational Spaces: Borders, Border Zones, and Prisons

The tensions between forces of disorder and those of governance that are at the core of the twenty-first-century security paradigm play themselves out with different degrees of intensity in different regions and different nations. Perhaps nowhere, though, is this tension as obvious as at national borders, which are the only places for monitoring and regulating global flows. Borders are confrontational spaces par excellence because they are where the dynamics of globalization, the imperatives of the global space of flows, and the demands of global trade confront the emphasis on national space and the claims of sovereign governments to determine what and who enters or leaves national territory. As one observer has noted, borders are where "the strategy of state territoriality is dramatized and state sovereignty is paraded. It is also here that many countervailing strategies contesting state territoriality are clustered. The struggle between these strategies continually reproduces, reconstructs, or undermines borders."[23] The forces of governance at national borders are represented by customs officials, immigration service personnel, and border guards. The forces of disorder and danger are represented by smugglers, illegal migrants, criminals, and terrorists, who see borders as both obstacles and opportunities. Borders are barriers to be overcome, but once they are overcome, all sorts of benefits accrue, whether job opportunities for illegal migrants or profits from illegal goods that increase in value when they are moved from one side of the border to the other. Smugglers exploit differential tax rates among countries (which explains why cigarette smuggling has become a major issue in Europe); they also seek to meet the demands for products that are illegal, regulated, prohibited, or stolen. Similarly, from a terrorist perspective, borders are merely the outer shell of protection for potential targets. Simply by obtaining access to the sovereign territory of the target state, terrorists have successfully surmounted a major obstacle. Moreover, dark networks are able to use four major techniques to defeat control efforts: concealment, deception, facilitation or corruption, and circumvention.

Border problems are particularly acute when they involve contiguous spaces juxtaposing different forms and levels of governance. Such areas develop their own character and dynamic, determined by legal systems and levels of economic development. Cross-border flows are a function not only of supply and demand, but also of asymmetries in legal and regulatory systems, currency exchange rates, and price differentials between the two sides of the border. Consequently, border zones become magnets for illegal flows that exploit asymmetries and disparities of value.

In some instances, borders are undermined by official state policies, through the deliberate creation of spaces to facilitate flows with little or no attention to the nature and content of these flows. Such spaces, typically known as free-trade zones, are poorly regulated, give priority to facilitation rather than inspection, and are attractive to those operating in gray or black markets. The United Arab Emirates, for example, because of its emphasis on free trade, has become the transshipment zone of choice for proliferation networks such as that of the Pakistani nuclear materials merchant A. Q. Khan, as well as of criminal and terrorist networks trying to move assets to safer locations. Other free-trade zones also facilitate various forms of trafficking.

The other dangerous spaces in which states and the forces of disorder often clash are prisons. In many parts of the world, the paradox of prisons is that they are simultaneously a monument to state power and an expression of the limits of that power. Although the formal power structure imposes a degree of outer controls, within these the prisoners have enormous latitude. In some cases, incarcerated leaders of criminal organizations continue to run their illicit businesses from prison. It used to be argued that prisons were places where people obtained master's degrees in crime; now some prisons have become the de facto corporate headquarters for criminal businesses that continue to operate in the outside world. This seems to have been true, for example, of La Palma maximum-security prison in Mexico where, until his extradition to the United States in January 2007, Osiel Cardenas continued to run the operations of his drug-trafficking organization, known as the Gulf Cartel, and direct hostilities against his archrival, Chapo Guzmán. In a similar vein, Louise Shelley has suggested that some of the business of trafficking in nuclear material in the former Soviet Union is run from Georgian prisons.[24]

Prisons are also Petri dishes of radicalization. This is particularly the case in European prisons, where foreigners in general and Muslims in particular are heavily overrepresented. Foreigners account for 34 percent of the German prison population and more than 28 percent of the Italian prison population, "far in excess of the foreign component of the general population."[25] In France, twenty-five thousand of forty-five thousand prisoners are Muslim—

more than six times the proportion of Muslims in France's overall population.[26] In Spain, 60 percent of new prisoners are foreigners, with Muslims making up 12 percent of the overall prison population.[27] Consequently, prisons offer enormous opportunities for terrorists to "recruit specialists whom they need to run their networks—specialists in fraudulent documents, arms trafficking, etc. They use concepts that justify crime, that transform it into redemption. The prisons of today are producing the terrorists of tomorrow."[28] Perhaps the most notable example is Jamal Ahmidan, a Moroccan drug trafficker, who was radicalized in a Moroccan prison and subsequently became the key figure in the implementation of the 2004 Madrid bombings.

Similarly, ties of friendship and affiliation that develop in prison are often perpetuated when prisoners are released, in some cases leading to unlikely and unexpected forms of cooperation among criminal organizations of different ethnicity. Equally plausible is a close connection between terrorists and criminals, especially where the latter have converted or become radicalized. Networks formed on the inside can prove very formidable on the outside.

### Concentrated Spaces, Zones of Social Exclusion, and Feral Cities

In international relations and political science, the state remains the basic unit of analysis. Yet if we think of spaces that are highly concentrated in terms of population, creativity, industry, finance, and the like, the focus moves from states to cities. This is not surprising. The large-scale movement of population from rural to urban areas over the latter half of the twentieth century was enormous. Yet it has also brought with it an increased number of dangerous spaces that will become even more dangerous as urbanization intensifies.

Cities have always been engines of economic growth; repositories of wealth, power, and entrepreneurship; and centers of culture, scholarship, and innovation. But they have also been breeding grounds of disease, concentrations of poverty and crime, and drivers of instability and revolution. Moreover, the future development of cities is more likely to be accompanied by instability rather than order. In some cases, they will even degenerate into what Richard Norton has termed "feral cities."[29] The attributes of such cities include the absence of social services, high levels of disease, and large-scale environmental degradation. What makes this particularly important is that in the next few decades there will be more cities, more large cities, and more globally connected cities. Big cities mean big problems, and globally connected cities mean global problems. The advent of meta-cities (those with

a population of more than twenty million); the increased number of mega-
cities (more than ten million), which is projected to reach twenty-three by
2015 (with nineteen of them in the developing world);[30] and the rapid growth
in the number and size of smaller cities will create major environmental haz-
ards, generate immense law and order problems, and strain infrastructures
that are already overstretched. In some cases, the stresses and strains will
prove overwhelming.

The problem is not just size; it is also the growth of slums in cities. The UN-
Habitat report *The State of the World's Cities 2006/7* noted that slums could
be the "emerging human settlements of the 21st century." Indeed, the report
also noted that "urbanization has become virtually synonymous with slum
growth, especially in sub-Saharan Africa, Western Asia, and Southern Asia."[31]
Characterized by lack of durable housing, sufficient living area, access to water
and sanitation, and security against eviction, slums typically have minimal
services from the state, which is often completely absent. This creates an enormous potential for pernicious interactions between urban growth on the one
side and economic crises, high levels of unemployment, and weak and inadequate governance on the other.[32] Although cities provide new opportunities,
the zones of social and economic exclusion will expand enormously during
the next two decades. Few cities in the developing world will have the capacity
to generate sufficient jobs to meet the demand of their growing populations.
Among those who suffer disproportionately from unemployment are youths
and young men. The problem here is that "underemployed, urbanized young
men are an especially volatile group that can easily be drawn into organized
crime."[33] They also provide the main recruitment pool for street gangs, terrorists, rioters, predatory criminals, and the like. In other words, the youth bulge
that is still growing in many parts of the developing world is likely to turn
into an unemployment bulge, with unfortunate and dangerous consequences,
that will transform many more cities into highly dangerous spaces. This is
even more likely where there is a stark juxtaposition of spaces characterized
by ostentatious wealth and spaces dominated by poverty and resentment. In
an increasing number of cities, therefore, survival will take precedence over
the rule of law, alienation and anger will be rife, and the criminal economy
will loom large. At the same time, it is worth emphasizing that most of those
urban spaces characterized as ungoverned or lawless areas are, in fact, subject
to alternative forms of governance, which tend to be either bottom-up or an
uneasy combination of bottom-up and top-down.

The other problem with cities is that the growth of connectivity makes them likely to emerge as super-hubs in the licit global economy; many cities have also become well-connected nodes in the networks of flows constituting the illicit global economy—and are consequently able to act as both hubs for and transmitters of illegal activities. Bangkok is a regional center of arms and human trafficking, Johannesburg is a magnet for illicit activities of all kinds, and Lagos is the global center for the ubiquitous 4-1-9 fraudulent e-mail solicitations from Nigerian criminals. Perhaps even more disturbing, connectivity facilitates the spread of emerging or reemerging diseases. Cities are not only incubators for diseases that result in national epidemics, but also key nodes in rapid and efficient global transportation networks that could fuel a global pandemic. This became evident with the outbreak and spread of severe acute respiratory syndrome (SARS). In this case, one of the transmission vectors was a woman, unaware that she was a carrier of the virus, who traveled from Beijing to Toronto via Vancouver. As one commentary noted, "she became a member of a small group who created an incredible chain of events that would be felt in 24 countries and affect the health of more than 8,000 people. By the time the SARS crisis had abated in less than fifteen weeks, 774 people would die, hundreds of thousands were quarantined, many would lose their livelihood, and entire health care systems would be on the verge of paralysis. A siege mentality set in as cities lost the capability to contain the threat."[34] New variants of influenza could be far more devastating. As slums increase, so do the dangers. Unfortunately, the prospect for a global pandemic moving from one globally connected city to another is an inevitable result of the mixture of globalization, urbanization, poverty, and the phenomenon of dangerous spaces that characterizes the twenty-first century. This mix is also closely connected to the space of dangerous flows.

### The Space of Dangerous Flows: Illicit Commodities, Dirty Money, and Digital Signals

One of the characteristics of contemporary global politics is the vast increase in flows of all kinds. This is as true of trade—where the intermodal container has had a profound effect in facilitating the movement of goods and commodities—as it is of the Internet, which facilitates the almost instantaneous flow of information and communications in digital form. There is nothing new about flows per se. Differences exist, however, in the scale, diversity, velocity, ease, and low cost of contemporary flows. The downside involves the flows of illicit and often dangerous goods such as drugs, arms, and even nuclear material and the use of the Internet for various forms of crime, ranging from child pornography to identity theft and fraud, and for terrorist recruiting, fundraising, and communications.

In the case of flows of dangerous goods, the expansion of licit trade and the massive growth of container shipping have transformed the global trading system into a smuggler's paradise, in which criminal opportunities continue to expand faster than constraints on criminal activities. The issue is partly volume but also largely diversity, which confronts those who attempt to stop smuggling with two kinds of problems: finding needles in haystacks, and finding needles in stacks of needles. The needle in the haystack problem is one of discovery—of finding smuggled products amidst the vast amount of licit products that are imported and exported; the needle in the stack of needles problem is one of the identification and differentiation of illicit products from licit. The potential consequences of failure are chilling. As the author of a major study on containers has noted, "Containers can be just as efficient for smuggling undeclared merchandise, illegal drugs, undocumented immigrants, and terrorist bombs as for moving legitimate cargo."[35] Given the scale of the task, even the growing exploitation of inspection and detection technologies is unlikely to render inspection and monitoring significantly more effective.

Dangerous flows affect security at various levels. The trafficking of stolen nuclear material, especially from the former Soviet Union, could help terrorists acquire some kind of improvised nuclear or radiological device, while the sale of nuclear production technology and knowledge along the lines of the Khan network facilitates nuclear proliferation by states. Trafficking in arms to conflict zones undermines conflict prevention, conflict management, and the reestablishment of a stable and enduring peace. It also highlights the limits of Westphalian management mechanisms, where states are incapable of stemming the flow of arms and ammunition to conflict zones: embargoes on arms supplies without effective enforcement mechanisms simply push up prices and encourage transnational arms traffickers to circumvent the sanctions and thereby perpetuate the conflict. Trafficking in people is a fundamental violation of human rights and a direct threat to human security. Drug trafficking also undermines security, both in consumer states, where the competition for drug markets becomes violent, and in production states such as Colombia, Burma, and Afghanistan, where the proceeds fund insurgency and warlordism. In short, the space of flows has become a very dangerous space indeed.

Although the space of physical flows is particularly dangerous, the space of digital flows also has a dark side, as Ronald Deibert and Rafal Rohozinski highlight in Chapter 13. Yet, to describe cyberspace as a completely ungoverned space would be a mistake. The Internet has rudimentary forms of governance, including rules, regulations, and norms of behavior. To one degree or another, Internet service providers are regulated by governments, and there are informal bodies that determine the procedures and priorities that enable the Internet to continue functioning effectively. Nevertheless, for many reasons cyberspace can still be understood as a dangerous space. First, the Internet is a truly global construction and, as such, is inherently transnational in scope and operation. Territorial demarcations and borders have little relevance to the massive yet rapid flows of signals through cyberspace, yet most laws and regulations relating to the Internet are national, imperfect, and incomplete. It is not surprising, therefore, that the dark side of the Internet both mirrors and contributes to the dark side of globalization. Epidemiology is as relevant on the Internet as it is in a world concerned about the next pandemic of infectious disease. Tracing the origin, spread, and mutation of computer viruses and developing the software equivalent of vaccines and antibodies are critical to maintaining the efficiency and usefulness of the Internet. So, too, is education against the peculiar combination of spam and fraud that has become endemic in recent years. Early forms of hacking were the equivalent of teenage joy riding; computer crimes now include activities such as phishing, pharming, identity theft, and extortion, which are more akin to organized carjacking than ill-considered pranks. There is growing evidence not only that traditional organized crime is increasingly involved in various kinds of cyber crime, but also that illicit opportunities on the Internet have encouraged the emergence of novel forms of organized crime: virtual criminal organizations that meet all the criteria for categorization as organized crime apart from the use of violence and corruption.[36] Ironically, virtual criminal organizations do not need to resort to violence and corruption largely because of the high degree of anonymity the members enjoy in cyberspace.

The other space that is important to criminals and terrorists is the space of global financial transactions. The global financial system is sometimes described as an electronic commons "owned" by the people using it. Money is transmitted rapidly and easily from one node on the network to another with very limited oversight or regulation.[37] During the 1970s, competitive deregulation led to a race to the bottom that culminated in the 1980s and early

1990s in "the commercialization of state sovereignty."[38] As Bill Maurer notes in Chapter 11, tax havens were expanded into offshore financial centers and bank secrecy jurisdictions, which used their legal systems to provide "corporations and individuals with anonymity and shelter from their home governments."[39] Ronan Palan's comment that tax havens are "like the sovereign equivalent of parking lot proprietors: they could not care less about the business of their customers, only that they pay for parking their vehicles there" highlights the slippery slope that led jurisdictions to provide protection for the proceeds of crime or corruption.[40]

Concern over money laundering in the 1990s resulted in modest efforts to reestablish control mechanisms, while the international Financial Action Task Force's "name and shame" campaign forced the most egregious culprits to reconsider sheltering criminal proceeds. Such efforts intensified after the terrorist attacks of September 11, 2001, as the United States increasingly targeted terrorist finances. Even so, the global financial space remains only partially reregulated. Steps have been taken to negate laundering opportunities stemming from deregulation of global finance, and efforts to combat money laundering are constantly being strengthened. Yet, it is difficult to avoid the conclusion that the main effects have been to make money laundering more complicated and risky and to force launderers to become increasingly flexible and imaginative. The mechanisms change but flows of dirty money continue.

## Conclusion

This survey of dangerous spaces is far from exhaustive. It does suggest, though, that dangerous spaces present two inextricably related challenges: implosion and contagion. In many cases, even weak governance perpetuates itself without a major deterioration in the situation. In some instances, however, a tipping point will push a state from weak to failing or a city from stability into ferality. The problem is that such implosions are not self-contained; their consequences radiate outwards in ways that pose major challenges to security and stability. The challenge for governments, therefore, is to devise effective preventive strategies. The problem is that the very weakness of so many states that has facilitated the emergence of ungoverned, alternatively governed, and contested spaces also makes it impossible for states to reassert control. Perhaps the major conclusion to draw from this is that preventive strategies are unworkable and that the only alternative is mitigation. Yet it is not clear how consequences can be mitigated without also halting or even reversing globalization. Ironically, if globalization is thrown into reverse, the economic consequences are likely to push even more states into crisis or even collapse. In the final analysis, therefore, perhaps the best outcome is for alternative forms of governance to evolve in ways that enhance the protection and security they provide while reducing their predatory characteristics. If this happens, then state decline might be less of a threat and more of a blessing as people once again embrace forms of governance that are bottom-up rather than top-down, that are organic and local rather than imposed and distant, and that reflect indigenous impulses rather than alien domination. Unfortunately, such an outcome could all too easily prove elusive or even illusory.[41]

## Notes

1. James Rosenau, *Turbulence in World Politics* (Princeton, NJ: Princeton University Press, 1990).

2. Robert D. Kaplan, "The Coming Anarchy," *Atlantic Monthly* 273:2 (February 1994): 44–76.

3. Gregory Laurent Baudin O'Hayon, "Big Men, Godfathers and Zealots: Challenges to the State in the New Middle Ages," PhD diss., University of Pittsburgh, 2003; Philip Cerny, "Terrorism and the New Security Dilemma," *Naval War College Review* 58:1 (Winter 2005): 11–33; Mark Duffield, "Post-modern Conflict: Warlords, Post-adjustment States and Private Protection," *Civil Wars* 1:1 (Spring 1998): 65–102. See also Hedley Bull, *The Anarchical Society* (New York: Columbia University Press, 1977).

4. Duffield, "Post-modern Conflict," 70.

5. Cerny, "Terrorism and the New Security Dilemma."

6. Rosenau, *Turbulence in World Politics.*

7. Enrique Desmond Arias, *Drugs and Democracy in Rio de Janeiro* (Chapel Hill: University of North Carolina Press, 2006).

8. See Warwick E. Murray, *Geographies of Globalization* (London: Routledge, 2006).

9. This is derived from Castells's notion of social exclusion. See Manuel Castells, *End of Millennium* (Oxford: Blackwell, 1998), 72.

10. H. Brinton Milward and Jorg Raab, "Dark Networks as Organizational Problems: Elements of a Theory," *International Public Management Journal* 9:3 (2006): 333–60.

11. Peter Andreas, *Border Games: Policing the U.S.-Mexico Divide* (Ithaca, NY: Cornell University Press, 2000), 22.

12. Nikos Passas, "Globalization and Transnational Crime: Effects of Crimino-

genic Asymmetries," in Phil Williams and Dimitri Vlassis, eds., *Combating Transnational Crime* (London: Frank Cass, 2001), 22–56.

13. Charles Tilly, "War Making and the State as Organized Crime," in Peter B. Evans, Dietrich Rueschemeyer, and Theda Skocpol, eds., *Bringing the State Back In* (Cambridge: Cambridge University Press, 1985), 169–91, especially 170–71.

14. Robert H. Jackson, *Quasi-States: Sovereignty, International Relations, and the Third World* (Cambridge: Cambridge University Press, 1990).

15. Joel Migdal, *Strong Societies and Weak States* (Princeton, NJ: Princeton University Press, 1988).

16. This is a theme in Diego Gambetta, *The Sicilian Mafia: The Business of Private Protection* (Cambridge, MA: Harvard University Press, 1993), and has been applied to Russia by Federico Varese, *The Russian Mafia* (Oxford: Oxford University Press, 2001).

17. Robert I. Rotberg, ed., *State Failure and State Weakness in a Time of Terror* (Washington, DC: Brookings Institution, 2003), 5–6, 7, 9.

18. Dangerous spaces can also arise when a state deliberately creates differentiated internal spaces with discriminatory laws and policies such as South African townships during apartheid. The focus here for the most part, however, is dangerous spaces that arise primarily from weakness or neglect.

19. Richard Shultz and Andrea Dew, *Insurgents, Terrorists and Militias: The Warriors of Contemporary Combat* (New York: Columbia University Press, 2006).

20. William Reno, *Warlord Politics in African States* (Boulder, CO: Lynne Rienner, 1999).

21. For more on the power of tribe or clan legitimacy to trump the state, see Chapter 5 in this volume.

22. Shultz and Dew, *Insurgents, Terrorists and Militias*, 53.

23. Willem van Schendel, "Spaces of Engagement: How Borderlands, Illicit Flows, and Territorial States Interlock," in Willem van Schendel and Itty Abraham, eds., *Illicit Flows and Criminal Things: States, Borders, and the Other Side of Globalization* (Bloomington: Indiana University Press, 2005), 38–68, at 45.

24. Louise Shelley, "Growing Together: Ideological and Operational Linkages between Terrorist and Criminal Networks," Threat Convergence: New Pathways to Proliferation? Expert Series, Fund for Peace, Washington, D.C., 2006, available at http://www.fundforpeace.org/web/images/pdf/shelley.pdf.

25. Ian M. Cuthbertson, "Prisons and the Education of Terrorists," *World Policy Journal* 21:3 (Fall 2004): 15–22, at 17.

26. Frank Viviano, "French Prisons: Extremist Training Grounds," *San Francisco Chronicle*, 1 November 2001, A4, available at http://www.sfgate.com/cgi-bin/article .cgi?f=/c/a/2001/11/01/MN148693.DTL.

27. Tracy Wilkinson, "Spain Acts against Prisons Becoming Militant Hotbeds," *Los Angeles Times*, 2 November 2004, available at http://articles.latimes.com/2004/nov /02/world/fg-spain2.

28. Alain Grignard, quoted in Sebastian Rotella, "Jihad's Unlikely Alliance," *Los Angeles Times*, 23 May 2004, A1.

29. Richard Norton, "Feral Cities," *Naval War College Review* 56:4 (Autumn 2003): 97–106.

30. UN-Habitat, *Urbanization: Facts and Figures,* available at http://www.unhabitat .org/mediacentre/documents/backgrounder5.doc.

31. UN-Habitat, *State of the World's Cities 2006/7* (London: Earthscan, 2006), 19, 11.

32. See Thomas Homer-Dixon, *The Ingenuity Gap* (New York: Random House, 2000).

33. Thomas Homer-Dixon, "Standing Room Only," *Toronto Globe and Mail*, 9 March 2002, A17 (print edition). Also available as "Why Population Growth Still Matters," at http://www.homerdixon.com/download/why_population_growth.pdf.

34. Lloyd Axworthy, Arthur L. Fallick, and Kelly Ross, *The Secure City: Protecting Our Cities from Terrorist, Environmental, Other Threats in the 21st Century,* report by the Liu Institute for Global Issues, University of British Columbia, 31 March 2004, p. 14, available at http://www.ligi.ubc.ca/?p2=/modules/liu/publications/view .jsp&id=60.

35. Marc Levinson, *The Box* (Princeton, NJ: Princeton University Press, 2006), 7.

36. David Bonasso and Douglas Brozick, "Virtual Organized Crime," paper presented to class on Transnational Organized Crime, Graduate School of Public and International Affairs, University of Pittsburgh, Spring 2006.

37. Joel Kurtzman, *The Death of Money* (New York: Simon and Schuster, 1993), 92.

38. Ronen Palan, "Tax Havens and the Commercialization of State Sovereignty," *International Organization* 56:1 (2002): 151–76.

39. Ibid., 151.

40. Ibid.

41. Phil Williams, *From the New Middle Ages to a New Dark Age: The Decline of the State and United States Strategy*, Strategic Studies Institute, U.S. Army War College, 2008.

PART II

ALTERNATIVE SOCIAL
GOVERNANCE ON THE MARGINS
OF TERRITORIAL SOVEREIGNTY

# 3 Persistent Insurgencies and Warlords

*Who Is Nasty, Who Is Nice, and Why?*

## William Reno

Rebels in Sierra Leone's 1991–2002 war amputated the limbs of noncombatants, mined diamonds, and looted communities. Fighting in Somalia has continued in the absence of a central government since 1991. Nigeria's Delta region features kidnapping and the organized theft of oil. Warfare of this sort presents a frightening image of a "new age" of conflict. Journalist Robert Kaplan wrote of his visit to West Africa: "I saw young men everywhere—hordes of them. They were like loose molecules in a very unstable social fluid, a fluid that was on the verge of igniting," in a landscape of bandit-driven war with fighters devoid of civic concerns, unable to grasp the logics of fighting in organized formations or mobilizing popular support.[1]

Many deeper analyses of the relationship between state breakdown and war point to demographic and environmental pressures that "drive societies into a self-reinforcing spiral of violence, institutional dysfunction, and social fragmentation," leading to unchecked factional fighting.[2] Political entrepreneurs protect vulnerable communities on the basis of ethnic or sectarian affiliations, which further fragments the wider political landscape as "protectors" compete with one another to control illicit commercial networks to attract "new warriors" who fight for a personal share of this wealth. This establishes a "new retrograde set of social relationships . . . in which economics and violence are deeply intertwined within the shared framework of identity politics."[3]

The collapse of institutions that can control and discipline armed individuals leaves all groups vulnerable to attacks from competitors. No authority capable of enforcing agreements or imposing settlements remains, which makes preemptive attacks less risky than seeking cooperation.[4] This competitive situation favors the skills of violent and self-interested individuals. People who loot and exploit rackets attract fighters faster and in greater numbers than the ideologue or community organizer, who has to take time for political education. This leaves even those who lament this situation with little option but to flee or seek protection from one of these predatory commanders.[5] Given this imposing structure of incentives, such a state of affairs can be expected to produce conflicts that show little variation in the behavior and organization of fighters once the pattern becomes established.

While the rise of predatory and self-interested warlords typifies wars of state collapse, some communities manage to avoid the worst effects of this violence. Home guard militias in Sierra Leone drew fighters from the same social groups that produced marauding "new warriors." Local strongmen who previously demonstrated no hesitation to serve their own interests over those of the wider community instead used their roles in illicit diamond mining—the so-called conflict diamonds identified as a major factor in promoting wanton violence—as a tool to control their fighters. Northern Somalia, despite its violent prewar politics and its share of predatory politicians and armed gangs, produced peace and a working administration without significant outside aid. Nigeria's Niger Delta region shows variable patterns of violence, with some communities raising militias to protect them from ill-behaved "liberation fighters," state security forces, and avaricious local politicians.

These variations in the micro-politics of warfare in fragile or collapsing states point to two broad questions. First, how and why do some local community authorities implement their own versions of order? Put differently, why do young people with guns obey unarmed local authorities in some instances, while they follow their own interests at the expense of community order in seemingly similar circumstances? Second, why do resources, especially those from illicit commercial networks, fuel fragmentation and entice self-interested predators in so many cases, yet become tools for the more comprehensive control of violence on behalf of wider community interests in others? In short, why does governance—in this case, community control over armed youths—develop in some places that share all of the elements of risk that lead to ungoverned spaces?

This chapter stresses the social contexts in which resources are used during the course of these wars. It largely accepts the conclusions of many scholars that the circulation of resources in the absence of constraining state institutions generates incentives for violent predation among armed groups at the expense of wider community interests. But the important instances in which this does not happen offer a lens for understanding the ways in which local social relationships shape how resources are used. The following section explains how and why such a variation develops. The evidence is informed by the author's field research in Sierra Leone, the Niger Delta, and Somalia. The conclusion underlines the practical importance of this variation in the micropolitics of war in collapsing states.

## Explaining Variation

The collapse of formal state institutions produces an intense fragmentation of political and military power, just as many scholars predict. It is useful to start with a closer examination of this behavior to figure out exactly who participates in these opportunistic schemes, given that the bulk of the public affected by the resultant wars typically prefer peace to violence. This examination also helps to identify the mainsprings of the alternative strategies of political entrepreneurs who pursue order and cooperation.

Most political entrepreneurs who emerge in these conflicts played important roles in prewar politics. The design of these prewar networks of authority is critical in establishing linkages between people and resources; those that survive the transition to wars go on to shape fragmentation and predation, as they also shape cooperation and consolidation. Such networks influence how political entrepreneurs recruit and coordinate followers because they incorporate social capital or the capacity of individuals and organizations to use connections of reciprocity and exchange to accomplish their goals. Social capital played very important roles in prewar politics, especially in states that had very weak institutions. This weakness encouraged prewar rulers to co-opt the available social capital for their own uses. The different configurations of this social capital, and the ways in which it was incorporated into or marginalized from states that eventually collapsed, help to explain variations in the organization and exercise of wartime violence.

In very poor countries, patronage is not simply a "Tammany Hall"–style distribution of bureaucratic appointments and state assets to political supporters.[6] Tammany Hall patronage has two main features that distinguish it from patronage in collapsing states. First, it draws resources for distribution to clients from a productive economy that provides state revenues. Rather than controlling the economy itself to generate patronage resources, officials often find that they can do better if they make deals with private businesses. In this kind of system, businesses often manipulate the interests of state officials rather than the other way around. The second feature is that state institutions play key roles in distributing patronage to clients. These patronage systems are more hierarchical and less networked.[7]

In sub-Saharan Africa, many state treasuries are too small and bureaucracies too weak to buy the support of diverse groups of powerful people and communities. Moreover, intense efforts to turn bureaucracies into tools of patronage during the 1960s and 1970s played a big role in undermining national finances. For example, government revenues in the late 1980s in Sierra Leone stood at about 10 percent of gross domestic product, or about $80 million, a typical budget for a rural county in the American Midwest. During the five years before Congo's (formerly Zaire's) civil war broke out in 1996, state revenues amounted to between 3 and 4 percent of the measured economy. Overall, in the mid-1990s, the domestic revenue of thirteen of Africa's forty-six sub-Saharan states was less than 10 percent of their gross domestic product,[8] a "tax effort" comparable to England in the late seventeenth century and well short of the 38.4 percent average for contemporary members of the Organization for Economic Co-operation and Development.[9]

As a partial alternative to outright theft, rulers manipulate their own courts to shield clients from prosecution. Resources gathered in this fashion come from commerce that is considered illicit under the country's laws. But the prerogatives of sovereignty—giving foreigners privileged access to national territory, keeping deals secret, and supplying official documents such as passports, for instance—give a comparative advantage to rulers who tap illicit economies as a tool of patronage. The use of commercial channels overcomes the problem of controlling sub rosa transactions that are ostensibly beyond the reach of state institutions and brings them within the grasp of patronage-based political networks. It also brings people who are otherwise treated as outlaws, with all of their commercial connections and techniques, into the ruler's political network.

Much more than the Tammany Hall–style operation, this kind of patronage employs social capital that can be turned to commercial pursuits in illicit and often violent economies. It seeks alliances with power brokers who operate in realms beyond day-to-day politics and recruits people who are adept at operating in these clandestine commercial circuits. Often, the evolution of these patronage networks in collapsing states brings outlaws into the corridors of power. In other cases, the politically connected simply displace old-fashioned outlaws. The pursuit of political authority in this manner results in what some scholars call the "criminalization of the state" (from a perspective based on global norms of governance). Subversion of the rule of law supplements actors' uses of state office for private accumulation in clandestine economies and to dominate other people from whom they extract resources.[10] Rather than focus on personal enrichment, however, the present analysis emphasizes the use of this strategy to control people and their transactions that are otherwise beyond the reach of formal state agencies.

This kind of political network includes a much wider array of clients than does Tammany Hall–style patronage. People who hold no state office and even foreigners often occupy key positions. In the 1980s, Sierra Leoneans called an Afro-Lebanese businessman the "White President" in recognition of his indispensable role in commercial rackets that sustained presidential power.[11] A European businessman managed timber, mining, and arms-trafficking operations for Liberia's President Samuel K. Doe (1980–1990), then provided the same services to Doe's successor, Charles Taylor (1997–2003).[12] As foreign governments started directing aid to nongovernmental organizations (NGOs) in the 1980s, entrepreneurs, some of whom were also state officials, created fake NGOs to receive foreign aid.[13] Networks of this sort incorporate strongmen and local politicians who preside over local illicit rackets, often with the help of armed local youth, that they may use to challenge those who became their patrons or simply to weather poor economic conditions. Although some of these people are criminals from the perspective of legal norms, all bring valuable social capital to the network. Criminal gangs, armed youth, illicit market operators, private businesspeople, and social activists (or those running fake NGOs) bring particular sets of skills and connections. As the evidence below shows, these skills and connections influence who fights and how networks fragment.

As an indication of how power is exercised in this kind of system, members of these networks often occupy multiple roles that would raise questions of conflict of interest in states with stronger institutions. This author has encountered people who produce multiple business cards—as a businessperson, state official, and head of an NGO, for example. Family ties and shared hometown origins often emerge as significant network links. Less obvious connections also appear. The U.S. East Coast, for example, became a crossroads for personal contacts and commercial activities that linked Liberian warlord Charles Taylor to overseas Liberians, U.S.-based organizations, and public relations services whose job was to sway U.S. officials in his favor, even as he fought a civil war in Liberia during the 1990s and supported the Revolutionary United Front (RUF) insurgency in Sierra Leone.[14] Niger Delta networks link religious fraternities and secondary school and university classmates, so that particular classes and professors at Nigeria's University of Port Harcourt, both intentionally and unintentionally, became network nodes at the elite level.[15] Overall, the broad social reach of these networks helps to blur the boundaries between the public and private realms. Public space diminishes as a political network displaces formal state institutions, while sprawling patronage networks dominate social space that previously was beyond the reach of political authorities in the capital.

The tendency of these networks to occupy social space previously out of reach of the state, such as in clandestine economies, may explain the dearth of mass-based insurgencies against such deeply corrupt governments. As the networks replace formal state institutions as the basis of authority, they occupy what Eric Wolf calls "fields of leverage," where people previously found resources to challenge their oppressors.[16] Ironically, the collapsing state's political network is surprisingly strong in its societal influence, even if it ultimately fails to prevent its own fragmentation.

This kind of authority often develops where rulers face threats of violent removal. A coup in Sierra Leone in January 1996 finally succeeded after three failed attempts had been beaten back during the previous two years. The civilian successor faced at least three attempts before his overthrow in May 1997, when he was removed in a joint rebel invasion and military revolt. The last ruler of a united Somalia came to power in a coup, faced several coup attempts and two major military revolts, the latter successful, and then made a failed attempt to fight his way back into power in 1991. Since gaining its independence in 1960, only four Nigerian presidents have come to office through peaceful constitutional means; the rest have come to power amidst violence.

The fragmentation of social patronage networks leads to war in collapsing states. The ruler's subordinates bring their own social capital to these networks, which they then supplement with the connections and resources they acquire through their association with the state. Insider deals, illicit rackets, and personal ties to overseas partners give them access to resources that they can convert into weapons and support for fighters when war breaks out. But as noted above, not every community experiences patronage politics in the same way. Degrees of proximity to centers of patronage shape prewar social relationships and determine which preexisting social relationships are destroyed, preserved, or strengthened and refashioned. Local strongmen who supported the losing sides in old political battles often attract the suspicion of the winners. In Somalia, for example, northern elites were largely forced out of power in the 1969 coup. Sierra Leone's 1967 coup left supporters of its target excluded or in subordinate positions in later networks. Parts of the Niger Delta backed the losing side in Nigeria's 1967–1970 civil war to the detriment of their later fortunes.

Many who failed to attain the good graces of rulers had to find their own ways to exploit illicit commercial opportunities and to shield them from the "official" rackets of the capital-based patronage network. This required that enterprising, and often greedy and violent, local operators deal with community leaders who commanded enough popular support that they could direct local people to conceal, and if necessary, fight to protect, these transactions. Often, this protection was found in customary practices such as vendetta and interclan mediation, and in religious institutions. Strongmen had to tie their fortunes to local social networks that placed a high value on trust, reciprocity, and social obligation. In return, they often were required to deliver benefits such as material wealth and protection to the communities and leaders who shielded them against the predators in the capital. Ultimately, these reciprocities in flows of resources bind political entrepreneurs to local community interests and later become the tools for controlling the behavior of fighters during wartime in ways that are quite different from the actions of those with strong ties to the capital.

The key to explaining variations in armed groups' behavior thus lies in mapping the direction and intensity of connections in these patronage networks. This chapter offers two propositions through which to generalize about the relationship between patronage political networks and the organization and behavior of armed groups during wartime. First, where capital city–based networks and "official" illicit economies are most established, communities face the greatest risks of fragmentation and intercommunal violence. These prewar networks and their wartime fragmentation ease the entry of political entrepreneurs with self-interested goals (warlords) or new agendas (for example, Islamic internationalists) from outside these areas. Second, where local elite groups occupy marginal positions in prewar capital city–based networks, they tend to establish practices and relationships that constrain political entrepreneurs during wartime. The mutual dependence of political entrepreneurs and local actors reduces risks of intracommunal violence, promotes the formation of protective armed groups, and shields informal and illicit economic resources from outsiders and aggressive local actors.

A key feature of these propositions is that the physical nature of resources and the personal motivations of individuals involved in conflict, whether fighters or commanders, do not necessarily differ to any great degree in wider conflicts. One finds greedy commanders, angry fighters, and clandestine economies across collapsing states. The cause of variation in the organization and behavior of armed groups in conflicts lies in how the social context of resource mobilization and uses of violence, particularly within pervasive prewar patronage networks, shapes the way people assert authority. Participants in these different social structures of patronage may be much alike in their personal desires, norms, and cultural backgrounds. The key difference lies in their communities' relationships to the elite networks of the prewar collapsing state.

## The Evidence

Variations in patterns of violence emerge in the wars of state collapse included in this study. In Sierra Leone, investigators found that RUF insurgents attacked one child (aged fourteen or younger) for every 3.89 adults attacked in the surveyed population. Community militias, organized primarily in the southern part of the country under the banner of the Civil Defense Forces (CDF), attacked one child for every 11.83 adult victims. This was more discriminating than Sierra Leone's army, whose attacks produced one child victim for every 9.14 adult victims.[17] These figures indicate the extent to which different armed groups either were inclined to attack or were unable to prevent fighters from attacking people who clearly were civilians. This author observed similar patterns in Nigeria's Niger Delta in the course of field research. The most violence-prone communities tend to be those whose local officials and traditional leaders live in the region's commercial and administrative capital. Armed groups in these communities have a considerably greater tendency to clash with other armed groups and to attack members of their own communities. Armed youth in communities that have resident chiefs, especially chiefs with less business in the regional capital, appear to be more disciplined in their uses of violence and are more consistent in applying it against outsiders and state security services.[18]

There does not seem to be a great difference in the social origins of fighters or in the opportunities to loot resources within wider wars. Yet in Sierra Leone, as CDF and RUF fighters mined alluvial diamonds, the former were considerably less prone to attack rival miners or local communities. Militias throughout the Niger Delta have opportunities to kidnap foreigners and to extort money from foreign oil companies through threats against oilfield infrastructure, but not all do. Moreover, the Niger Delta provides instances in which local fighters preyed upon their home communities and then turned into protectors of those same communities. But in a closer look, one finds showdowns between prewar insider elite groups and political outsiders. Among the latter, local institutions of governance rather than resources and relationships from old patronage networks become primary instruments for mobilizing and controlling fighters. The careers of key individual wartime leaders highlight their social relationships and access to resources for mobilizing fighters; these careers also illustrate links between the micro-politics of warfare in collapsing states and the two broad propositions above.

### The Liberia–Sierra Leone–Côte d'Ivoire Nexus

The apparent uninterest of Sierra Leone's RUF in the welfare of the communities from which it drew fighters is puzzling at first glance. It is the group's seeming irrationality that attracted Robert Kaplan's concern about volatile "loose molecules." Moreover, Foday Sankoh, the RUF's leader, was no political insider, which would seem to violate the propositions above. Born in 1933, he was fifty-eight years old when the war began in 1991. He had joined the colonial army in 1956, rose to the rank of corporal, and then went to work at the government-run television station. After a 1971 coup attempt, Sankoh was judged to have been too friendly to the coup plotters when they appeared at the television station and was arrested. After his release from prison, Sankoh was remembered by his neighbor as a "strange, funny man." Others recall Sankoh flying into rages and threatening vendettas, while local student activists found him to be "undisciplined" and erratic.[19]

While Sankoh was no Sierra Leone insider, his connections to Charles Taylor put him in direct contact with Liberia's extensive patronage networks. Taylor also started as a critic of government. While studying in the United States, he staged a protest of Liberian President William Tolbert's

1979 visit to New York. Taylor and his associates occupied Liberia's United Nations mission and jeered the president. Rather than pressing charges, Tolbert invited Taylor, who had earned his degree from a college in Massachusetts, to return to Liberia and take up a position in government. Virtually upon his arrival in Monrovia, coup leaders murdered President Tolbert and replaced him with Sergeant Samuel K. Doe. But fortunately for Taylor, one of his friends, Thomas Quiwonkpa, was among the coup leaders. Taylor got his government position after all and became head of the Liberian government's chief procurement arm, a plum source of opportunities for skimming contracts and demanding bribes from suppliers. These commercial and personal connections proved invaluable to him when he launched the invasion of the National Patriotic Front for Liberia (NPFL) into Liberia from across the Côte d'Ivoire border in 1989.

Taylor fell out of favor with Doe when Quiwonkpa led a failed coup attempt in 1985. Taylor headed to Libya, where he met the disaffected Sankoh, who helped him search for partners and a place from which to launch an attack on Doe's regime. Taylor gained the support of the president of Côte d'Ivoire, Félix Houphouët-Boigny, who nursed his own grudge after Doe's coup plotters killed his son-in-law, the son of the murdered Liberian president. Taylor also had the benefit of his friendship with an exiled official from Tolbert's administration, who was married to Tolbert's daughter and was a friend of Houphouët-Boigny. To make matters even more interesting, Houphouët-Boigny's daughter, widow of the murdered son of the murdered Liberian president, later married Blaise Compaore, who was commander of Burkina Faso's army until he became president of Burkina Faso in 1987 after killing his boss . . . and so on. Thus it comes as no surprise that Compaore became a major supplier of arms and fighters to Taylor's NPFL and Sankoh's RUF.[20]

Taylor and Sankoh circulated in the same groups of West African dissidents, apparently meeting in Burkina Faso and Libya. Sankoh agreed to gather a Sierra Leonean contingent to help Taylor overthrow President Doe in Liberia. In return, Taylor would help Sankoh's group invade Sierra Leone and install Sankoh as president. Sankoh appeared to have gotten a good deal, as Taylor's NPFL took control over most of Liberia by the middle of 1990 and welcomed Doe's former business partners, including some foreigners, to join him.[21] According to United Nations investigators in 2000, a Dutch businessman was "responsible for the logistical aspects of many of the arms deals involved in arms trafficking between Liberia and Sierra Leone," in return for concessions in mining and timber operations.[22] By then, Taylor commanded a sprawling patronage network as the basis of his authority. In 2001 and 2002, for example, he personally controlled about $200 million in annual proceeds from business operations, between two and three times the entire government budget,[23] and used his official position to decree for himself "sole power to execute, negotiate and conclude all commercial contracts or agreements with any foreign or domestic investor for the exploitation of the strategic commodities of the Republic of Liberia."[24]

### Sierra Leone's Patronage Systems

Connections to Taylor's network and its resources insulated Sankoh's RUF from the need to negotiate with local populations for support. In any event, Sankoh did not appear to have the temperament to build a base of community support in Sierra Leone. Thus the RUF attracted a different kind of fighter. Krijn Peters found in interviews of ex-combatants that many RUF members were rural youth who had been abused by local chiefs, the main administrative authorities in rural Sierra Leone. He contrasted these with CDF recruits: "Although coming from rural communities, similar in many ways to RUF conscripts, and army irregulars, most of the Kamajor [CDF] youth fighters were not alienated from their villages and differed greatly from the footloose RUF. . . . They were to a large extent under the control of the village or town chiefs, who were playing a key role in recruitment."[25]

This contrast points again to the key role of the standing of local politicians in their communities and in the wider national system of political patronage. Areas of concentrated RUF mining activity and violence in Sierra Leone had previously been dominated by the post-1967 ruling party.[26] The president, Siaka Stevens, had installed his political supporters from among local political bosses and business leaders in an "official" illicit diamond mining economy. Some prospered when they were invited to join the president's ventures with foreign diamond traders and commercial rackets, including "official smuggling" in violation of increasingly draconian economic requirements of the International Monetary Fund. Freed from the social obligations that some of them once owed to local youth, these local bosses recruited miners and political muscle from around the country, youth who "were prepared to support any 'big man'" who gave them access to some of the material benefits of their political standing.[27] The RUF, appearing on the scene after 1991, looked to these youth like a new patron that offered an attractive opportunity for upward mobility. This RUF core continued to recruit prewar gangs and politicians' militias, consisting of "urban disenchanted youth . . . significantly removed from the civilian population. Their aberrant recreational pursuit of smoking marijuana and their disregard for traditional authority structures made them appear as 'social deviants' to others in the community"[28]

This pattern of recruitment contrasted with CDF practice and illustrates the second proposition, that marginality to prewar networks is linked to local success in promoting order and control over armed youth. CDF support came mostly from areas that produced Sierra Leone's first ruling party before the 1967 coup. This region then received the brunt of the new regime's violence, especially in the Kenema diamond mining areas, where some politicians and local leaders refused to back the new rulers. According to historian Alpha Lavalie, these leaders organized antiregime militias based on a male initiation society prevalent among the region's dominant ethnic group.[29] Members included local chiefs who had been the targets of regime violence before the war and who mobilized religious authorities to initiate young men into the militia. (Lavalie, who became a leader of the Eastern Regional Defense Committee militia in Kenema for about a year before he was killed by a landmine in 1993, was acutely sensitive to the social context in which violence was used.)

This religious organization and the militias that later joined it incorporated methods to manage the youth who had migrated to the Kenema area. Since local chiefs were on the margins of prewar capital-based patronage networks, they had to shield their involvement in illicit diamond mining from the regime. They mobilized youth, including some from other parts of the country and even abroad, to operate and protect their mines. Local leaders had to rely on their customary powers as "landlords" to grant to newcomers the status of a protected client,[30] as they had no access to the state security services used by their well-connected counterparts to the north. This relationship involved reciprocities of protection, each guaranteeing the safety of the other from the predations of the higher authorities. Once the RUF and other marauders began to plague the region, these local social institutions underpinned community defense. Their authority extended over people who were not originally from those areas, owing to the fact that the outsiders had to seek local patrons who were themselves vulnerable to threats from politicians in the capital.

## The Niger Delta

Predatory militias with close ties to prewar patronage networks also appear in Nigeria's Niger Delta region. Mujahid Dokubo Asari, head of the Niger Delta Peoples' Volunteer Force (NDPVF), was a close associate of Diepreye

Alamieyeseigha, governor of Bayelsa State, who was arrested in London on 15 October 2005 in possession of one million pounds sterling in laundered funds. The governor's abrupt return to Nigeria (disguised in women's clothes) resulted in his arrest on corruption charges. Some believe that the NDPVF was responsible for the robbery of a bank and the killing of eight police officers in Port Harcourt in January 2006.[31] Despite their patron's legal troubles, however, Asari and the NDPVF supported him in hopes of a favorable outcome in the 2007 election, in which Alamieyeseigha backed the unsuccessful Vice President Atiku Abubakar. Asari also was arrested on treason charges in November 2005. Local suspicions held that the two strongmen were targeted because they opposed President Olusegun Obasanjo's bid to stand for a third term. Opposition continued through new groups that, along with those linked to the governor of Delta State, are suspected of involvement in the theft of oil from foreign-controlled pipelines. As of 2006, foreign firms estimated losses of one hundred thousand barrels per day, or more than $200 million per month.[32] A spokesman for the Movement for the Emancipation of the Niger Delta, which is responsible for kidnapping foreign oil workers, demanded the release of Asari and Alamieyeseigha.[33]

Their ties to politicians also expose these militias to political faction strains. Governor Alamieyeseigha's palace guard, the Bayelsa Volunteers, "provided employment for youths who had hitherto been engaged in piracy and kidnap of oil workers." Once the governor had been arrested, the group's commander (who also was the deputy superintendent of police) switched his support to the new governor, engaging in battles with their old associates that included exchanges of gunfire and the dynamiting of the commander's home.[34]

In contrast, a few Delta communities have managed to insulate themselves from this predatory style of violence. Unlike Sierra Leone, few communities in the Delta are truly peripheral to Nigeria's sprawling networks of political patronage. Instead, the strongest cases of local control over fighters appear in places where customary social institutions have remained insulated through other means. In one instance, this manifested as female-led NGOs working for "good governance." The descendants of female traders and religious leaders who played prominent roles in the 1929 anticolonial Women's War, these contemporary NGO leaders complain of marginalization in Nigeria's male-dominated political system; at the same time, they manage to retain authority in the region's traditional Egbesu religious institutions. Like CDF's connections to initiation ceremonies and customary "landlord-tenant" reciprocities in Sierra Leone, Egbesu provides these women (in alliance with other local leaders) with the social authority and resources to mobilize, arm, and discipline young men to protect their communities.[35]

## Somalia's Civil War

Patterns of violence in Somalia's war illustrate the two core propositions as well. Areas in the south that have been focal points of violence since 1991 were previously favored by President Siad Barre's patronage network. This patronage benefited from the nearly $4 billion (in 2008 dollars) in foreign aid that Mogadishu received over a decade beginning in the late 1970s.[36] Much of the food and development aid from overseas was distributed to pro-Barre communities and militias.[37] Donor-supported commercial farming and irrigation projects in the south, and the externally financed "privatization" of state-run agricultural projects, ended up in the hands of key pro-Barre politicians.[38] As the land was distributed to powerful regime supporters, local people were turned into hired labor. This disrupted the customary role local authorities played in mediating conflicts over resources and weakened their control over local youth. The appearance of wage labor opportunities, tied to political support for men who did not come from the region, gave enterprising young men opportunities to ignore what some saw as onerous burdens of community expectations concerning their behavior.[39]

These agriculture projects became bases of operations for regime supporters and their militias. Young men from urban areas were drawn to the region to enjoy the more direct support of their patrons. Both proregime and antiregime militia leaders set up plantations to employ followers who were later organized to fight in the 1990s. One practical benefit of these projects for these strongmen lay in their location. As young supporters arrived from other parts of the country, they shed the social strictures that governed their behavior in their home communities. Sanctions for the misuse of violence, such as a vendetta against family members if the crime was committed in their home communities, were much harder to apply against these followers. Thus, young men who were removed from their home communities generally would be more willing to use violence on behalf of their patrons, with the assurance that they would not suffer the usual social consequences for it.

The northern areas faced a different situation. As centers of support for the political elite before the 1969 military coup, and the source of many leaders of an anti-Barre insurgency in the late 1970s, this region received little largesse from the capital-based establishment. Local elites faced difficulties penetrating Barre's political network and overcoming his outright hostility toward the region. In May 1984, Barre's supporters used their militias to aggravate local conflicts over grazing rights, which resulted in fighting that killed more than five hundred people. A visitor to the region wrote, "Male Ogadeeni refugees [who were allied with Barre's political networks] have been encouraged to take over the remains of Issaq [northerner] shops and houses that are now ghost towns."[40]

Barre also invited his supporters to join a significant "official" illicit economy that he helped to create through the passage of draconian economic policies in the 1980s. His willingness to selectively protect lawbreakers made some of his political allies very rich, while it also undermined a heretofore thriving informal and clandestine international trade in the north. This forced northerners to find alternative ways to protect their clandestine trades, which to their eyes were perfectly legitimate. Moreover, they had to manage the transfer of remittances of relatives who worked overseas—several hundreds of thousands out of a northern population of about two million—outside of the very unfavorable formal currency exchange structure. Overall, this involved an annual income of several hundred million dollars.[41] These constraints forced local businesses to turn to customary authorities such as clan leaders to guarantee their transactions. In contrast to the south, this strengthened customary institutions that later played key roles in controlling and disciplining armed youth.

This discipline appeared in the Somali National Movement (SNM), the insurgency that drew a lot of anti-Barre northerners into its ranks. It was suddenly thrown out of its Ethiopian base and forced to return to Somalia in 1988 when Ethiopian President Mengistu Haile Mariam came to an agreement with Barre. Forced to confront Barre's security forces and army, and in desperate need of finances, the SNM turned to both clan elders and the business leaders who had the backing of these authorities. The inclusion of customary authorities as mediators in the commercial and political affairs of the SNM has had a large effect on northern society: financial backers have greater confidence that their assets will not be confiscated by the political authorities and are thus more willing to invest; elders are included in the post-1991 political establishment as members of the (unrecognized) Republic of Somaliland's *Guurti*, or House of Elders; and the control of remittances limited political entrepreneurs' access to resources. The economists Paul Collier and Anke Hoeffler find that diaspora remittances are a risk factor in promoting violence and factionalization in conflicts.[42] But remittances (like "conflict diamonds" in Sierra Leone) can also contribute to order, provided that these resources are channeled through networks that were insulated from the old prewar patronage network.

Overall, the cases of Liberia, Sierra Leone, Nigeria, and Somalia illustrate the link between patterns of wartime violence and local elites' positions in prewar patronage networks. They offer a serious view of the informal relationships and practices that shape how people control and use resources. This analysis of wartime violence reflects how politics worked in these places well before fighting began: the tendency of political entrepreneurs to operate outside formal state institutions, and patronage's networked, as opposed to hierarchical, quality. Here is where the sinews of power and the key actors are found.

## Conclusion: The Practical Significance of Variation

These examples of variation in the behavior of armed groups illustrate the importance of preconflict political ties, particularly in the realm of the distribution of patronage resources, in shaping these outcomes. They show how close ties to political patronage networks have enabled local strongmen to "privatize" their access to resources in the sense of gaining personal control over them once the capital-based patronage network begins to fragment. Their direct control over resources enables these strongmen to finance and field their own armed groups without much regard for local community interests or standards of behavior for armed youth. In contrast, those who were more marginal to capital-based patronage networks already had long experience in negotiating with local notables to help them hide and protect their dealings from rivals in the capital and from prosecution by state security services. These ties, based upon recognition of reciprocities in exchange for cooperation, evolve in wartime as constraints on leaders of armed groups. While constraining some from the capacity to react quickly to threats or opportunities to expand their power elsewhere in the conflict zone, these ties offer at least the prospect that such armed groups can acquire popular support as protectors of local order. A key observation of this analysis is that armed groups often follow this seemingly virtuous path as a result of constraints on their behavior more than from a plan.

There are good practical reasons to care about this micro-politics of wars in collapsing states. These wars fit Martin van Creveld's generalization that intervention forces that "beat down the weak" will lose the support of bystanders.[43] When fighting fragmented groups, it is hard to distinguish enemies from the often well-armed surrounding population. Local noncombatants get hit while weak adversaries attack "collaborators" and undermine the efforts of peacekeepers to provide security and services.[44] This is especially true where real lines of authority do not correspond to formal titles and offices. Moreover, as the evidence above shows, simple labels such as "illicit economies" or even "conflict diamonds" are not always accurate guidelines for determining what activities and which armed groups promote order and what activities fuel predation and disruption.

One option would be to ignore these wars. But in the wake of the Al-Qa'ida attacks on New York and Washington, D.C., on September 11, 2001, U.S. President George W. Bush declared: "The events of September 11, 2001, taught us that weak states, like Afghanistan, can pose as great a danger to our national interests as strong states . . . poverty, weak institutions, and corruption can make weak states vulnerable to terrorist networks and drug cartels within their borders."[45] Britain's Foreign Secretary Jack Straw connected collapsing states to a growing security threat: "After the mass murder in the heart of Manhattan, no one can doubt that a primary threat to our security is now posed by groups acting outside formal states, or from places where no state functions at all. It is no longer possible to ignore misgoverned parts of a world without borders, where chaos is a potential neighbour anywhere from Africa to Afghanistan."[46]

These and other events highlight the need to understand what these wars are all about, who fights them, and why. Figuring out who will fight to maintain or establish local order, versus those who undermine it, involves identifying and understanding the complex networks of clan, family, and illicit markets that are not visible to satellites or unmanned spy planes. This information can be difficult to find as many of the key players, including ones that turn out to share outsiders' interests in stability, do not speak English. Moreover, quite a few may have committed serious human rights violations, although they will argue, sometimes convincingly, that they acted only to protect their communities. Some do not welcome visitors, especially official ones, or they try to manipulate their visitors, protesting that they help out in the war on terror (for example, the Alliance for the Restoration of Peace and Counter-Terrorism in Somalia) in hopes of getting outside assistance for their internal struggle for power. Overall, these different groups demonstrate the diversity of organizations that can provide local stability and governance. A flexible approach to them would aid the goal of supporting those who contribute to locally legitimate order rather than undermine it.

## Notes

1. Robert Kaplan, *The Coming Anarchy* (New York: Random House, 2000), 5.

2. Thomas Homer-Dixon, *Environment, Scarcity, and Violence* (Princeton, NJ: Princeton University Press, 1999), 5.

3. Mary Kaldor, *New & Old Wars: Organized Violence in a Global Era* (Stanford, CA: Stanford University Press, 1999), 106–7.

4. Rui de Figueiredo Jr. and Barry Weingast, "The Rationality of Fear: Political Opportunism and Ethnic Conflict," in Barbara Walter and Jack Snyder, eds., *Civil Wars, Insecurity, and Intervention* (New York: Columbia University Press, 1999), 261–302.

5. Jeremy Weinstein, *Inside Rebellion: The Politics of Insurgent Violence* (New York: Cambridge University Press, 2007).

6. Tammany Hall refers to the period between 1854 and 1934 when New York City and state politics were dominated by a patronage machine that comprised the Democratic Party, the mayor's office, and a fraternal organization known as the Society of St. Tammany. Its most notorious leader was William Marcy "Boss" Tweed, who manipulated elections and embezzled tens of millions in public dollars during his tenure as party boss. See David Wiles, "'Boss Tweed' and the Tammany Hall Machine," http://www.albany.edu/~dkw42/tweed.html.

7. William Riordan, *Plunkitt of Tammany Hall: A Series of Very Plain Talks on Very Practical Politics* (New York: Signet Classics, 1995).

8. Janet Stotsky and Asegedech Woldemariam, "Tax Effort in Sub-Saharan Africa," International Monetary Fund, Washington, D.C., September 1997, 5–7.

9. John Brewer, *The Sinews of Power: War, Money and the English State, 1688–1783* (Cambridge, MA: Harvard University Press, 1988), 30.

10. Jean-François Bayart, Stephen Ellis, and Béatrice Hibou, *The Criminalization of the State in Africa* (Oxford: James Currey, 1999); Geoffrey Wood, "Business and Politics in a Criminal State: The Example of Equatorial Guinea," *African Affairs* 103:413 (2004): 547–67.

11. Author's observations in Sierra Leone from 1989. See also "Sierra Leone: Rape," *Africa Confidential* 25:24 (28 November 1984): 1–4.

12. Stephen Ellis, *Mask of Anarchy: The Destruction of Liberia and the Religious Dimension of an African Civil War* (New York: New York University Press, 1999), 170.

13. Christine Messiant, "The Eduardo Dos Santos Foundation; or, How Angola's Regime is Taking over Civil Society," *African Affairs* 100 (2001): 287–309.

14. Taylor attended university in Boston in the 1970s and returned to the U.S. East Coast in the 1980s during his exile from Liberia. National Patriotic Front for Liberia (NPFL) overseas support groups and an NPFL-supported "foreign ministry" built upon these networks; documents in author's possession.

15. Author's observations during field research, 2005; Yomi Oruwari, "Youth in Urban Violence in Nigeria: A Case Study of Urban Gangs from Port Harcourt," Institute of International Studies, University of California, Berkeley, 2006, 5–7.

16. Eric Wolf, *Peasant Wars of the Twentieth Century* (Norman: University of Oklahoma Press, 1999), 290.

17. "Report of the Truth Commission: Summary of Findings," Sierra Leone Truth Commission, Freetown, October 2004, 19.

18. Author's interviews with officials and activists in the Akassa region of the Niger Delta, May–June 2005.

19. Lansana Gberie, *A Dirty War in West Africa: The RUF and the Destruction of Sierra Leone* (London: Hurst, 2005), 47–48.

20. For details, see General Prince Yomi Johnson, *The Rise & Fall of President Samuel K. Doe* (Lagos: Soma Associates, 2003), 38–49. Yomi Johnson started out as a Liberian army officer, joined Taylor, became the leader of his own faction, reinvented himself as an evangelical preacher, and then became a member of Liberia's Senate.

21. The author has collected correspondence between Taylor's NPFL and foreign businesses.

22. United Nations Security Council, "Report of the Panel of Experts Appointed Pursuant to Security Council Resolution 1306 (2000), Paragraph 19, in Relation to Sierra Leone," United Nations, New York, December 2000, 36.

23. United Nations Security Council, "Report of the Panel of Experts Appointed Pursuant to Security Council Resolution 1395 (2002), Paragraph 4, in Relation to Liberia," United Nations, New York, 11 April 2002, 11.

24. "Annex 1: Strategic Commodities Act: An Act to Designate Certain Natural Resources, Mineral, Cultural and Historical Items as Strategic Commodities," Liberian House of Representatives, Monrovia, 2000, n.p.

25. Krijn Peters, "Re-Examining Voluntarism: Youth Combatants in Sierra Leone," Institute for Strategic Studies, Pretoria, South Africa, 2004, 10.

26. Sierra Leone's first peaceful election, in 1967, was abruptly undone by a military coup. Civilian rule, if not democracy, was restored in 1968 under the All People's Congress Party, which ruled for most of the next three decades. Humphrey J. Fisher, "Elections and Coups in Sierra Leone, 1967," *Journal of Modern African Studies* 7:4 (1969): 611–36.

27. Roger Tangri, "Conflict and Violence in Contemporary Sierra Leone Chiefdoms," *Journal of Modern African Studies* 14:2 (June 1976): 314.

28. Patrick Muana, "The Kamajoi Militia: Civil War, Internal Displacement and the Politics of Counter-Insurgency," *Africa Development* 22:3 (1997): 79.

29. Alpha Lavalie, "SLPP: A Study of the Political History of the Sierra Leone People's Party, with Particular Reference to the Period 1968–78," master's thesis, Department of History, University of Sierra Leone, 1983.

30. Vernon Dorjahn and Christopher Fyfe, "Landlord and Stranger: Change in Tenancy Relations in Sierra Leone," *Journal of African History* 3 (1962): 391–97.

31. "Mystery Kidnappers," *Africa Confidential* 47:3 (3 Feb 2006): 5–6.

32. "Showdown in the Delta," *Africa Confidential* 47:6 (17 March 2006): 1–2.

33. Lauren Ploch, "Nigeria: Current Issues," Congressional Research Service Report RL 33964, Washington, D.C., 2008, 17.

34. Anietie Ekong, "Under Siege," *The Week*, 12 December 2005, 12.

35. Author interviews and visits to Port Harcourt and environs in 2005 and 2006.

36. John Sommer, "Hope Restored? Humanitarian Aid in Somalia," Refugee Policy Group, Washington, D.C., 1994, 7.

37. Jonathan Tucker, "The Politics of Refugees in Somalia," *Horn of Africa* 5:3 (1984): 22.

38. Jamal Abdalla Mukarak, *From Bad Policy to Chaos in Somalia* (Westport, CT: Praeger, 1996), 126.

39. Michael Roth, "An Analysis of Land Tenure and Water Allocation Issues in the Shalambood Irrigation Zone, Somalia," University of Wisconsin Land Tenure Center, Madison, 1987.

40. I. M. Lewis, "The Ogaden and the Fragility of Somali Segmentary Nationalism," *Horn of Africa* 13 (1990): 59.

41. Vali Jamal, "Somalia: Understanding an Unconventional Economy," *Development & Change*, 19:2 (1988): 239.

42. Paul Collier and Anke Hoeffler, "Greed and Grievance in Civil War," Centre for Economic Policy Research, London, 2002.

43. Martin van Creveld, "Power in War," *Theoretical Inquiries in Law*, 7.1 (2006): 1.

44. Ibid., 6–7.

45. "The National Security Strategy of the United States of America," the White House, Washington, D.C., March 2006, http://www.strategicstudiesinstitute.army.mil/pdffiles/nss.pdf.

46. Jack Straw, "Order Out of Chaos: The Challenge of Failed States," in Mark Leonard, ed., *Re-Ordering the World: The Long-Term Implications of September 11* (London: Foreign Policy Centre, 2002), 98.

# 4 Non-state Actors and Failed States

*Lessons from Al-Qa'ida's Experiences in the Horn of Africa*

## Ken Menkhaus and Jacob N. Shapiro

The Horn of Africa has been an important area of operations for Al-Qa'ida and the jihadi movement since the early 1990s.[1] An East African Al-Qa'ida cell was established in Kenya in 1992 and was responsible for the terrorist attacks on U.S. embassies in Nairobi and Dar es Salaam in 1998. More recently, as the Somali jihadist movement Al-Shabaab has gained strength and the 2007–2008 Ethiopian military occupation of Somalia was portrayed as a Christian attack on a Muslim country, top Al-Qa'ida figures such as Ayman al-Zawahiri and Osama bin Laden have highlighted Somalia in their taped messages to supporters. In early 2007, Zawahiri called for attacks on Ethiopian forces in Somalia using "ambushes, mines, raids and martyrdom-seeking raids to devour them as the lions devour their prey."[2] Finally, the physical presence of foreign Al-Qa'ida advisors in Somalia in support of Al-Shabaab demonstrate that Al-Qa'ida is elevating Somalia as an item on the group's global agenda. The degree to which Al-Qa'ida has actually established a foothold in the region—and its longer-term objectives in Somalia and the Horn of Africa—remains the subject of significant debate among analysts and policymakers. Much of this debate has focused on the potential threat of terrorism in the region and the significance of the linkages between Al-Qa'ida and Al-Shabaab. Insufficient attention has been paid, however, to the operational challenges that Al-Qa'ida and other groups have faced when carrying out activities in the Horn. While Al-Qa'ida has been successful in weak states like Kenya, it has for years faced difficulties operating in failed states like Somalia.

To date, the details of terrorist activities in the Horn of Africa have been largely misunderstood. A number of analysts, for example, have argued that Al-Qa'ida has deep, longstanding ties to Islamic militants in Somalia and could draw on these ties to use Somalia as a staging ground for further attacks.[3] A closer look at the available evidence helps to provide a more nuanced portrait of Al-Qa'ida's experiences in Somalia and Kenya. It turns out that the links in the recent past were actually quite tenuous, at least as described in Al-Qa'ida's internal correspondence. Common assumptions about the Horn as an operational environment and base of support have been overstated. In particular, the anarchic conditions in Somalia that many believe serve Al-Qa'ida's purposes have turned out to be as challenging for Al-Qa'ida as for the Western organizations seeking to help the country.[4] Moreover, the radical Islamist movements in the region with which Al-Qai'da has sought to partner had, and continue to have, divergent agendas from those of Al-Qa'ida. In the 1990s, Somali Islamists were split over the use of political violence. By 2009, divisions within radical Islamist movements in Somalia over tactics, leadership, external linkages, and broader objectives meant that Al-Qa'ida operatives there have invariably been at odds with much of the movement. Most importantly, Somali hard-line movements have demonstrated a much greater commitment to a Somali nationalist platform and much less commitment to Al-Qa'ida's global jihadist agenda.

Within Somalia, a failed state allegedly ideal for terrorist organizations, Al-Qa'ida struggled to build a coalition during the 1990s. The group had little success forging alliances with local militias in Somalia, its involvement in attacks against Western forces in Somalia was tangential at best,[5] and its operatives were exposed to constant risk of detection and arrest by Western counterterrorism efforts.[6] Although Somalia provided occasional passage and temporary refuge to Al-Qa'ida operatives, the country's lawlessness and isolation, which many cite as ideal for Al-Qa'ida's efforts, were seen by the group itself as constraining its ability to create a secure base for operations.

By contrast, Al-Qa'ida has been relatively successful in Kenya. Kenyan counterterrorism efforts, supported by generous Western assistance, have until recently been ineffective. Al-Qa'ida operatives in Kenya moved freely into Somalia during the 1990s, conducted attacks against the U.S. embassy in 1998, and continued to launch attacks against Western targets as late as 2002. Extensive U.S. support to the Kenyan government to counter Al-Qa'ida's activities appears to have enjoyed some successes, most notably in improved capacity to patrol border areas. But those successes have come at a cost. They have increased the sense of alienation and anti-Americanism within the country's minority Muslim community, which feels it is being unfairly targeted by security measures meted out by the predominantly Christian, highlander security sector in Kenya. While only a tiny fraction of the Kenyan Muslim population actively supports terrorist activities, angry and marginalized Muslim communities are much more likely to provide "passive support" for Al-Qa'ida cells operating in their midst by not alerting authorities to suspicious activities. Moreover, the wider Kenyan population, Christian and Muslim alike, does not place as much priority on counter-terrorism as does the United States, seeing it primarily as a problem for the United States. For the Kenyan government, its stance against terrorism is partly a function of its desire to attract substantial Western military assistance and increase its leverage with Western donors. Neighboring Ethiopia has been even more adept at emphasizing its strategic partnership role in counterterrorism to garner Western aid and mute Western criticism of its increasingly harsh, authoritarian rule.

From 1992 to 2006, evidence from the Horn of Africa clearly demonstrated that the region's weak states, not its failed ones, provided the greatest potential terrorism threat. In weak states, groups like Al-Qa'ida found a target-rich environment where they were protected from Western counterterrorism efforts and yet were not significantly interdicted by the state's corrupt law enforcement and intelligence apparatus. Meanwhile, in failed states like Somalia, Al-Qa'ida suffered from logistical constraints, a hostile set of local political actors, and relatively unrestricted Western counterterrorism efforts.

Dramatic changes in Somalia since 2006—including the rise and fall of the Islamic Courts Union, the Ethiopian military occupation, the ensuing armed insurgency, and the ascent of a powerful coalition of hard-line Islamist militias, some with direct links to Al-Qa'ida—may be altering this equation. As of 2009, foreign Al-Qa'ida advisors are actively involved in support of Al-Shabaab inside southern Somalia. It is impossible to predict whether Al-Shabaab and its Islamist allies will consolidate control over Somalia, and whether in that event Al-Qa'ida will use Somalia as a significant safe haven. If this scenario does occur, however, it does not challenge the main thrust of this chapter. Instead, it reminds us of the four very distinct political settings that Al-Qa'ida must navigate: (1) weak states that are unwilling or unable to police against Al-Qa'ida, (2) strong states with the commitment to police against terrorist activities, (3) collapsed or failed states that present large areas of ungoverned space, and (4) allied states, or polities in which a local ally of Al-Qa'ida is able to exercise direct control over some or all of the country (such as the Taliban in pre-2002 Afghanistan). Both weak states and allied states, we argue, constitute enabling environments for Al-Qa'ida, though in very different ways. By contrast, failed states do not.

The remainder of this chapter fleshes out these points as follows. First we discuss why failed states are a relatively poor haven for terrorists. Then we describe the details of Al-Qa'ida's mission in Somalia and examine why Al-Qa'ida, like Western analysts, thought that failed states such as Somalia would be useful to its plans for global jihad. Next we focus on why Al-Qa'ida's assumptions were wrong and how its operations during the 1990s in Somalia failed. Finally, we conclude with a series of policy recommendations.

## Failed States: An Unsafe Haven for Terrorists

Do failed states actually serve as an effective safe haven for terrorists? There are a number of reasons to suspect not. In the first place, areas without functioning state institutions do not provide safety for their residents. This security vacuum creates problems for the terrorists, too.[7] As a result, terrorist strategists do not think such spaces are very useful.[8] Two documents are instructive on this point. The first, from Somalia, identifies a five-point strategy to unite Somali forces and create an Islamic national front.[9] The authors argue for (1) expulsion of the foreign international presence, (2) rebuilding of state institutions, (3) establishment of domestic security, (4) comprehensive national reconciliation, and (5) economic reform and combating of famine. This approach parallels that of a June 2005 Zawahiri letter addressed to Abu Musab al-Zarqawi in Iraq.[10] In that letter, Zawahiri argues that jihad in Iraq should proceed incrementally, according to the following phases: (1) expel the Americans from Iraq; (2) establish an Islamic authority or emirate, then develop it and support it; and (3) extend the jihad wave to the secular countries neighboring Iraq.

Notice that what is important to these thinkers is not the existence of a security vacuum but what comes next: establishing functioning state institutions under jihadi control.[11] What made Afghanistan so useful to Al-Qa'ida from 1995 onward was not an absence of state institutions, but the fact that Al-Qa'ida could operate under the protection of a sovereign state, shielding its infrastructure from potential attack by Western forces. Operating in a security vacuum, where training camps and the like can be more readily attacked directly by the United States and indirectly by local allies, is much less attractive.[12] In fact, existing security vacuums have not proved to be viable bases for exporting attacks abroad. No major international attacks have been supported out of Afghanistan, Iraq, or Somalia since the U.S. military operations began in 2001. From this perspective, policymakers should be concerned with ungoverned spaces only so far as they are allowing terrorists to operate openly and at reasonable expense.

The Horn of Africa does not afford terrorists such benefits. Al-Qa'ida and like-minded groups have had four problems operating there. The first was that the lack of government-enforced order in many areas imposed what was effectively a tax on all operations. This tax came in two forms: the need to provide security against local bandits,[13] and the increased cost of getting personnel and resources into poorly governed areas.[14] The second problem was the unreliability of local allies.[15] Not only were Somali Islamists and would-be allies of Al-Qa'ida frustratingly clannish and internally divided, they also embraced a much more local, rather than global, set of objectives. The third problem was that the better an area was for training, the more remote and sparsely populated it was and thus the harder for basic sustenance needs to be met.[16] The final problem was the challenge of getting fiscal resources in place. Financial services in the region were weak during the early to mid-1990s, and groups did not seem able to effectively use the emerging *hawala* system of remittances, which in subsequent years came to provide key financial services in weakly governed areas of the Horn.

In fact, these problems were so bad that after then–Al-Qa'ida operations chief Mohammed Atef (also known as Abu Hafs) visited the training camps that his personnel had established in Lu'uq, Somalia, he wrote back to his superiors and suggested: "We found out that it is difficult to do this in the areas that we visited because of dangers pertaining to security. This is why it is preferred that the courses be done by you in Khartoum. As a result this will save us transportation expenses and others."[17] Through 2006 there was little reason to think this region had become any more hospitable to jihadis since Abu Hafs rendered his judgment.[18] Since then the situation may have changed as Al-Shabaab established effective control over substantial territory in the southern half of Somalia, potentially easing some of the problems Al-Qa'ida faced during earlier periods.

## Why Terrorists Choose Failed States

In 1992, Osama bin Laden moved his operations to Sudan and immediately initiated a series of business projects in and around Khartoum.[19] By the end of 1992, he began openly discussing the issue of U.S. troops in Somalia. Together with his religious advisor, Mamdouh Salim (aka Abu Hajer al-Iraqi), bin Laden began a campaign to recast the "far enemy" of Islam as the United States, which he saw as the main international thief of Muslim oil wealth, occupier of the holy land, and embodiment of corrupt Western values.[20] Unable to operate in Saudi Arabia, Al-Qa'ida turned to Somalia as a possible base from which to strike the Americans and drive them out of the Middle East.[21]

We can think of Al-Qa'ida as a firm that produces terrorism against Western nations, specifically the United States. Just as firms locate themselves where they can minimize costs and maximize production and profits, Al-Qa'ida chose operational venues that it expected would minimize security costs and allow it to conduct attacks at minimal expense. The Horn of Africa presented important production advantages on both scores. Al-Qa'ida leaders like Abu Hafs clearly expected that Somalia would provide a low-cost recruiting ground where a disaffected and isolated people would gladly come under the Salafi banner. With no functioning government and a poor Muslim populace, Somalia appeared on the surface to be another Afghanistan, an area that would provide a safe haven and whose population would willingly fight to expel foreign occupiers. Reality turned out to be far different from these expectations.

The Sudanese government provided safe harbor for operational planning, thus easing security concerns. Additionally, the Sudanese economy was very weak during the early 1990s, so labor was cheap. Bin Laden hired more than five hundred people in Sudan and "those employees who were actual members of Al-Qa'ida received a monthly bonus between $50 and $120."[22] The Horn of Africa also presented Al-Qa'ida with opportunities to strike against the United States. Bin Laden, still angered by the "continued presence of American troops in Saudi Arabia," felt compelled to take action against U.S. forces that were present in Somalia as part of a United Nations peacekeeping mission.[23] Al-Qa'ida leaders also thought Somalia would present a good environment in which to produce attacks against the United States and continue to grow its movement. They expected security costs to be low because of the lack of a central government, and, on account of the pervasive poverty, they looked forward to a large pool of recruits. Neither expectation was met.[24]

Al-Qa'ida's reasons for venturing into the Horn of Africa appear obvious. Analysts rarely reverse the question, however, and ask whether individuals from the Horn of Africa would want to be part of Al-Qa'ida and the broader Salafi-jihadi movement. In Somalia, those with the skills for militancy are in demand as the lack of a central government has led to a proliferation of militias. In this competitive labor market, Al-Qa'ida had to provide a sufficient compensation package to attract good recruits. While the average Somali's economic prospects were, and still are, undoubtedly very bad, it is not clear that this was true for those who would make good terrorist recruits. Moreover, groups like Al-Qa'ida cannot match the substantial nonmonetary benefits that accrue to those who join clan militias.

Al-Qa'ida's religious doctrines were intended to provide members with an attractive set of spiritual benefits should they perish in pursuit of the cause. Relying on these spiritual benefits as part of the compensation package had the added value of serving as a screening mechanism for "true believers" that eased the organizational challenges that plague all militant organizations.[25] The challenge for groups like Al-Qa'ida is that other local institutions also provide valued nonpecuniary benefits. Competition from these groups made Al-Qa'ida's recruitment efforts much more difficult than the group anticipated. In many cases, the individual motivations of local Somali residents diverged from the group motivations and core tenets of Al-Qa'ida. This meant there was a mismatch between the value of the nonpecuniary compensation package Al-Qa'ida thought it was offering and what local Somalis perceived as the benefits to joining Al-Qa'ida. The result was poor recruitment and excessive operational costs.[26]

### Al-Qa'ida's Mission to Somalia

The mission of what we will call Al-Qa'ida–Somalia began in late January 1993 when Abu Hafs designated a team of veterans to conduct operation MSK (from an Arabic word meaning "holding" or "grabbing"). These veterans immediately began preparing for deployment to Africa. Beginning on 4 February 1993, Al-Qa'ida members departed for Nairobi, Kenya. Abu Hafs tasked them to "1—Find a location for military operations that would replace Afghanistan. . . . 2—[T]he location must be near the Arab region. . . . 3—[A]ttempt to help the brothers in Somalia and Ogaden."[27] Al-Qa'ida believed that Somalia would provide another safe haven for its operations, allow it to target the United States in both Somalia and the Arabian Peninsula, and provide a steady flow of recruits. None of these hopes came to fruition.

The first elements of Al-Qa'ida–Somalia departed from Peshawar, Pakistan, through Kenya en route to Somalia. Upon arriving in country, Al-Qa'ida–Somalia began establishing three training camps with the agreement of the General Islamic Union, the Somali militant group better known as Al-Ittihad al-Islami (AIAI).[28] AIAI was, in the early 1990s, a newly created Somali Islamist movement that had sought to gain control of key seaports and other towns in the aftermath of the fall of the government of Siad Barre in 1991. The movement succeeded in holding the town of Lu'uq for five years but was driven out of other locations by more powerful clan-based militias. AIAI initially was a diverse movement, divided by ideology, tactics, leadership, and clan. This eventually produced open splits over issues such as the use of terrorist attacks against the Ethiopian government in 1994–1995. By the late 1990s, AIAI has ceased to exist as a functional movement but lived on as a loose network of "alumni," some of whom reemerged to play roles in the Court of Islamic Council (CIC, formerly the Islamic Courts Union).[29]

The first two camps were established in Lu'uq and Bosaso, and a third was established later in the Ogaden region. In Nairobi, Al-Qa'ida's "Team Green," led by Saif al-Islam, received new members from bases of operation in Pakistan and Sudan.[30] Al-Qa'ida–Somalia used an air infiltration route from Wilson Airport in Nairobi;[31] a water route from Lamu, Kenya; and at some point an overland route from Djibouti across the Ethiopian Ogaden region.[32] Al-Qa'ida's Africa Corps operations appear to have been headquartered in Khartoum from 1993 to 1994. Cells operating in the region maintained communications with personnel in camps in Afghanistan as well.[33]

Over a roughly eighteen-month period, Al-Qa'ida found more adversity than success in Somalia. In order to project power, Al-Qa'ida needed to be able to promote its ideology, gain an operational safe haven, manipulate underlying conditions to secure popular support, and have adequate financing for continued operations.

In pursuit of its first objective, Al-Qa'ida–Somalia tried to promote its ideology through propaganda and by establishing administrative offices in each military training program. The Salafi message, however, largely fell on deaf ears. While the military training was of value to members of AIAI, it did not ensure their loyalty to the greater jihadi movement. Al-Qa'ida–Somalia likewise failed to achieve its second objective as it faced constant security headaches in the seemingly anarchic environment of clan-dominated Somalia. Making matters worse, the challenges of long, insecure lines of logistics seriously hampered operations. Gaining local support was no easier. At one point Al-Qa'ida operatives were so frustrated that they listed going after clan leaders as the second priority for jihad after expelling Western forces.[34] Internal discussions identified the lack of adequate communications equipment as an obstacle to building a coalition among Somalia's diverse Muslim clans.[35] Finally, insufficient financing ultimately made operations impossible to sustain on a long-term basis.[36]

## Why Al-Qa'ida–Somalia Failed

Three larger themes emerge from this analysis. First, Al-Qa'ida leaders greatly underestimated the costs of operating in Somalia. Second, they overestimated the value to Somalis of their version of jihad, of the nonpecuniary benefits they were offering. Third, where Al-Qa'ida did find success in Somalia, it was by providing local order and not ideological motivation. By providing security, Al-Qa'ida fulfilled the functions normally reserved for clan militias.

The low operational costs expected by the Somali franchise never materialized. Abu Hafs, the overall expeditionary leader, repeatedly discusses the high costs of operating in Somalia, writing about a "brother" who "is in desperate need for the monies because he did not receive the amount of $21,600."[37] These high costs were encountered both within Somalia and en route. Abu Hafs cites Kenya as an expensive route of transit for mujahideen and lists Djibouti as having an "abnormal high cost of living," where "Brother Khaled has no money . . . [and] his debts reached $4000."[38]

The Harmony database documents suggest two reasons for this pattern. First, getting in and out of Somalia was very expensive. Abu Hafs refers to this problem in stating, "the operation pertaining to the transfer of the brothers from Nairobi to Luuq will be costly: $150 for rent per person, and the roadways are not good."[39] Accounting documents reveal that shipping and transportation costs consumed a vast amount of the group's resources.[40] The very reasons that Al-Qa'ida sought Somalia—an isolated safe haven for preparing and conducting terrorist operations—also made it nearly impossible to sustain operations.[41]

Second, the poor security environment and unreliable allies effectively imposed a tax on all operations. For example, getting into the Ogaden region of Somalia apparently came at great risk and with large financial costs. Abu Bilal describes movement through this area with an Islamist group: "I was saying to the leader of [the] caravan that the road is dangerous (unintelligible) let us choose another road, and he was saying that all these tribes here are Somali and are sympathetic to us."[42] Shortly after this discussion, the group became engulfed in a roadside ambush. According to Abu Bilal, they ultimately won this skirmish but still sustained casualties. The route from Djibouti through the Ogaden to Somalia proved difficult because the Islamist tribes lacked both vehicles that could traverse the terrain and "a good and sharp guide of the region."[43]

In addition to these shipping costs, Al-Qa'ida sustained continual leakage through extortion from local clans and unintended losses during transportation as convoys and clan movements fell victim to banditry.[44] Cultural misunderstandings between the Arab Al-Qa'ida operatives and the Somali population routinely enter the equation, leading Saif al-Islam to bitterly criticize the Somalis:

> [E]ven though the thorny trees I described have sap and gum, no one uses them for anything. All the people there prefer to subsist off wheat and camel milk, and because of this, they are stingy and greedy. There are some stories so you can know about these people, such as the one about the man who left his wife to die of hunger because he wouldn't slaughter a camel from his herd of more than 100. If they see a caravan of fair-skinned people [Arabs] approaching them, they will welcome them if the caravan looks rich. You would think this is so they can offer the caravan some hospitality, but it is exactly the opposite.[45]

An additional, somewhat surprising expense was incurred because of Somali clan leaders' parochial concerns. Although many Somali clan leaders wanted to expel foreign occupiers, their first goal was always the security of their clan against local competitors. Abu Hafs routinely ran into difficulties building consensus among Somali leaders to focus on foreign occupiers instead of other Somalis. He had to spend scarce resources to create and maintain alliances between the tribes. Saif al-Islam complains, "we had Abd al-Salam [in the Revolutionary Council], who had taken $20,000 from Abu Fatima (aka Abu Hafs) on behalf of the council! As for military affairs, they didn't even have any maps with enemy locations and movements."[46]

While the costs for operating in Somalia were greater than expected, the value of Al-Qa'ida's compensation package to the locals was much lower than expected. The two major practical benefits Al-Qa'ida offered to local allies were money and military training. The group's accounting records reveal that funding went to expected expenses such as individual salaries, personal loans, and a host of equipment needs such as socks, shoes, dishes, and camels.[47] Saif al-Islam outlines that meeting basic needs for "every individual will cost $1.50 daily–$45 monthly. . . . [T]herefore the camp force (30) will cost $13,500 per month."[48] But operating his camp for three months will cost a minimum of $130,000, and "this does not cover the administration, media and the tribe's expenses."[49] Clearly, Al-Qa'ida had to do more than just offer training; it had to directly pay "tribe's expenses."

Indeed, pecuniary benefits were the anchor for gaining support from the locals. Omar al-Sumali, aka Saif al-Adl, the expeditionary commander for Ras Kamboni, begs for resources with which to provide pecuniary benefits: "Give this locality a chance by supporting it financially and supplying good personnel. The potential is very good. We should move very quickly, and seize this opportunity for Jihad. It is a good locality, from which we can establish the expected (base for) work in Somalia."[50] The idea seems to have been to use money to gain a foothold and then to begin preaching and ideological outreach so that nonpecuniary benefits would motivate the locals to support the jihad.

Al-Qa'ida expected it to be quite easy to win over the locals with money; after all, their country was poverty stricken. Once on the ground, however, Al-Qa'ida's leaders realized that they had competition. In the unstable environment of early 1990s Somalia, business leaders were a threat to Al-Qa'ida's ability to recruit. Saif al-Islam explains how "a man came from Jarbo with money to distribute to the people, especially the tribal Sheikhs. . . . [H]e said that, 'we don't want political parties in our countries, and weapons either. . . . Our best interests are not being followed because the Islamic Union is here.'"[51] Saif responds by recalibrating the Al-Qa'ida strategy, establishing new "priorities of the jihadist effort: (which is) specify the primary enemy (the businessmen), and postpone [efforts against] other groups."[52] By eliminating businesspeople, Saif sought to reduce the cost of the pecuniary benefits he must offer to gain local recruits. Essentially draining an area of all outside financial support is seen as a way to increase Al-Qa'ida's leverage in recruiting individual terrorists and co-opting other groups to its cause. The group, however, clearly recognized that to maintain the loyalty of the people, such a strategy must be followed by "supervision of liberated areas and securing of lives, funds, and property of all members of the populace."[53] Only much later in Iraq, in the face of the "Sunni awakening," would Al-Qa'ida learn that placing itself in direct competition with local business interests was guaranteed to trigger a backlash.

Once financial benefits gained a foothold, the group planned to use the ideas of Salifism and violent jihad to provide nonmonetary motivations for continued support. Al-Qa'ida encountered two unexpected challenges, however, in winning the hearts and minds of Somalis. First, overtaking traditional Sufi doctrine proved difficult.[54] Second, to the extent that membership in an Al-Qa'ida cell meant breaking with the interests of one's clan—a calculation that varied from case to case—individual recruits often found the opportunity cost of joining Al-Qa'ida too high.[55] Predictably, the foreign Al-Qa'ida operatives found themselves stymied by the continued loyalty of Somali recruits to their clan; at one point Abu Bilal complained at length that "each member of the movement is fanatically attached to his tribe."[56]

At that time (1993), clan affiliation was one of the only sources of physical protection and access to resources in Somali-inhabited East Africa; under those circumstances, it would have been risky for a Somali to forsake clan identity in the name of a newly arrived ideology. For Al-Qa'ida and for the AIAI movement, the persistence of clannism made it exceptionally difficult to build and maintain an Islamist coalition. Already in the early 1990s, separate AIAI wings divided by clan were emerging in the region. This afforded members the ability to maintain (uneasy) ties to the clan while serving in an Islamist movement. Even so, the risks of joining operations in which AIAI collaborated with Al-Qa'ida were high, as a new recruit could not be certain (1) that he would not be punished for joining what was perceived in the clan as a rival leadership to traditional clan elders, (2) that Al-Qa'ida would not be overwhelmed by rivals from within the clan or betrayed by a rival neighboring clan, or (3) that Al-Qa'ida would continue to operate in Somalia for the long term, especially if foreign interventions were eliminated.

In the final analysis, Al-Qa'ida's efforts to move into Somalia fell short for many of the same reasons that Western interventions there failed. Al-Qa'ida did not understand the political, economic, and social dynamics of the country. The costs of this misunderstanding were felt in two ways. First, the lack of any form of governance created excessive operational costs for Al-Qa'ida in Somalia. Instead of finding a safe haven like the tribal areas of Pakistan, Al-Qa'ida in Somalia found a lawless land of shifting alliances, devoid of Sunni unity. Second, Somali allies ultimately placed a lower-than-expected value on the compensation package Al-Qa'ida had to offer. The group could not provide benefits sufficient to overcome local loyalties. Although Al-Qa'ida was successful in buying its way into a few clans, the primacy of tribalism in Somalia ultimately frustrated the group's efforts to develop a unified coalition against foreign occupiers. In Somalia, local competition trumped jihad.

### Al-Qa'ida and Somali Islamists

Al-Qa'ida did find indirect success in certain distinct areas and thus provides data for analyzing the threat from foreign terrorists operating in Somalia today. In the one area in Somalia where Al-Qa'ida may have established an enduring presence, it did so by providing local order. Omar al-Sumali won one village over by providing security and then immediately began ideological efforts. He writes, "we already formulated a political program for the Bajuni and the region . . . [and] next week we will ask Sheikh Hassan to adopt the plan."[57] Al-Qa'ida was apparently able to provide effective law and order near Ras Kamboni, presumably working through AIAI. The Bajuni, a tribal population of the east African coast, residing in the vicinity of Ras Kamboni, actually requested that Al-Qa'ida operatives "stay and govern, and secure the city." As Omar al-Sumali explains, the Bajuni "have noticed that the presence of the brothers prevented the highwaymen from entering the city, and the fishermen began coming to the shore to spend the night in the city . . . [T]hey told our people that they do not want them to leave. They await the arrival of our wives and children. They freely gave fish to our people, and our people guarded the well while reading the Koran, and helped the fisherman get water."[58] Significantly, there has never been evidence that the Bajuni have been active supporters of Al-Qa'ida or AIAI. Their interest in maintaining an Al-Qa'ida presence on the coast was driven by a desire to use the group to protect them from the predatory attacks and extortion they suffered at the hands of nearby factional militias. In this sense, the Bajuni were simply adhering to the time-honored logic of "the enemy of my enemy is my friend."

Today, Ras Kamboni and the entire lower and middle Jubba regions are considered a safe haven for regrouping Islamist militias. Since the late 1990s, numerous reports suggested that Ras Kamboni served periodically as a terrorist training camp and that jihadis from outside Somalia came and went from the area.[59] Interviews with a Kenyan fisherman and other local witnesses revealed that there were people in Ras Kamboni who "were not locals, but rather, Arabs and other more 'European-looking type people' but who were Muslims."[60] This was at no time a large-scale presence, however.

Despite the apparent local successes of Islamic militants, the dangers of creating fixed operational sites in a failed state were dramatically illustrated during the recent Ethiopian invasion into Somalia. On 8–10 January 2007,

U.S. forces conducted a series of air raids on the area around Ras Kamboni in an attempt to kill Al-Qa'ida operatives seeking sanctuary there.[61] Those raids failed to kill any of the "high value targets" the United States sought but served as a reminder that counterterrorism operations can be launched with fewer diplomatic and political complications in areas of state collapse where no sovereign state authority has jurisdiction over the territory. This is yet another reason why zones of state collapse are less attractive as sites of Al-Qa'ida operations than they appear to be.

## Conclusions and Key Policy Recommendations

Al-Qa'ida's efforts to establish a presence in Somali-inhabited areas of the Horn of Africa and use them as a base for attacks against Western targets were largely a failure from 1992 to 2006. The group's only significant successes in the Horn were in Kenya, where the state's poor governance capacity combined with relative stability to create a favorable operational environment. In Somalia, unfavorable operating conditions prevented Al-Qa'ida from achieving any of its significant objectives.

Al-Qa'ida initially failed in Somalia for three reasons. First, its arguments about fighting a foreign occupier did not resonate with locals because it, too, was seen as a foreign force. Second, its leaders significantly underestimated the costs of operating in a failed state environment. Third, it could not recruit at a sufficient level to sustain operations because the benefits of membership were simply too low to induce high levels of local participation.

Since 2006, events in Somalia have progressed with the ascent of a powerful coalition of hard-line Islamist militias, some with direct links to Al-Qa'ida. As of 2009, foreign Al-Qa'ida advisors are actively involved in support of Al-Shabaab's efforts to consolidate control over Somalia. This involvement does not challenge the main thrust of this chapter. That Al-Qa'ida operatives are working to help a local ally exercise direct control over substantial territory (as the Taliban did in pre-2002 Afghanistan), rather than simply setting up training camps and logistical bases amidst the chaos, is consistent with our argument that failed states are not an effective operational base.

The key strategic lesson from our analysis of Al-Qa'ida's experiences in the Horn of Africa is that *the threat from terrorists operating in weak states is greater than from those operating in failed states*. This implies the need for a much greater focus on supporting counterterrorism in Kenya than has been the case so far. At the operational level, we conclude that effectively reducing terrorist threats requires carefully tailored policies that only rarely involve a direct foreign military intervention. In weak states like Kenya, direct military involvement may not be an option. A foreign military presence in weak states can actually discredit government counterterror efforts and risks creating incentives for the host government to tolerate low levels of terrorist activity. In failed states like Somalia, empowering local authorities and clans who can police their territory and compete with terrorist organizations for local support may yield great dividends in fighting terrorism. Maintaining and demonstrating the ability to judiciously strike emerging terrorist targets of opportunity also reduces these regions' value as safe havens.

Until recently, the prospects for a serious terrorist threat to emerge in the Horn of Africa seemed quite low, with the notable exception of target-rich Kenya. The region consistently proved much less hospitable to foreign jihadis than conventional wisdom suggested. The political dynamics unleashed in Somalia since 2006 have, however, altered this equation. Al-Shabaab in particular has a powerful interest in regionalizing and globalizing the war inside Somalia. To the extent that it can portray itself as a Somali liberation movement battling foreign meddlers (specifically Ethiopia), it can engage Somali nationalist sentiments and thereby win local support. Al-Shabaab's prospects are much dimmer when it must play in a strictly domestic political context based on its Islamist agenda; few Somalis support its draconian social policies and links to Al-Qa'ida. As a result, Al-Shabaab has every interest in drawing regional states into the Somali quagmire. The threat of an Al-Shabaab terrorist attack in Kenya, Ethiopia, or Djibouti is thus much higher. External actors responding to Al-Shabaab terrorist threats or attacks must take into account that their countermeasures will have important political consequences inside Somalia and must be cognizant of the dangers of unintended consequences.

## Notes

Throughout this chapter we refer to documents from the Department of Defense Harmony database (hereinafter Harmony). The Harmony database collects documents related to al-Qa'ida activities that have been captured or discovered by the Department of Defense. Some of these have been declassified and used as part of analytical documents produced by the Combating Terrorism Center at the U.S. Military Academy at West Point. Originals, translations, and summaries of the documents we use are available at http://www.ctc.usma.edu/harmony/harmony_docs.asp.

1. We use the term "jihadi" as it is widely used in both the Western counterterrorism community and the Arab media. See William McCants, ed., "The Militant Ideology Atlas," Combating Terrorism Center report, U.S. Military Academy, West Point, 2006: 5, http://ctc.usma.edu/atlas/atlas.asp.

2. Ayman al-Zawahiri audiotape, 5 January 2007. Translation at "Al Zawahiri Audio Urges Somalis, Muslims to Fight Ethiopian Forces," Exposing the Enemy project, U.S. Central Command, http://www.centcom2.mil/sites/uscentcom1/What%20 Extremists%20Say/Al-ZawahiriAudioUrgesSomalis,MuslimsToFightEthiopianForces 2.aspx (no longer available online).

3. A typical example is James Phillips, "Somalia and al-Qaeda: Implications for the War on Terrorism," *Backgrounder* 1526 (Washington, DC: Heritage Foundation, 2002).

4. For a detailed analysis, see "Al-Qa'ida's (mis)Adventures in the Horn of Africa," Combating Terrorism Center report, U.S. Military Academy, West Point, 2007: chapter 3, http://ctc.usma.edu/aq/aqII.asp.

5. Lawrence Wright, *The Looming Tower* (New York: Alfred A. Knopf, 2006), 188–89.

6. For more on the myriad problems jihadi terrorists have faced in Somalia, see "Counter-Terrorism in Somalia: Losing Hearts and Minds?" *Africa Report* 95 (11 July 2005), International Crisis Group, Brussels: 9–13, http://www.crisisgroup.org/home /index.cfm?id=3555&l=1.

7. In a series of reports from Somalia in the 1990s, Mohammed Atef (also known as Abu Hafs) details the challenges of operating in a failed state. Prominent among these are problems with local bandits, the costs of corruption in neighboring states, and the ability of Western forces to act in ungoverned spaces. See Harmony, AFGP-2002-600104, AFGP-2002-600110, and AFGP-2002-800597.

8. For a thorough development of this argument by a very influential jihadi thinker, see Abu Bakr Naji, "The Management of Savagery," trans. William McCants, Combating Terrorism Center report, U.S. Military Academy, West Point, 2006, http:// ctc.usma.edu/publications/naji.asp.

9. Harmony, AFGP-2002-600053: 6.

10. See English translation of Al-Zawahiri letter to Al-Zarqaqi at http://www.fas .org/irp/news/2005/10/letter_in_english.pdf, accessed 13 August 2009.

11. A similar argument is made in Naji, "The Management of Savagery."

12. In 1996, for example, Ethiopian forces entered Somalia to conduct an offensive against Islamist forces in the Gedo region. In the same year, the Ethiopians used a local proxy force, the Secularist National Front, to take a number of towns where foreigners had been operating. Harmony, AFGP-2002-600110: 1–2.

13. In August 1994, Saif al-Islam wrote a journal of his trip to Somalia to establish training camps on behalf of Abu Hafs, a senior Al-Qa'ida military leader. Saif describes how it took a caravan of eighty local men to guard eight Arabs on the trip through the Ogaden region to Lu'uq, Somalia. Harmony, AFGP-2002-600104: 4.

14. In fact, the logistical challenges of moving from Kenya into Somalia were so

great that in January 1994 Al-Qa'ida operative Saif al-Adel suggested buying a boat for transportation and raising funds through fishing. The biggest challenge he notes is that because the locals can't be trusted, the group will have to train one of its own as a sailor. Harmony, AFGP-2002-600114: 1–2; AFGP-2002-600053: 5.

15. Harmony, AFGP-2002-800640.

16. For a description of some of the challenges of operating in Somalia, see Harmony, AFGP-2002-600104: 5. On the problems of moving during the rainy season in areas with few paved roads, see Harmony, AFGP-2002-600114: 5. In a March 1993 letter to "Brother Othman," Saif al-Islam describes the poor food in the Ogaden camps, even though the major expenditure was on food. Harmony, AFGP-2002-800621: 4.

17. Harmony, AFGP-2002-800597.

18. See, for example, Ken Menkhaus, *Somalia: State Collapse and the Threat of Terrorism* (New York: Routledge, 2004).

19. See Wright, *The Looming Tower*, 165.

20. Ibid., 170–75.

21. The first Al-Qa'ida attack was in December 1992 against U.S. troops in Yemen who were traveling to Somalia.

22. Wright, *The Looming Tower*, 169.

23. Ibid.

24. There is an important point here: terrorist organizations have a limited ability to understand their operational environment, even when they are operating as openly as Al-Qa'ida in the early 1990s.

25. An excellent overview of the economics of religious militancy is presented in Laurence R. Iannaccone and Eli Berman, "Religious Extremism: The Good, the Bad, and the Deadly," *Public Choice* 128 (2006):109–29. For a discussion of agency problems in terrorist organizations, see Jacob N. Shapiro, "The Terrorist's Challenge: Security, Efficiency, Control," Ph.D. diss., Stanford University, Stanford, CA, 2007.

26. The application of a labor economics perspective to militant recruitment in this case was inspired by Clinton Watts, "Jihadi Seeking Challenging Martyrdom Opportunity; Will Travel," Combating Terrorism Center working paper, U.S. Military Academy, West Point, May 2007.

27. Harmony, AFGP-2002-600104: 1.

28. For detailed background on AIAI, see "Al-Qa'ida's (mis)Adventures," Appendix A-I.

29. "Somalia's Islamists," *Africa Report* 100 (12 December 2005), International Crisis Group, Brussels.

30. Harmony, AFGP-2002-600104: 2–4.

31. This facility is used primarily for small aircraft making local and regional flights, including tourist charters.

32. Harmony, AFGP-2002-600113: 1–3.

33. See Harmony, AFGP-2002-800081, which shows the routes that Al-Qa'ida members took to and from South Asia.

34. Harmony, AFGP-2002-800600: 2.

35. For a thorough analysis of the underlying conditions that worked to the disadvantage of Al-Qa'ida throughout its campaign in Somalia, see "Al-Qa'ida's (mis) Adventures," chapter 3.

36. For detailed accounts of Somali training camps, see Harmony AFGP-2002 -600053, AFGP-2002-600104, AFGP-2002-800597, and AFGP-2002-800640.

37. Harmony, AFGP-2002-800597: 9.

38. Ibid., 11.

39. Harmony, AFGP-2002-800597: 10.

40. Harmony, AFGP-2002-800621: 4.

41. Harmony, AFGP-2002-600104: 17.

42. Harmony, AFGP-2002-800640: 7.

43. Ibid.: 6.

44. Harmony, AFGP-2002-800573.

45. Harmony, AFGP-2002-600104: 7.

46. Harmony, AFGP-2002-600104: 19.

47. Harmony, AFGP-2002-800573.

48. Harmony, AFGP-2002-800621: 13.

49. Ibid.

50. Harmony, AFGP-2002-600113, 7. Ironically, other Al-Qa'ida communications from Ras Kamboni complain bitterly about the intolerable conditions there.

51. Harmony, AFGP-2002-600104: 21.

52. Ibid.: 23.

53. Harmony, AFGP-2002-600053: 3.

54. Harmony, AFGP-2002-600104: 21.

55. Similar issues largely stymied AIAI efforts to build independent forces. Where that group did establish militias in Somalia, they often emerged as internal rivals to clan-based factions with whom they shared a common lineage identity. In essence, clans found themselves with a factional militia and an Islamist movement. Clan elders who were loathe to see armed conflict break out within the lineage tended to discourage clashes between the two, but relations were invariably very poor.

56. Harmony, AFGP-2002-600104: 5.

57. Harmony, AFGP-2002-600113: 3.

58. Ibid.

59. Interview with a Kenyan fisherman, 28 September 2001. See "Al-Qa'ida's (mis) Adventures," Appendix C-I for additional interviews with locals.

60. Ibid.

61. "Somalia says al-Qaida embassy bombing suspect believed killed," *Guardian*, 10 January 2007, http://www.guardian.co.uk/world/2007/jan/10/alqaida.usa1, accessed 28 April 2008.

# 5　A Fortress without Walls

*Alternative Governance Structures on the*
*Afghanistan-Pakistan Frontier*

## Ty L. Groh

Ungoverned spaces represent the modern equivalent of an invisible fortress—
a fortress without walls—capable of staving off the siege of governments attempting to assert sovereignty. Although these areas have no physical walls
that provide sanctuary to their often problematic inhabitants, there is a de
facto barrier that has led many states to spend, and arguably waste, precious
resources trying to establish authority within them. What constitutes this in-
tangible barrier that prevents even the strongest states from extending their
authority in certain areas of the world?

To answer this question, this chapter develops two themes highlighted in
Phil Williams's analysis in Chapter 2. First, Williams suggests that spaces considered ungoverned, according to generally accepted norms of sovereignty, are
not necessarily lawless and devoid of governance, but rather possess a competing governance structure. This chapter argues that an alternative governance
structure represents a fortress without walls, offering those within an intan-
gible, yet effective, defense against both the establishment of a central rule of
law and the writ of state sovereignty. Second, Williams proposes that problems
occur "when the state fails to fill these spaces with appropriate, adequate, and
accepted legal and regulatory measures." This chapter further maintains that
when the state and those living within an ungoverned space have different
opinions about what constitutes lawful governance or a legitimate use of force,
the state's efforts to impose its rule of law tend to shift from building legitimacy in the region to establishing order and maintaining the level of violence

at or below an acceptable threshold. This shift often leads to counterproductive strategies that isolate and/or overly accommodate those who would be governed and ultimately reinforce the existing alternative governance structure.

Focusing on the efforts of modern states—imperial Britain, Pakistan, and the Soviet Union—to establish a centralized rule of law in the Pashtun tribal areas of Afghanistan and Pakistan, this chapter offers an explanation for why modern states, using a variety of strategies ranging from violent suppression to accommodation, have failed to establish sovereignty in this region in the past. Customary tribal law, called Pashtunwali, and central governments have long clashed in what Joel Migdal characterizes as a battle to determine "who will set the rules."[1] The ability to say, with authority, what is and is not lawful is an important method for instituting change and maintaining control over a society.[2] The presence of an established, competing tribal law challenges state authority and fuels strong opposition to any attempt at superseding it.[3] More specifically, this chapter argues that the normative and organizational governance structures that characterize Pashtunwali have significantly hindered the efforts of central states to assimilate, co-opt, or divide and conquer the Pashtuns. Furthermore, history shows that state policies that have attempted to incorporate and accommodate certain normative and organizational aspects of Pashtunwali have been most successful in engendering Pashtun loyalty.

Afghanistan's and Pakistan's tribal regions loom large in policymakers' conceptions of ungoverned spaces, as they are widely labeled safe havens for terrorist groups such as Al-Qa'ida, insurgents, drug traffickers, and arms smugglers. As a spokeswoman for the International Security Assistance Force in Afghanistan remarked in 2006, "when there are areas of ungoverned space, where the rule of law is not in operation, it becomes a breeding ground for insurgent action."[4]

To appreciate the challenge of instituting a central rule of law in tribal regions, it is important to understand some of the sources of resistance. Although in many cases geography might partially explain the success of tribal resistance, this chapter focuses on the normative and organizational governance structures entailed in Pashtunwali. Pashtunwali establishes the grounds for both moral and legitimate authority among its constituents. In most cases, the source of conflict with the state lies in the vastly different conceptions of what determines acceptable behavior. Resolving these conflicts is difficult because the organizational governance structure embodied in Pashtunwali is self-enforcing and nonhierarchical. Thus, it is nearly impossible for a state to execute any kind of divide-and-conquer strategy, or to empower a small number of individual Pashtuns to mediate with the state in a binding and meaningful way. For these reasons, the Pashtun areas represent a hard case for establishing centralized rule of law. To promote a better understanding of the normative and organizational governance structures of the Pashtuns, the next section offers a brief description of Pashtunwali and the ways it contributes to the persistent Pashtun resistance to state authority.

## Pashtunwali and Ungoverned Spaces

The Pashtuns represent one of the largest ethnic groups in the world, with an estimated 41.3 million members living predominantly in Afghanistan and northwest Pakistan.[5] Having a tribal culture, they identify themselves in terms of familial ties and commitments. Social, political, and economic activities mostly take place at this level, which effectively prevents government-oriented institutions from gaining a foothold in tribal areas.[6] The Pashtun region has long been a crossroads for countless conquerors because of the rough and often deserted terrain that makes it nearly impossible to defend; yet no state has ever truly been able to conquer it.[7] The nineteenth-century imperial contest known as the Great Game found both Great Britain and Russia unable to subject the Pashtuns to either state's authority.[8] Even today, the Federally Administered Tribal Areas (FATA), a heavily concentrated Pashtun region in northwestern Pakistan, remains exempt from most aspects of Pakistani law. Although many Pashtuns live in urban areas in both Pakistan and Afghanistan, the vast majority live in rural areas and are the focus of this chapter.

Aside from geography, the organizational structure of Pashtun society makes the Pashtuns difficult to subjugate. Charles Lindholm characterizes Pashtun society as segmentary, "a subtype of what are technically known as 'acephelous' or headless societies."[9] Segmentary societies, unlike purely headless (nonhierarchical) societies, have some internal organization and stratification, but power and influence remain widely distributed. Tribal elders, or *Maliks*, serve as administrators under a tribal chief, or *Khan*.[10] For the most part, these positions of leadership are hereditary.[11] Under Pashtunwali, most decisions are based on a consensus of tribal members, and any form of leadership is contingent upon promoting the interests of the tribe. Although there are some slight differences in the internal organization of various Pashtun tribes, the exception to the practice of ruling by consensus occurs only when an external threat arises. In such a case, Pashtun tribes combine their strength and appoint a leader whom they follow without question. All grievances existing within the tribe are effectively put on hold, and a form of military-like order is established under the skilled and experienced leader to allow the group to focus on fighting the common enemy.[12]

Pashtunwali also provides a source of resistance in a normative sense. Lindholm suggests that segmentary societies band together not only when they are physically threatened, but also when they feel they are losing influence over their own way of life. Pashtuns are intent on preserving their way of life.[13] Offers of social or economic progress as an incentive to accept state authority are often meaningless. For example, one Pashtun *Malik* told a British administrator that the aim of any social or political system should be to produce "a fine type of man. Therefore, let us keep our independence and have none of your law and order and your other institutions but stick to our customs and be men like our fathers before us."[14] Only a life lived in accordance with Pashtunwali can produce a fine Pashtun man

Pashtunwali translates as "the way of the Pashtuns." First and foremost, it is about honor, or *nang*. *Nang* is not based on morality or justice as defined in Western societies, but rather stems from a close, unquestioning observance of Pashtunwali. This difference has created a great deal of tension between Pashtuns and the states that have attempted to establish their rule of law over that of Pashtunwali. Action that must be taken to preserve *nang* but contradicts or breaks the laws of a state would seem perfectly acceptable to a Pashtun. Even more troubling from the state's point of view, Pashtunwali would demand such an action regardless of the consequences.[15]

The main tenets of Pashtunwali include *badal*, *nanawatai*, and the *jirgah*. *Badal*, often considered the strongest pillar of Pashtunwali, demands that a Pashtun seek revenge or retaliation for any slight against his stature. Similar to the premise of "an eye for an eye," the injury or insult determines the nature of the response. This becomes problematic when, for example, *badal* requires killing someone to avenge an insult. The state would consider such an act murder, but a Pashtun would see it as an appropriate means of settling the issue. Another problem related to *badal* is that in Pashtun society, like other segmentary societies, custom dictates that some form of restitution can be offered as a settlement to avoid bloodshed.[16] When the state seeks to imprison an individual for wrongdoing, a Pashtun would not see this as justice. Restitution, not incarceration, is considered a just penalty.

*Nanawatai* requires a Pashtun to risk both life and property to shelter and protect any person, friend or enemy, who asks for sanctuary. *Melmastia,* somewhat related to *nanawatai,* demands that a Pashtun offer any traveler or guest food, shelter, and protection if requested.[17] These two tenets of Pashtun-wali demand, not merely condone, the harboring of a person wanted by the state. The fact that people would lie, not to protect themselves but to maintain their honor, makes it extremely difficult for states to apprehend fugitives who make their way into areas governed by Pashtunwali. For this reason, Western officials find Pashtun regions particularly troubling today.

*Jirgah* refers to a council. Pashtuns use a truly Greek form of democracy that gives all those entitled to participate in the *jirgah* an equal voice and an equal opportunity to be heard. Although more eloquent and passionate individuals hold greater sway over the council, any action to be taken must consider the interests of the tribe or the clan first and those of the individual second.[18] No individual truly holds the ability to speak for others, so bargaining often must take place at an individual level. This makes it very difficult for the state to gain meaningful support because a *jirgah* will likely reject any policy that benefits only a few individuals. In addition, when the *jirgah* perceives that the interests of the state are superseding the interests of the tribe or clan, it will often vote to renege on any agreement previously made.[19]

In all respects, a Pashtun must adhere to the code to maintain his identity as a Pashtun.[20] If a Pashtun breaks the code of Pashtunwali, he has one of two options: either he suffers humiliation and the loss of his honor, or he is ostracized and forced to flee the tribal area. Being ostracized puts an individual Pashtun in a very dangerous position because he no longer has familial or tribal ties to protect him from being robbed or killed.[21] Therefore, all Pashtuns living in ungoverned spaces take the observance of Pashtunwali very seriously. The combination of normative and organizational governance structures inherent in Pashtunwali has plagued modern states for nearly two centuries, despite a wide variety of state strategies designed to establish sovereignty.

## The Failure of Modern States to Supplant Tribal Governance

Great Britain, the Soviet Union, and Pakistan have all attempted various strategies to establish sovereignty in the Pashtun tribal regions, ranging from pure accommodation—letting Pashtuns live undisturbed under Pashtunwali—to violent suppression by destroying those unwilling to give up Pashtunwali. In all cases, these three states failed to accomplish their objective. The following case studies detail the policies that were used and the reasons for their failure.

### Great Britain

The British Empire wanted to tame the Pashtun region primarily to protect its interests in India. Russia's steady expansion toward India in the nineteenth century spawned the era of the Great Game, in which the two rivals sought control over the "buffer zone" of Persia, Afghanistan, and Tibet. Great Britain originally intended simply to extend its rule of law in India into the Pashtun hinterland, but failure after failure forced the British to slowly modify their policies and eventually led to pure isolation and accommodation for the Pashtun tribes. In the end, the British never managed to supersede Pashtunwali.

During this period, India was ruled by the Indian Penal Code (Act No. 45 of 1860), which was based on British law and suppressed any competing forms of law or custom. When the British began to establish settlements in the Pashtun region in the nineteenth century, British authorities instituted the Indian Penal Code there, assuming that the code was sufficient to extend British authority to all regions and ethnic groups. The Pashtuns, however, did not recognize the code as a fair representation of the law. Thus, when the penalty for breaking a law according to the code was not justified by Pashtunwali, the Pashtuns either ignored it or evaded it.[22] Further complicating the situation, the British simply failed to understand that Pashtunwali demands compensation for a victim rather than the punishment of an offender.[23] Incarceration meant that neither revenge nor compensation could be obtained, so Pashtuns often elected to rectify the situation without government assistance.

The fiercest resistance to British authority came from the Pashtun tribes living in the rugged hills surrounding settled areas.[24] The hill tribes were skilled warriors unaccustomed to the idea of central authority and were often in conflict with neighboring tribes.[25] Actions associated with these conflicts such as theft, or murder stemming from *badal*, were acceptable under Pashtunwali but were considered lawlessness by the British.[26] The hill tribes were especially troublesome because they were so inaccessible that it was nearly impossible to bring them to justice.

The Indian Penal Code failed to bring order to the region because the Pashtuns did not recognize it as a just governance structure. This failure led the British to narrow the scope of their policy. Under the Close Border Policy of 1846, the British sought to segregate settled areas on the frontier from the pastoral Pashtun communities found in the surrounding hills.[27] British authorities made no attempt "to advance into the highlands, or even to secure the main passages through the mountains such as the Khyber Pass."[28] In addition, the Close Border Policy tried to contract services from more resistant hill tribes in an attempt to co-opt them. In exchange for their cooperation, the tribes would receive a stipend for their services.

The years under the Close Border Policy witnessed a steady escalation of tribal violence. During the first twenty years, the British conducted eleven punitive expeditions to enforce their authority, and twelve more during the next five years.[29] They had failed to learn from their mistakes with the Indian Penal Code, or to recognize the significant differences between British notions of justice and the normative governance structure of Pashtunwali. Segregating the plains tribes from the hill tribes did not make the imposed alternative to Pashtunwali more desirable; the Pashtuns were not willing to exchange their traditional identity for better access to trade and empty promises of security. After thirty years of failure and frustration, the British abandoned the Close Border Policy and began to experiment with new policies aimed at achieving some form of compromise.

Recognizing the need to appeal to the Pashtuns' sense of justice, in 1901 the British enacted the Frontier Crimes Regulation (FCR). Under this policy, criminal or civil cases occurring in the settled areas were subjected to a hybrid system of British law and tribal custom. British administrators would appoint a jury of several *Maliks* to preside over a case; "[the jury] was not bound by law of evidence, and was expected to arrive at its decision through its own methods."[30] Under FCR, many more individuals were brought to justice, and order in the settled areas improved. Leveraging the legitimacy of village *Maliks* and incorporating Pashtunwali into the official system of law enabled the British to create a more successful, albeit hybrid, code.

In 1879, Russian diplomatic efforts in Afghanistan once again began to challenge British interests. To strengthen the buffer between India and Afghanistan, the British began to expand their influence along the Afghan border under a renewed Forward Policy, which sought to bring more Afghan territory under British India's control. This policy aimed to co-opt the tribes within designated settlement areas. In exchange for an annual allowance, tribes accepted responsibility for border security and agreed to deny sanctuary to those the British considered outlaws.

In conjunction with the Forward Policy, the British also introduced Indirect Rule and the Maliki System. Indirect Rule allowed tribes to manage their own affairs and required British administrators to settle any official grievances through tribal custom.[31] The Maliki System selected Pashtun agents within the settled areas to communicate with transborder tribes. Under this policy, *Maliks* signed agreements acknowledging British authority. In turn, British agents were assigned to administer their respective tribal region through the *Maliks* in hopes of strengthening British authority. The British would pay out allowances for good behavior or demand reparations for deviant behavior directly to or from the *Maliks*.[32] Under these policies, the British sought to maintain an acceptable level of violence in the region by training and employing local militias, paying out high subsidies to problematic tribes, attacking other tribes, and building rail lines to improve commerce and speed response to breaches of peace. As the Forward Policy pulled the British deeper into Pashtun regions, the progressive nature of British policy failed to stem Pashtun resistance; tribal raids against settlements under British control increased from 56 in 1907, to 99 in 1908, to 159 in 1909.[33] The evolution of British policy gradually moved away from its original purpose of establishing British-style rule of law. The longer the British remained in the region and the deeper they pushed, the greater the Pashtuns' incentive to cause trouble and in return solicit greater subsidies to refrain from violence or payments to prevent it.

For nearly a hundred years the British adopted a number of different policies to secure Pashtun areas on the northwest frontier of India. Although more progressive policies marginally improved the level of civil order in the region, implementation of the accommodating FCR and Indirect Rule bolstered the normative governance structure under Pashtunwali. Although together these policies increased the number of people being brought before tribal courts, the Pashtuns were not afraid to intimidate the *Maliks* or seek revenge against them should they rule in a manner that either appeared solely to serve British interests or conflicted with Pashtunwali. In the end, the British left the region and left Pashtunwali as the supreme law of the land.

### Pakistan

Pakistan has been in a constant struggle to establish itself as an autonomous, unified state since its partition from British India in 1947. State security and state capacity have been the two considerations most responsible for directing Pakistan's policies in the Pashtun regions.

Immediately after partition, the newly formed government of Pakistan lacked sufficient resources or legitimacy and therefore sought order and stability mainly through the reenactment of past British policies. The new government reinstated the British Maliki System and the 1901 version of the British FCR, both of which are still in effect today.[34] It also reinstated the British program of allowances and subsidies and initially allowed Pashtunwali to serve as the rule of law in the tribal areas in exchange for a commitment from Pashtun leaders to become part of Pakistan and to assist the state when called upon to do so.[35]

The government's first step to make the transition away from Pashtunwali incorporated a shift from accommodation to co-optation beginning in 1951. A strategy of "peaceful penetration" that promoted and facilitated developmental projects such as health care, clean water, education, and communications in the tribal areas steered clear of competition with the existing alternative governance structure and sought only to demonstrate the advantages of closer relations between the tribal areas and the central government.[36] Despite the small scale of the original program, the development sparked some tribal integration and incorporated some of the tribal areas into the Northwest Frontier Province (NWFP).[37]

A dramatic change in government policy came in 1955 with the enactment of the One Unit Plan. This policy combined the NWFP, Balochistan, Sindh, and the tribal areas into one province called West Pakistan, through which the government intended to foster a common identity for the people living there.[38] The One Unit Plan, however, failed to inspire a sense of unity among the different ethnic groups. The Pashtuns felt that the plan threatened to subsume the Pashtuns, Baloch, and Sindhis into a single political group dominated by the Punjabis. Furthermore, the One Unit Plan directly contradicted the existing organizational governance structure under Pashtunwali that makes decisions based on a consensus and generally favors the majority of Pashtuns. Instead of persuading Pakistani Pashtuns to align with Islamabad, it inspired a renewed sense of Pashtun nationalism. This feeling was exacerbated by the fact that Afghan Pashtuns began raising the notion of a free and independent Pashtunistan, a country that would protect and promote Pashtun identity, values, and customs.[39] Not surprisingly, when the continuation of the One Unit Plan was later subjected to popular referendum, it was overwhelmingly voted down.[40]

Following the failure of the One Unit Plan, provincial administrations were reinstated, and in 1970 the Pashtun regions were converted into the

FATA, consisting of seven different agencies: Mohmand, Kurram, Khyber, Bajaur, Orakzai, and North and South Waziristan. Pakistani troops were sent into the FATA along with teachers and medical services. Between 1972 and 1977, new projects providing water, education, roads, electricity, and industry in the FATA and the NWFP appeared to marginalize Afghanistan's repeated attempts to gain support for Pashtun nationalism. Pakistan, however, supplied all these development programs with no demand for change from the Pashtuns, and Pashtunwali remained the recognized law of the land.[41] The Pashtuns accepted this policy wholeheartedly because it provided them with social benefits and required nothing in return. The appeal of an independent Pashtunistan faded as Pashtuns realized that their lives were significantly better with the support of the state of Pakistan.[42] Once again, Islamabad began to make inroads with the Pashtuns and sparked an increasing degree of cooperation. This approach, however, was never carried to fruition in the sense that neither the normative nor organizational governance structure in the region was challenged by Islamabad's rule of law. Unfortunately, these efforts would be overcome by events, making it impossible to determine whether or not they would have had a reasonable chance at establishing a central rule of law.

When the Soviet Union invaded Afghanistan in 1979, Pakistan, out of necessity, shifted its policy in the FATA to concentrate on funneling weapons and money to the Pashtuns in the transborder region to fight against the Soviets. Islamabad reverted back to accommodative and isolative policies that allowed the Pashtuns essentially to govern themselves. As a result, the government of Pakistan created and fostered the conditions that have led to the persistent and problematic ungoverned space found along the Pakistan-Afghanistan border. The open border and the acceptance of Afghan refugees led to problems of overpopulation, unemployment, pressure on grazing land, and reduced law and order, giving rise to militancy and terrorism.[43] As "jihad, drugs, and gun running became the main source of livelihood for the local people," an alternate economy grew within the FATA and reduced Pashtun dependence on government subsidies and allowances.[44] In addition, leaders of the resistance were able to carve up the region into fiefdoms and isolate themselves from Islamabad's authority.[45]

Once the Soviets left Afghanistan, Pakistan continued to accommodate the Pashtuns in hopes of gaining more influence in Afghanistan and preserving Pakistan's strategic depth with India.[46] A friendly neighbor on Pakistan's western border would allow Pakistan to focus on its eastern border. The rise of the predominantly Pashtun-led Taliban movement gave Pakistan confidence that Afghanistan, under Taliban rule, would protect Pakistan's strategic depth.[47] This led to Pakistan becoming one of only three states that recognized the Taliban regime.[48] The Pakistan-Afghanistan border remained open and further fused the connections among the Pashtuns living along the border.

The Pakistani government's decision to sacrifice the integration of the Pashtuns living in the FATA in exchange for greater security and increased influence in Afghanistan created a power vacuum in the region that was filled by leaders of the different mujahideen factions. Once the Soviet threat was removed, interethnic and intertribal rivalries dominated the struggle to control Kabul. Pashtuns focused their allegiances regionally, reinforcing Pashtun identity and marginalizing their perception of inclusion and affiliation with the state of Pakistan.

Until the terrorist attacks of September 11, 2001, the government of Pakistan remained satisfied with isolating the Pashtun region and supported the pro-Pashtun Taliban government of Afghanistan, while the organizational and normative governance structures that prevented the establishment of state authority within the FATA were reified with the tacit approval of Islamabad.

## The Soviet Union

From the beginning, it appeared that the Soviet Union was intent on forcing the diverse, fragmented, multiethnic population of Afghanistan to conform to the Soviet communist mold. Suppression became the primary tool for establishing Soviet authority. The social policies of the Soviet Union's puppet regime, the People's Democratic Party of Afghanistan (PDPA), aimed to eradicate ethnic and religious identities, in stark opposition to the well-established customs of the different ethnic groups, especially the highly independent Pashtuns. Education, property rights, and law enforcement were all intended to bolster Soviet/communist control. Predictably, most Afghans resisted Soviet and PDPA efforts to establish their authority.

For ten years, the Soviet Union invested significant resources to acquire Afghanistan as another satellite communist state. Using a strategy of suppression, the Soviets forcefully seized control of Afghanistan's three major cities, Kabul, Kandahar, and Herat; sought to eliminate individuals opposed to Soviet authority; and infiltrated existing national and local governments to suppress any urban uprisings or resistance.[49] As a result, the Soviets managed to rid the major cities of resistance and gained some measure of control over the infrastructure of governance in urban areas. Although the Soviets enjoyed early success in subduing the Afghan resistance outside the cities, it was only a matter of weeks before resistance forces (predominantly Pashtun) regained control of the countryside and established footholds in the areas surrounding Kabul.[50]

While the Soviets were consolidating their hold on the urban areas during the early stages of the invasion, they also made an attempt to gain control of the eastern region of Afghanistan where Pashtuns dominate.[51] At this point, however, the Soviets did not seek to supersede the existing Pashtunwali governance structure but only to eliminate any form of resistance in rural areas. Understanding that the Afghanistan-Pakistan border area was far too large to control with the number of Soviet soldiers deployed to Afghanistan, Moscow attempted to create a "no-man's land" between the two countries by bombing and clearing the main supply routes from Pakistan on both sides of the border.[52] This strategy had two objectives: to rid the border area of resistance fighters, and to intimidate Pakistan into stopping its support for the resistance.[53] The Soviets also conducted overt attacks on refugee areas in Pakistan. These efforts failed to hinder Pakistani support and only served to stiffen the Afghan resistance. Large amounts of external support from Pakistan, the United States, and Saudi Arabia, in the form of military training and the distribution of more sophisticated weapons (most notably antiaircraft missiles), was provided to the mujahideen because of these attacks.[54]

The Soviet strategy to pacify the frontier through the use of force, moreover, only enraged the population. Although it seems that burning crops and villages, intimidating the people, and occasionally engaging the mujahideen (when they could be found) would possibly have weakened the resistance over time, the mujahideen continued to grow in strength because of the collateral damage inflicted on those who were not directly involved.[55] The normative aspect of Pashtunwali that demands revenge required ambivalent Pashtuns who had suffered from Soviet attacks to join the mujahideen. The Soviets also failed to grasp the common practice of segmentary societies to put aside internal enmity toward a collective enemy.

The failure to suppress resistance in rural areas led the Soviets to institute massive reforms in the distribution of land to gain the support of the peasants and redefine the normative rule of law in the region. The Soviets took land from the *Khans* (who often were relatively wealthy landowners) and gave it to younger, poorer men, a tactic by which they hoped to inspire cooperation and support for the communist regime. The younger farmers resisted the re-distribution of land, however, because it violated both the normative (it was not considered just) and organizational (it was not a collective decision of the tribe) governance structures of Pashtunwali and thus threatened Pashtun society.[56] In response, the Soviets forced the changes onto the tribes through physical intimidation and by attacking elements of Afghan custom such as "burning religious books, tearing the veils off women and mocking villagers at prayer."[57] This predictably did not engender respect for Soviet rule of law.

The organizational governance structure under Pashtunwali foiled numerous Soviet attempts to co-opt Pashtun Afghans. In the few cases where Pashtun leaders were successfully co-opted through bribery, those leaders typically lost the support of their followers.[58] When the Soviets tried to play on the divisions in tribal or ethnic factions, many of these groups would often pledge their loyalty to the Soviets in exchange for money and weapons, only to renege on their commitment later and rejoin the mujahideen.[59] Moscow repeatedly failed to grasp the common practice of segmentary societies to put aside internal enmities in the face of a collective foe. Therefore, most Soviet successes in gaining the support of tribes on the Afghan frontier were temporary and only valid until they no longer served the tribe's interests.

By the time Soviet President Mikhail Gorbachev ordered troops to begin withdrawing in 1988, the Soviet Union was no closer to gaining control of Afghanistan than it had been immediately following the invasion. The Kremlin's complete disregard for the competing governance structure that existed in rural Afghanistan, and its commitment to suppress rather than co-opt or accommodate those opposed to Soviet rule, made it impossible for the Soviet Army to subdue the resistance without greater resources. Ultimately, the Soviets failed to conquer Afghanistan because Moscow and the Soviet people lost the political will to succeed. The mujahideen, with the aid of the United States, Saudi Arabia, Pakistan, and Iran, succeeded in making the war too costly for the Soviets with too little benefit.

## Beyond the Pashtun Case

This chapter has focused on identifying the barriers that impede the establishment of state authority in Pashtun areas and the policies states have used to circumvent those barriers. From these cases, four conclusions can be drawn that may apply to other situations in which a state desires to expand its authority into an ungoverned space. First, suppression does not create an environment that contributes to the state's authority. If the state continually has to suppress its people, it is not fostering its legitimacy among them. Under such a policy, the state remains outside society and will likely fail to supplant, in a positive way, local customs with state institutions or a central rule of law. This can be seen in both the British and Soviet cases. Under the British, the Pashtuns did not recognize as illegal many acts considered illegal in British law. Under both the British and the Soviets, suppression only caused the Pashtuns to retreat farther into the hinterland to escape temporary enforcement measures. Neither state had sufficient resources to force the Pashtuns to submit permanently to centralized laws.

Although suppression may allow the state temporarily to control the region and establish some order, the endurance of that control will depend on the amount of resources the state is willing to commit to its maintenance. Control becomes a function of the state's capacity, which in turn depends on both the resources available and the state's ability to maintain its political will, characterized by both popular and political support. Such policies do not establish state authority, though they may, given sufficient capacity and will, establish a semblance of order.

Second, neither isolation nor accommodation creates authority. In both cases, the critical link between the people and the state is broken. To establish and maintain authority, a state must create an atmosphere in which offers of personal security and welfare are not interpreted as carrots intended to change the people's way of life, but as benefits chosen freely and worth the sacrifice of certain aspects of the people's lives. At the same time, a state should promote a sense of representation and/or participation in the government. This extends a state's identity to its people and assures them that their acceptance of the state's authority comes with the ability to shape some of its policies. These are not easy tasks, however, and it is impossible to predict the time required to accomplish them.

Third, if a state's capacity is limited, for either fiscal or political reasons, its policies should focus more on the accommodation side of co-optation (but without giving in completely to accommodation, for the reasons stated above). Unfortunately, this means a state should allow itself more time to establish policies intended to expand state authority. If a state pushes too hard or too fast, its people will likely resist or make larger demands than can be met. In either case, the state's limited capacity would cause such policies to fail.

Fourth, states should understand the difference between establishing order versus establishing authority. Policies designed to establish only order tend to ignore integration and could lead to isolation, accommodation, or even suppression. The incorporation of this concept into policy is obviously problematic. Without order, government representatives attempting to adhere to the previous three recommendations may face unacceptable levels of violence in the ungoverned space. Acknowledging the difficulty involved in implementing this proposition, a state should be willing to accept some resistance and unrest in order to achieve the level of integration necessary to establish its authority. In the Pashtun case, sensitive issues emerged when the imposition of a centralized rule of law entailed the loss of cultural or political autonomy. Therefore, a state that incorporates some cultural aspects of the ungoverned tribe into the rule of law may minimize resistance. In addition, connecting government policy with the tribe's participation adds a level of legitimacy. Although this may seemingly slow the process of incorporation, establishing centralized laws over an existing governance structure likely warrants "slowing down to speed up."

In summary, analysis of the three case studies above produces the following four broad points that should strongly be considered by any state engaging a group living in an ungoverned space: (1) suppression fosters resistance instead of authority; (2) neither isolation nor accommodation generates state authority; (3) limited capacity requires more accommodative co-optation and more time; and (4) policies must focus on establishing authority, not simply establishing order. Although these findings do not sufficiently encompass all the considerations necessary for creating a policy to extend state authority in tribal regions, they do provide a starting point for the development of such policies.

## Notes

The views expressed here do not reflect the views of the U.S. Air Force or the U.S. Department of Defense but are solely the views of the author.

1. Joel Midgal, "Strong Societies, Weak States: Power and Accommodation," in *Understanding Political Development*, ed. Samuel Huntington, Myron Weiner, and Gabriel Almond (Boston: Little, Brown, 1987), 391–437.

2. Lawrence Rosen, "Law and Social Change in the New Nations," *Comparative Studies in Society and History* 20:1 (1978): 3–4.

3. Olaf K. Caroe, *The Pathans* (New York: St. Martin's Press, 1958); John C. Griffiths, *Afghanistan* (New York: Frederick A. Praeger, 1967); Louis Dupree, *Afghanistan*

(Princeton, NJ: Princeton University Press, 1978); Rosen, "Law and Social Change," 3–4.

4. Commander Susan Eagles, quoted in Pamela Constable, "New Attacks Foment Fear in Afghanistan," *Washington Post*, 13 April 2006: A16, http://www.washington post.com/wp-dyn/content/article/2006/04/12/AR2006041201823.html.

5. Tribal population estimate from Central Intelligence Agency, "The World Factbook," as of 2009, http://www.cia.gov/cia/publications/factbook/index.html.

6. Dupree, *Afghanistan*, 415.

7. Ibid., xiii.

8. The Great Game entailed a battle for supremacy over Central Asia between the British and Russian empires from 1813 to 1907. For more information, see Peter Hopkirk, *The Great Game: The Struggle for Empire in Central Asia* (New York: Kodansha America, 1994).

9. Charles Lindholm, "The Segmentary Lineage System: Its Applicability to Pakistan's Political Structure," in *Pakistan's Western Borderlands: The Transformation of Political Order,* ed. Ainslie T. Embree (New Delhi: Vikas, 1977), 41–66.

10. Charles Allen, *Soldier Sahibs* (New York: Carroll & Graf, 2000), 96; Caroe, *Pathans*, 395.

11. James W. Spain, *People of the Khyber: The Pathans of Pakistan* (New York: Frederick A. Praeger, 1963), 49.

12. Caroe, *Pathans*, 395.

13. Lindholm, "Segmentary Lineage System," 60.

14. Caroe, *Pathans*, 397.

15. Allen, *Soldier Sahibs*, 119.

16. Lindholm, "Segmentary Lineage System," 41–66.

17. Spain, *People of the Khyber*, 47.

18. Henry Bellew, *A General Report on the Yusufzais* (1864), quoted in Allen, *Soldier Sahibs*, 94–97.

19. This happened often during the Soviet invasion of Afghanistan. Tribes would receive arms or money from the Soviets on one day and then turn around and start fighting against the Soviet forces the next. M. Hassan Kakar, *Afghanistan: The Soviet Invasion and the Afghan Response, 1979–1982* (Berkeley: University of California Press, 1995), 177.

20. Griffiths, *Afghanistan*, 46–47.

21. Niloufer Qasim Mahdi, "Pukhtunwali: Ostracism and Honor among the Pathan Hill Tribes," in *Ethnology and Sociobiology* 7 (1986): 153.

22. Paul E. Roberts, *History of British India under the Company and the Crown*, 3rd ed. (London: Oxford University Press, 1952), 352.

23. Ibid., 355.

24. Settled areas were places where the British had established security and transportation to provide for the welfare of the people living in the settlement.

25. Caroe, *Pathans*, 395.

26. Roberts, *History of British India*, xiii.

27. Caroe, *Pathans*, 346.

28. Ibid., 329.

29. Ibid., 348.

30. Ibid., 372.

31. Ibid., 399.

32. Akbar S. Ahmed, *Religion and Politics in Muslim Society: Order and Conflict in Pakistan* (Cambridge: Cambridge University Press, 1983), 18.

33. Dupree, *Afghanistan*, 431.

34. Azmat Khan, "FATA," in *Tribal Areas of Pakistan: Challenges and Responses*, ed. Pervaiz Iqbal Cheema and Maqsudul Hasan Nuri (Islamabad: Islamabad Policy Research Institute, 2005), 88.

35. Rashid A. Khan, "Political Developments in FATA: A Critical Perspective," in Cheema and Nuri, *Tribal Areas of Pakistan*, 26–28; James W. Spain, "Political Problems of a Borderland," in Embree, *Pakistan's Western Borderlands*, 11–12.

36. Khan, "Political Developments in FATA," 30.

37. Spain, *People of the Khyber*, 159.

38. Author interview with Brigadier General (ret.) Feroz Khan on 2 March 2003, Monterey, California.

39. Leon B. Poullada, "Pushtunistan: Afghan Domestic Politics and Relations with Pakistan," in Embree, *Pakistan's Western Borderlands*, 133.

40. Khan, "Political Developments in FATA," 29.

41. Spain, "Political Problems of a Borderland," 12.

42. Khan, "Political Developments in FATA," 36–37.

43. Maqsudul H. Nuri, "Soviet Withdrawal: Security Implications for Pakistan," in Cheema and Nuri, *Tribal Areas of Pakistan*, 130.

44. Khan, "Political Developments in FATA," 39.

45. Ibid.

46. Strategic depth is defined as the proximity of the state's strategic security assets to its enemy. For more information, see Peter R. Lavoy and Stephen Smith, "The Risk of Inadvertent Nuclear Use between India and Pakistan," Center for Contemporary Conflict, 3 February 2003, http://www.ccc.nps.navy.mil/rsepResources/si/feb03/southAsia2.asp.

47. Owen B. Jones, *Pakistan: Eye of the Storm* (New Haven, CT: Yale University Press, 2002), 2.

48. "Pakistan's Support for the Taliban," U.S. Department of State, daily press briefing, http://www.state.gov/r/pa/prs/ps/2001/3739.htm (no longer available online).

49. Jeri Laber and Barnett Rubin, *A Nation Is Dying, 1979–1987* (Evanston, IL: Northwestern University Press, 1988), 77.

50. Kakar, *Afghanistan: The Soviet Invasion*, 74.

51. Edward Girardet, *Afghanistan: The Soviet War* (New York: St. Martin's Press, 1985), 33–34.

52. Ibid., 34–35.

53. Bruce J. Amstutz, *Afghanistan: The First Five Years of Soviet Occupation* (Washington, DC: National Defense University Press, 1986), 144; Girardet, *Afghanistan: The Soviet War*, 37.

54. Milan Hauner, *The Soviet War in Afghanistan: Patterns of Russian Imperialism* (Philadelphia: University Press of America, 1991), 93–94.

55. Henry S. Bradsher, *Afghanistan and the Soviet Union* (Durham, NC: Duke University Press, 1985), 211.

56. Girardet, *Afghanistan: The Soviet War*, 110.

57. Ibid.

58. Amstutz, *Afghanistan: The Soviet Occupation*, 148.

59. Kakar, *Afghanistan: The Soviet Invasion*, 177.

PART III
   ALTERNATIVE MODES OF
   SECURITY PROVISION IN
   ZONES OF URBAN EXCLUSION

# 6 Understanding Criminal Networks, Political Order, and Politics in Latin America

Enrique Desmond Arias

By June 2007 paramilitary organizations have come to dominate the *comunas nororientales* (administrative districts) of Medellín, Colombia, an area that until recently had been a major site of conflict in Colombia's generations-old civil war. During 2005 and 2006, paramilitary groups, through negotiations with the state and by defeating Revolutionary Armed Forces of Colombia (FARC) militias in the area, established dominance over the local shantytowns. In doing so, they not only pushed the guerillas out of many of the neighborhoods, but they also took over neighborhood civic groups, in the process forcing many residents who did not agree with their political program to leave. The paramilitaries who operated in this area formed part of a larger military-political structure that is connected with the Corporación Democracia, a political interest group that coordinates the wider demobilization process in Medellín, negotiates the national truth and reconciliation process for some paramilitary groups, and makes demands of the government to effectively distribute resources to the areas of the city dominated by their affiliates. The paramilitaries have been very successful in establishing local dominance and, through such programs as the city's participatory budgeting initiative, gaining control of the state resources flowing into the neighborhood and using them to enhance their status.

The role of violent actors in maintaining local order and providing social services is nothing new in Medellín, where guerillas and drug traffickers have long engaged in these types of activities. Moreover, the political work of the paramilitaries at the local level reflects a wider trend in Latin America, in which armed groups collaborate with state officials to maintain systems of local governance in exchange for state resources and the support of politicians. This process is equally clear in Rio de Janeiro, Brazil, where drug dealers and vigilante groups regularly act as clientelist interlocutors in poor neighborhoods and share the space of governance with public authorities. These two cities, in which most of the fieldwork on which this chapter is based was conducted, are but a small fraction of the areas of Latin America affected by persistent criminal and political violence, but they illustrate the trends toward the provision of governance by armed illicit actors, often in cooperation with licit actors, in ungoverned urban spaces.

The analysis of conflict in Latin America, however, lags substantially behind our understanding of political institutions in the region. In general, scholarship focuses on democratic processes and treats the growing wave of violence that affects most of the major countries in the region as a failure of policy or a failure of political institutions. This chapter argues that conflict in Latin America stems not from state failure or the failure of policy, but rather from historically based political practices, institutional design, and economic processes that enable armed actors to work effectively with the government and share in local governance. We see in Latin America a new system of governance, elsewhere called "violent pluralism,"[1] in which armed groups are incorporated into wider political processes and become part of the political system. The nature of this system of governance is determined by the interaction between sites of institutional strength and weakness, flows of goods, and historical social factors that give rise to different types of organizations and relationships. The chapter will explore how these varied factors come to bear on the structure of governance in urban ungoverned spaces such as those found in Rio de Janeiro and Medellín.

## Violence and Conflict in Latin America Today

For the past generation, scholarship on the Western Hemisphere has focused principally on the process of democratization and the consolidation of democratic regimes and institutions. During the initial wave in the 1980s of research on democratization, studies focused principally on the complexities of getting the military out of government and popular demands for the establishment of a responsive political system.[2] As the literature grew over the course of the 1990s, more work focused on the particulars of the institutions that have been established, the ways they operate, and specific things about Latin American governments that can be tweaked to promote effective governance. As a result, articles in major political science journals have focused on such issues as federalism, parliamentarism, economic development, and legislative voting.

The return to democracy, however, coincided with a substantial upsurge in violence throughout the hemisphere. By the time the Argentine dictatorship fell in 1983, Miami was awash in cocaine. The development of the drug industry in Colombia during the late 1970s spurred a restructuring of the local conflict around illegal goods that enabled the growth of numerous armed groups there.[3] The internationalization of the cocaine trade and its transshipment through other countries led to a growth in violence around the hemisphere. These conditions were aggravated by the difficult financial situation in which many governments in the region found themselves during the debt crisis of the early 1980s, when they experienced substantial inflation and, with pressure from international financial institutions, had to cut back on basic state services to the population.[4]

This shift in resources from the state to the cocaine trade led to the organization in many regional cities of effective criminal gangs that were able to buy high-powered weapons along with the protection of police and higher state officials. These gangs fueled growing murder rates and disorder throughout the region, a trend that was aggravated after 1995 by punitive immigration laws in the United States that led to the deportation of many Central American and Caribbean gang members and the emergence in some countries of the *maras* phenomenon.[5]

Scholarship on the region has struggled to keep up with these issues despite a number of articles and books on the subject published over the course of the 1990s. Most of this work, however, suggested that Latin America was suffering from a lawlessness that had emerged in the context of state failure.[6] The most sophisticated analyst on the topic, Guillermo O'Donnell, breaks the region down into blue, green, and brown areas that reflect different levels of state effectiveness: green areas are where the government works; brown areas are where gangs or other subnational authorities dominate outside the official rule of law; and blue areas fall somewhere in between.[7] O'Donnell has called for increasing attention to the question of state power; other scholars have studied violence by looking principally at problems of policing.[8] The notable exception to this pattern of scholarship is Colombia, where the ongoing civil war has forced scholars to look explicitly at questions of conflict dynamics rather than state institutions.[9] The literature in political science has given us a vision of Latin America in which states are expected to be working democracies and where crime and violence reflect the failure of the state to effectively guarantee democratic order. Violence, as a result, is seen as an absence of effective institutions rather than as the presence of an alternative system of order.

This limits our analysis of the region. Seeing conflict as a failure of the political order can only tell us that murders are a result of something the state has not done, such as effectively police neighborhoods or control police corruption. The issues facing Latin America, however, are much broader and deeper. Poor policing and state violence are a component of conflict in the region, but the heart of violence often lies in non-state armed groups that engage in a variety of illegal activities. Understanding this dynamic means we have to go beyond regarding the brown areas simply as places where the state does not function and instead see the different forms of existing order that intersect with and often support the formal political system in a number of ways.[10] A deeper understanding of the region will come only when we develop a stronger framework for looking at the systems of order that operate in ungoverned spaces.

## Reinterpreting Politics in Latin America

Violence is not a *failure* of Latin America's political systems but a *product* of those systems, and often an important factor in supporting their operation. To understand conflict and violence in Latin America and the Caribbean today, we need to shift our theoretical orientation from one focused on democratic institutions and their failure to one focused on the nature of conflict, broader structural issues, and the relationship between conflict and institutions. In this model, the question is not whether democracy and the state are succeeding or failing, but how space in the region is governed, the factors that support that governance, and the relationship between those involved in governance and the state. A deeper analysis of these historical, social, and structural issues can help us understand the broader trends in the region.

### Historical Factors
Susan Strange has suggested that we are seeing a worldwide retreat of the state.[11] This withdrawal, however, has not left a lack of governance, but rather the proliferation of new forms of governance through such groups as reinsur-

ance firms, accounting firms, and mafias, which serve to regulate spaces that states, for a number of reasons, have neither the resources nor the interest to directly govern. Governments are happy to let certain parts of national territory and the economy be controlled by other groups in order to economize resources and avoid conflict, in effect allowing ungoverned spaces to emerge and be filled by non-state actors.

In Latin America, the retreat of the state was driven by the twin pressures of the democratization process and the debt crisis. The fascistic dictatorships that led Latin America during the 1960s and 1970s usually supported aggressive state policies that actively repressed the left opposition and that inserted the government into economic decision making. Stagnant economies, the debt crisis, and exhaustion with state repression created an alliance between elements of the business elite, the middle class, and the political opposition to force a shift toward democratic systems of government. These new "pacted" governments dramatically decreased political repression, especially of the elite and middle class; supported the reduction of state intervention in the economy; and fostered a market-based regional economic system.[12]

This shift was, in a sense, nothing new in the region, which has long been characterized by a relatively high level of decentralization, with militaries focused more on suppressing dissidents than fighting foreign rivals, and states that had a mediocre ability to collect revenues.[13] The result is not so much the classic "weak" state found in Africa, but rather "medium strength" states that have long had the capacity to maintain order in major cities, engage in substantial national cultural projects, and sustain relatively effective large-scale bureaucracies but that delegate substantial amounts of state power to private actors in more isolated areas and only occasionally have had the capacity to support major industrial programs.

The retreat in state power that began during the 1980s represented a historic break with a previous government policy across the region, dating back to the early twentieth century, that was characterized by active government efforts to integrate the working class, develop the economy, and repress the political opposition.[14] With this shift, most state-building efforts in the region came to an abrupt halt, and governments found themselves without the resources or the political support for further activity. States allowed industries, foreign actors, nongovernmental organizations, civil society, and religious groups to take the government's place in leading the economy and providing services to the poor and other marginalized actors.[15] This retreat of the state created weakly or ungoverned spaces in poor areas and created an opportunity for armed groups to emerge and maintain order. Thus, the particular way in which old forms of state incorporation and building projects failed in the late twentieth century contributed to the structure of violence in Latin America and the Caribbean today.

Even though the cost-benefit calculus no longer favored a state presence, democratization in many countries led politicians to still seek out votes in poorer, less well-governed districts. In many cases, they would develop relationships with local strongmen, exchanging personal or state assets for votes.[16] This would further strengthen local armed actors and create a specific relationship between those actors and the state. Alternatively, in some cases armed local actors became so powerful that they had little use for political patronage from state officials and would provide a separate conduit for services in the area where they operated, or they would put up their own candidates for office.

This dynamic operates in the historic context of clientelism that exists in each country. The particular relationships between political parties and local populations that have evolved in each place will affect the types of violent relationships that emerge at the local level. Thus, in places with longstanding tight clientelist relations conditioned by specific historical circumstances, different patterns of violent practices and organizations may emerge than in places where a more distant relationship between political leaders and the population exists. Some of this, of course, is affected by the particular effects of nondemocratic or dictatorial predecessor regimes on the current political system. A decolonization experience, for instance, would affect the relationships between political parties and the population differently from democratization or a civil war.

This process also operates in relation to the structure of civil society that has emerged in a particular country or region. In places with a deep and robust civil society, armed groups will have to find ways of dealing with various civic actors that have their own power base in newly ungoverned areas, whereas in places with a more limited civil society, armed groups will be able to interpose themselves as the primary local civic actors.

Finally, the role of organized armed groups in ungoverned spaces also appears to be deeply linked to local landholding and economic patterns. Long-term conflict can often be generated by struggles over access to and control of land in rural areas. Likewise, norms and laws regarding land tenure in urban areas, particularly in informal areas, affect the extent to which local residents are dependent on armed actors. In places where individuals do not have a legal right to be on the land where they live, they may turn to armed actors to resolve local disputes and to protect their property rights.[17] Alternatively, armed groups may come to control certain types of residences, such as public housing projects. People who would like to live there may need a gang's permission for access to the area.[18] In essence, the ability of armed actors in urban areas to facilitate and deny access to spaces in which residents live and work reinforces their role in the alternative governance structures that have emerged in many poor or informal districts across the region.

## Institutional Factors

Local institutions affect how violence operates at the local level. How elections take place, the distribution of power through levels of government, and the types and quantities of resources state actors have to distribute to different districts help to structure when and where armed actors emerge and how they use violence.

Specific electoral structures can greatly contribute to the types of localized order that emerge. One of the driving factors affecting relations between politicians and armed actors is whether officeholders are elected from narrow single-seat districts or from wider multimember districts. In places where a single representative emerges from a particular constituency, control of the ballot boxes will be essential to putting a desired member in office, since gaining just one more vote may be enough to push a candidate into the lead. In multimember voting districts, the control of particular geographic space is less important. In these cases, armed actors and other political aspirants have more flexibility in choosing where they will seek votes and how they will achieve the territorial concentration that tends to favor election in these systems.[19] This flexibility means that intense and violent confrontations specifically for votes will be less likely. It does not mean that in the context of a civil war such as Colombia's there will be no military contests focused on controlling towns and votes, or that violence will never be used to win elections in particular places but, rather, that various types of violence will be employed intermittently rather than constantly.

In places where concentrated votes are needed to win election, one will tend to find tight relationships between politicians and specific armed actors that last for a relatively long period of time. Where votes can be gathered more diffusely, politicians are likely to maintain more distant relationships with criminals, since they will gain advantages by negotiating with different groups and can garner support in those places where local leaders make the smallest demands.

The distribution of power through the state is also important to how non-state governance occurs. Where power is principally concentrated in a national government, there will tend to be more competition to control the state itself by electing parties aligned with specific illegal actors. Alternatively, if an electoral path is not viable, illegal actors may formally reject that state system even though they will often maintain relations with members of it. Where power is more diffuse, there is more space for compromise, with illegal actors developing different types of relationships with different levels of political actors. This allows for a more subtle integration of illegal actors into the larger state system.

An important factor in this dynamic is how state and local resources are distributed and spending decisions are made. In places where municipal governments control a substantial amount of spending or control security, there will be a tighter relationship between illegal groups and this level of the political system. Alternatively, if these decisions are made at the national or state level, it is with these governments that armed actors will establish relationships. In the latter context, one will tend to find more powerful, well-organized armed actors as opposed to the municipal level, where lower-level criminals may attain political power.

Another important institutional factor is the question of where and how resources are distributed. In those cases in which large amounts of state resources are distributed through the decisions of individual politicians, relationships with armed groups will be particular and individualized. Alternatively, where resources are distributed through institutionalized mechanisms such as popular budgeting, armed groups may work to manipulate these mechanisms, and even alter their structure. In general, places with smaller and more disorganized criminal groups will tend to work principally through individual politicians, and places with larger and more organized groups will have the ability to work through specific institutions.

As discussed above, much of the political analysis of conflict and crime in Latin America focuses on institutional factors relating to criminal justice. Having ineffective or corrupt police forces will contribute to growing levels of violence and a greater role for criminal groups in governance. Ineffective policing or police abuse can impel large portions of the population to look to armed actors for protection. Disagreements between investigative and uniformed police forces can contribute to these problems. Evidence from Brazil also shows that poorly managed prison systems can increase the levels of crime and acts of mass violence against the population.[20]

## Economic Structure

The last major factor for determining the effect of crime and violence on governance in Latin America is the market flows of resources. The level of violence in places that have easy access to illegal resources will tend to remain high, whereas it will be lower in places with lower amounts of illegal resources.[21]

A large part of the violence in Latin America stems from the cocaine trade. Countries with high levels of cocaine production tend to experience greater violence and governance problems because both the state and traffickers will put a substantial amount of effort into maintaining control over the coca growing regions. The major coca-producing countries are all sites of substantial rural disorder and have experienced serious political instability in recent years. The resources flowing into countries that act as transshipment points create high levels of urban violence, with less effect on rural areas. Finally, locations of consumption will experience lower levels of violence. Table 6.1, which shows data from 1995 to 1998, illustrates this with regard to urban homicides. Colombia's cities, which combine the commercialization of the

**TABLE 6.1**  Urban homicides per 100,000 in Latin America, 1995 to 1998

| City | Homicide rate |
| --- | --- |
| Medellín, Colombia | 248.0 |
| Diadema, Brazil | 146.1 |
| Calí, Colombia | 112.0 |
| Belford Roxo, Brazil | 76.5 |
| Caracas, Venezuela | 76.0 |
| São Paulo, Brazil | 55.8 |
| Rio de Janeiro, Brazil | 52.8 |
| Lima, Peru | 25.0 |
| Santiago, Chile | 8.0 |
| Buenos Aires, Argentina | 6.4 |

SOURCE: Leandro Piquet Carneiro, "Violent Crime in Latin America: Rio de Janeiro and São Paulo," research report for the World Bank, 2000.

drug trade with nearby production, have the highest levels of homicide. Other Latin American cities on trade routes to North America and Europe also have high levels of homicide (Belford Roxo and Diadema are poor suburbs of Rio and São Paulo, respectively). Lima, Peru, which is not a center of drug commercialization but which is located in a country where drug production contributed to national violence, experiences mid-range homicide rates. Finally, Buenos Aires and Santiago, centers of drug consumption, have the lowest levels of homicides.[22]

Cocaine is not the only source of illegal funding. Other narcotics such as heroin and marijuana can play a role in organizing local illegal actors. Their effect will depend on their contribution to the role of narcotics in the local economy and the place of the country in the international division of illegal labor. Some mineral resources can also contribute to local conflicts. This is especially notable in Africa, where diamonds have helped support civil wars, and in Colombia, where emeralds have long supported conflict in parts of the country.[23] The existence of petroleum can contribute to conflict, too, but this operates in a very different way since a strong government usually takes the lead in supporting extraction. In Colombia, for example, the insurgent group Ejercito de Liberación Nacional extorts protection money from oil companies to *not* attack their pipelines.[24] Finally, armed groups can make money through other types of illegal activities such as the trade in human beings.

The effect of different types of illegal economic activities varies from country to country, depending on the particular role of that country in international crime and the particular historical context that exists in that country. Thus, for example, Mexico, Brazil, Jamaica, and the Dominican Republic are all drug transshipment sites but experience the problem of violence slightly differently. At the same time, Colombia, Peru, and Bolivia are the three largest producers of cocaine, and cocaine has contributed to violence and political instability in each country, but the individual history of each, and its place in the commercialization of drugs, has an effect on violence in the country.

A second major component of the way economic flows affect governance is through access to illegal arms. Violent groups with easy access to arms will generally play a larger role in local governance than groups that have more trouble getting access to weapons. The small arms flows from the United States, from a large domestic market, or as the result of a nearby conflict will contribute to the ability of armed actors to engage in local governance. Weapons play an important role in developing illegal activities, as they allow armed organizations to shift from primary illicit markets such as dealing drugs into illicit security markets. Selling protection, however, is the central social contribution of the state.[25] As armed organizations shift into the protection market, their role in governance will grow as they more distinctly supplant the state.

### Criminal Organization and Synthesizing Governance

The variety of roles that armed actors can play in governance often emerge as a result of relationships between armed actors and wider institutional, social, and economic factors. Illegal groups operate in specific ways on the paths of economic flows, within markets, and in relation to other elements of state and society.

Illegal armed actors can take on a variety of organizational structures, though the persistence of armed activity depends on the ways in which these groups are networked together and into social, economic, and political organizations. Depending on the factors discussed above, there may be larger or smaller hierarchical components to illegal organizational structures, but across the region illegal activities also reflect the role of networking in supporting ongoing illegal activities. Thus, even guerilla armies rely on semi-clandestine networks, contacts in the government, and other illegal actors to support their activities. In most cases these networks will survive the deactivation of a specific criminal or group, since the network structure will enable other illegal actors to step into their place.[26] These networks are embedded in the social, political, and economic processes discussed above. Thus, governments may work to arrest criminals, but the networks through which they operate mean that it is extremely hard to affect overall levels of crime.

Over time and across countries the internal structure of criminal organizations varies on the basis of local cultural and institutional factors, the particular nature of these groups' interactions with the wider political system, and the types of criminal activities in which they are engaged. Local drug gangs in Rio de Janeiro, for example, have distinct hierarchies and roles for members. These groups interact with other gangs through loosely structured but formally hierarchical commandos that in turn link into the wider criminal and institutional environment through networks.[27] Drug-trafficking organizations in Colombia adopt different forms of network structures to support the different forms of criminal activity in which they engage.[28] The cartels that formerly dominated criminal activities in cities such as Medellín operated as business associations that provided insurance to small carriers and facilitated corrupt payoffs on behalf of members.[29] No solid rule describes the structure of criminal organizations in the region except that they operate in networks with hierarchical nodes that change over time in reaction to changes in economic opportunities and institutional pressure.

Criminals play roles in governing space, negotiating political alliances, delivering political support, and enabling the illegal markets on which many in the informal sector depend for a living.[30] As such, armed actors work with state, social, and economic actors to build synthetic forms of governance; at certain times and places they resolve disputes and administer certain types of interactions. This administration is based within a political calculus that is related to the wider national law and norms but that also changes the practice of that law.[31] This leads to a constantly shifting structure that appears from the outside to be disorder or a lack of governance but, when looked at closely, reflects a changing system of network-based governance embedded in a social, political, and economic system. The following section suggests how these systems of governance operate in Colombia and Brazil.

## Analyzing Violent Governance in Colombia and Brazil

Colombia is a mid- to large-sized South American country that has experienced ongoing conflict for more than sixty years and where large armed groups wage a war against the state and each other, in both cities and the countryside, that is funded by narcotics revenues. Brazil is one of the world's largest countries in terms of both population and area. Rio de Janeiro, its former capital and second largest metropolitan area, and other major cities suffer from gang violence principally associated with the local drug trade. Despite these substantial differences there are also remarkable similarities between the countries along historical, social, economic, and political lines.

Illegal drug markets fund conflict in both countries. The large international demand for narcotics, and the particular value of cocaine, infuses a tremendous amount of resources into illegal marketplaces in Latin America. The conditions of violence in Colombia, however, differ from those in Brazil. Colombia is one of a handful of Andean countries that can produce large amounts of cocaine. The value of rural areas for coca production means armed groups maintain control of large regions of the country, and the dominant armed groups in each city use their urban operations to support wider political and military strategies. In other words, urban violence in Colombia is driven by rural processes. Rio de Janeiro, on the other hand, is a transshipment center where cocaine is moved out of Latin America into North America and Europe. As a result, rural violence in Brazil has only a tenuous link to urban violence, and each major metropolitan area has its own independent violent organizations. Major urban port cities are centers of violence, and gangs located in poor areas provide important support for moving the drugs abroad. This autonomous urban violence then connects into the political system through traditional clientelist networks. Table 6.2 summarizes the type of criminal activity and it effects on conflict in the two countries.

Each country experiences the problems of economic dependence and surplus labor. The unemployed in Rio de Janeiro and Medellín often seek economic opportunities in the informal sector. At times this causes them to depend on illegal armed actors for access to resources in violent clandestine markets. At other times, working outside the formal sector or living in a home to which they do not have title forces the poor to go to illegal actors to resolve local conflicts. The result is the same in each case: substantial portions of the population live outside the normal legal system because of poverty and as a result depend on strongmen for protection. This provides illegal armed actors with a limited amount of political legitimacy and an important social role.

The final element of wider economic processes that are important in each country is easy access to arms. In Colombia, the long-term conflict and drug trade provide access to large quantities of weapons from both the international illegal market in arms and the Colombian military, which supplies some paramilitary groups. Brazil's illegal arms generally come from the domestic arms industry and are often sold directly by police officers to gangs. The large volume of internal arms production gives Brazilians access to relatively powerful light combat weapons.

**TABLE 6.2** The international division of criminal labor and violence in Colombia and Brazil

| Country | Criminal activity | Effects on conflict |
| --- | --- | --- |
| Colombia | Production and commercialization | High levels of linked urban and rural violence; national scale violent actors |
| Brazil | Transshipment | High levels of urban violence unconnected to rural land conflicts; violence concentrated in port cities |

Elements of the political system in each country also affect the particular practices of violence that evolve in these places and the relationship between violence and governance. Colombia has a presidential system with large multimember voting districts and, today, relatively powerful municipalities. The power of armed groups and the relative wealth of municipalities promote heavily armed contests for control of population centers. The large multimember districts enable candidates to build relationships with particular neighborhoods and towns across the region to which they are aligned. Candidates must maintain strong contacts with the armed groups that dominate municipalities in their regions; these groups thus have succeeded in electing representatives to the national legislature.

While the Brazilian political system is very similar to Colombia's, the absence of a rural guerilla movement limits armed contestation over municipal governments. Although armed actors are critical to local political access in Rio de Janeiro, they are relatively weaker and, historically, have had fewer direct links to politicians once they have been elected, especially at the national level. With the advent of *milícias*—local vigilante groups, often tied to state officials, that have succeeded in electing representatives to municipal councils and state legislatures—this has begun to change. The result in the cases of both Colombia and Brazil has been that state resources are diverted to areas where armed groups with political representation have power. Table 6.3 illustrates this trend.

While the electoral system in each country differs, the bureaucracies in both suffer from similar problems. Each country has corrupt and inefficient security forces that are often aligned with armed actors. Bribe-taking by these groups or actual participation in illegal violent activities reinforces the power of armed groups in both countries, while corruption on the part of state security forces decreases their legitimacy and effectiveness among the population.

As a result of these factors, the implementation of order in these areas depends on collaboration between armed groups and the state. The type of collaboration that emerges is structured by the particularities of the local electoral system and the division of power between levels of government. In Colombia this plays out in the way that armed groups try to dominate municipal political processes. Brazil's armed groups vie to control access to their communities and, more recently, directly seek public office.

Violence does not emerge so much out of state weakness as it does out of the relationship between spaces of state strength and weakness. Armed ac-

**TABLE 6.3**  Political institutions and violence in Colombia and Brazil

| Country | Voting system / subnational system | Outcomes |
|---------|-----------------------------------|----------|
| Colombia | Large multimember districts, proportional representation | Development of multiple parties with relatively low party discipline. Some parties have direct ties to armed groups, but armed groups also have ties to members of other parties. |
| | Direct budgetary transfer to municipalities | Armed groups engage in intense conflict to control municipalities and openly work to control local budgetary mechanisms such as the Participatory Budgeting Program in Medellín. |
| Brazil | Large multimember districts, open-list proportional representation | Low party discipline in which many political leaders establish transient ties to armed actors to gain access to votes, and some successful cases of representatives of armed groups winning election as members of important political parties; residents of neighborhoods tend to identify with local leaders rather than politicians. |
| | Direct budgetary transfer to municipalities | Armed groups attempt to develop relations with municipal leaders to gain access to resources. |

tors engage in governance activities in ungoverned spaces within generally adequately governed states that exist in this region. They structure many of their activities around getting access to certain types of state resources and maintaining relations with public officials. The types of relationships that emerge, and the nature of the efforts to exploit these resources, depend on the institutional constraints of the political system and the historical legacies that have given rise to that political system.

## Roots of Violent Politics

Social and historical factors are the last constraints on the relationship between states and armed groups. The most important component in this mix is the particular way that the large-scale state-building and national incorporation processes of the twentieth century failed, and the ways in which that failure played out politically. In Colombia, that national incorporation process began in the 1930s and led to some degree of workers' rights in urban areas. As demands for social and economic justice spread beyond the major cities and into the countryside, land conflicts contributed to the interparty strife that drove *La Violencia* (1948–1958). This period of internecine war resulted in a stalemate between armed groups associated with the Liberal and Conservative parties, and ended in 1958 only with the formation of the coalition National Front, in which the two major parties agreed to cease hostilities in exchange for sixteen years of power sharing. This agreement among elites excluded the armed popular militias that had supported each party; these militias then evolved into the nuclei of the left-wing guerillas who participate in the current civil war. Their longstanding independence from major parties and their strong position in the countryside enabled them to become political players in Colombia, and to sit at the negotiating table with the government. The paramilitary groups that have evolved in response have achieved that same status.

Brazil developed a top-down form of corporatism, initiated during the *Estado Novo* period of authoritarian rule in the 1930s and held together at the federal level through the end of the dictatorship in 1945. This hybrid structure simultaneously excluded and abused elements of the urban poor even as it worked to maintain the basic corporatist social structures connecting the state to labor. With the debt crisis of the 1980s and the consensus to reduce state size during this same period, the Brazilian government substantially scaled back its safety net to the working classes in the industrial centers of Rio and São Paulo. This pushed many workers into the informal economy. More importantly, it undermined the very institutions that used to connect the state to different elements of the poor.[32] Thus, clientelism and an often abusive police presence emerged as the principal ties between the excluded population and the state. In Brazil, armed popular actors had never had a substantial political role, and, indeed, the state had brutally crushed what popular uprisings emerged in the nineteenth century. The criminals who stepped in to fill some of the resource gaps left by a retreating state in the 1980s and 1990s did so in an environment in which there was little history of links between popular armed groups and the state. As a result they had no accepted place in the political framework and instead interposed themselves on the clientelist relations that existed between shantytown dwellers and the state, as well as starting their own local patronage networks. Over the course of the 1980s and 1990s, drug dealers established semi-clandestine networks that inserted them into the political system as a new type of violent actor that provided patronage and controlled access to some parts of the urban area. During this time, they often depended on civic authorities to maintain their

**TABLE 6.4** Historic process and armed actors' role in governance
in Colombia and Brazil

| Country | Circumstances | Outcomes |
|---|---|---|
| Colombia | Strong ties between armed actors and state in 1950s that break down in 1960s and 1970s as drug economy provides independent resources to guerilla groups | Powerful autonomous armed actors with substantial national political standing and dominance over wide areas of national territory |
| Brazil | Armed popular actors traditionally destroyed by state; clientelism main link between poor and state | Armed groups with no legitimate political role; instead they work through clandestine connections and civil society to establish transient patronage relations with politicians and to work through the state bureaucracy to gain space to engage in violent activities. As a result, violence is not tied to elections, but rather to contestation over how government bureaucracies will operate. |

links with the state, since there was no accepted way for armed actors to connect directly to the government. As new armed groups have evolved and relations with the state have changed, these groups have been able to establish more regular ties to state government. Table 6.4 summarizes this process.

## Conclusion

Violent groups in Latin America are incorporated into the state through networks that tie them together with civic actors, bureaucrats, and politicians. The shape of these networks is determined by the historical legacy of how incorporation projects failed and the role of armed groups in those incorporation projects. In the case of Colombia, years of fighting and the resources available through drug production enabled these groups to establish themselves as independent political actors who could sit down and negotiate with the state and make formal political demands. By contrast, armed actors in Brazil had no accepted political space because they had no role in the incorporation process. Brazilian armed groups had to feel their way through the political system, initially by building contacts with the government through civic actors, and later by developing new types of political activity, including vigilantism, that enabled them to gain some political legitimacy.

This chapter has provided a multileveled analysis of the problems of governance in Latin America. Going well beyond the existing writing on this problem in political science, which tends to place the question of violence in Latin America squarely within the bounds of different forms of state failure, this chapter has demonstrated that violence in Latin America reflects not so much the failure of the state, but rather the way in which the state operates in conjunction with armed actors. Starting from a historical perspective, it shows that violence in different countries in the region is constrained by the particular ways that state-building and incorporation projects have changed or failed over the past thirty years, the ways that political institutions promote different types of conflict and engage violent actors in the governance process, and the ways that economic flows contribute to violence in particular places. This account provides a systematic way to look at violence in Latin America, not simply as a problem emanating from weakness in contemporary democratic regimes but rather as part of a wider historic, structural, social, and economic process that can be contextualized within the long process of state and social violence in the region.

## Notes

1. Enrique Desmond Arias and Daniel Goldstein, "Violent Pluralism: Understanding the 'New Democracies' of Latin America," in *Violent Democracies of Latin America*, ed. Enrique Desmond Arias and Daniel Goldstein (Durham, NC: Duke University Press, 2010).

2. See especially, Guillermo O'Donnell and Philippe C. Schmitter, *Transitions from Authoritarian Rule: Tentative Conclusions about Uncertain Democracies* (Baltimore, MD: Johns Hopkins University Press, 1986).

3. William Ramírez Tobón, "Las Autodefensas y el Poder Local," in *El Poder Paramilitar*, ed. Alfredo Rangel (Bogotá: Editora Planeta, 2005), 183.

4. Guillermo O'Donnell, "On the State, Democratization, and Some Conceptual Problems," *World Development* 21 (August 1993): 1361, 1364; see also, Felipe Agüero, "Conflicting Assessments of Democratization: Exploring the Fault Lines," in *Fault Lines of Democracy in Post-Transition Latin America*, ed. Felipe Agüero and Jeffrey Stark (Coral Gables, FL: North-South Center Press, 1993), 6.

5. Presentation by Honduran police at a conference on community policing in Latin America, John Jay College of Criminal Justice, New York, November 2006. The Mara Salvatrucha, known as MS 13, is an affiliation of extremely violent street gangs that has spread across the hemisphere from its origins among Salvadoran immigrants in Los Angeles.

6. A comprehensive example of this approach can be found in "Democracy in

Latin America: Towards a Citizens' Democracy," United Nations Development Program, New York, 2004, http://www.un-ngls.org/orf/democracy-undp-publication. htm; and Guillermo O'Donnell, "Why the Rule of Law Matters," *Journal of Democracy* 15:4 (2004): 42. On informal rules and police violence, see Daniel Brinks, "Informal Institutions and the Rule of Law: The Judicial Response to State Killings in Buenos Aires and São Paulo in the 1990s," *Comparative Politics* 36:1 (2003): 6–7; O'Donnell, "Why the Rule of Law Matters," 1355–69. On policing and violence in Argentina and Brazil, see Mercedes Hinton, "A Distant Reality: Democratic Policing in Argentina and Brazil," *Criminal Justice* 5:1 (2005): 75–100, esp. 90; Ronald E. Ahnen, "The Politics of Violence in Brazil," *Latin American Politics and Society* 49:1 (2007): 141–64, esp. 142. An interesting variant on this approach focuses on how state reforms can bring military perpetrators of violence to justice; on this, see Jorge Zaverucha, "Military Justice in the State of Pernambuco after the Brazilian Military Regime: An Authoritarian Legacy," *Latin American Research Review* 34:2 (1999): 43–74; Jorge Correa Sutil, "Judicial Reforms in Latin America: Good News for the Underprivileged," in *The (Un) Rule of Law and the Underprivileged in Latin America*, ed. Juan Méndez, Guillermo O'Donnell, and Paulo Sérgio Pinheiro (South Bend, IN: University of Notre Dame Press, 1998), 255–77.

7. O'Donnell, "On the State," 1361, 1364.

8. O'Donnell, "Why the Rule of Law Matters," 42.

9. Eduardo Pizarro Leongomez, *Una Democracia Asediada: Balance y Perspectivas del Conflicto Armado en Colombia* (Bogotá: Grupo Editorial Norma, 2004); Jenifer S. Holmes, Amin Gutiérrez de Piñeres, and Kevin M. Curtin, "Drugs, Violence, and Development in Colombia: A Department Level Analysis," *Latin American Politics and Society* 48:3 (2006): 157–84.

10. For a discussion of this approach, see Enrique Desmond Arias, *Drugs and Democracy in Rio de Janeiro: Trafficking, Social Networks, and Public Security* (Chapel Hill: University of North Carolina Press, 2006), 8.

11. Susan Strange, *The Retreat of the State: The Diffusion of Power in the World Economy* (Cambridge: Cambridge University Press, 1996).

12. For a discussion of pacted transitions, see O'Donnell and Schmitter, *Transitions from Authoritarian Rule*.

13. Miguel Angel Centeno, *Blood and Debt: War and the Nation-State in Latin America* (University Park: Pennsylvania State University Press, 2002).

14. Ruth Berins Collier and David Collier, *Shaping the Political Arena: Critical Junctures, the Labor Movement, and Regime Dynamics in Latin America* (Princeton, NJ: Princeton University Press, 1991), 6.

15. On the breakdown of state-society ties, see Rubem César Fernandes, *Private but Public* (Washington, DC: Civicus Press, 1995), 104–7. On this process in Ecuador, see Monique Segarra, "Redefining the Public/Private Mix: NGOs and the Emergency Social Investment Fund in Ecuador," in *The New Politics of Inequality in Latin America: Rethinking Participation and Representation*, ed. Douglas A. Chalmers, Carlos M. Vilas, Katherine Hite, and Scott B. Martin (New York: Oxford University Press, 1997),

515; also see Douglas A. Chalmers, Scott B. Martin, and Kerianne Piester, "Associative Networks: New Structures of Representation for the Popular Sectors," in Chalmers et al., *The New Politics of Inequality*, 543–82.

16. One of the most nuanced analyses of contemporary clientelism in Latin America can be found in Javier Auyero, *Poor People's Politics: Peronist Survival Networks and the Legacy of Evita* (Durham, NC: Duke University Press, 2000). For analyses specifically of violent clientelism, see Robert Gay, "The Broker and the Thief: A Parable (Reflections on Popular Politics in Brazil), *Luso-Brazilian Review* 36:1 (1999): 49–70; Colin Clarke, "Politics, Violence and Drugs in Kingston, Jamaica," *Bulletin of Latin American Research* 25:3 (2006): 420–40; Amanda Sives, "Changing Patrons, from Politicians to Drug Don: Clientelism in Downtown Kingston, Jamaica," *Latin American Perspectives* 29:5 (September 2002): 66–89; Andres Villareal, "Patronage Competition and Violence in Mexico: Hierarchical Social Control in Local Patronage Structures," *American Sociological Review* 67 (2002): 477–98; Kent Eaton, "The Downside of Decentralization: Armed Clientelism in Colombia," *Security Studies* 15:4 (2006): 533–62; and Enrique Desmond Arias, "Trouble en Route: Drug Trafficking and Clientelism in Rio de Janeiro Shantytowns," *Qualitative Sociology* 29:4 (2006): 427–45.

17. Hernando De Soto, "The Constituency of Terror," *New York Times*, 15 October 2001: A19.

18. This is the case in Jamaica. See Laurie Gunst, *Born Fi' Dead: A Journey through the Jamaica Posse Underworld* (New York: Owl Books, 1998), 79–80.

19. Barry Ames, "Electoral Strategy under Open-List Proportional Representation," *American Journal of Political Science* 39:2 (1995): 406–33.

20. Arias, *Drugs and Democracy in Rio de Janeiro*; Brinks, "Informal Institutions and the Rule of Law."

21. Mathew Brzezinsky, "Re-engineering the Drug Business," *New York Times Magazine*, 23 June 2002: 24–29, 46, 54–55; Leongomez, *Una Democracia Asediada*, 170–81; Tobón, "Autodefensas y el Poder Local," 181–91.

22. Table 6.1 is a shorter version of a chart taken from Leandro Piquet Carneiro, "Violent Crime in Latin America: Rio de Janeiro and São Paulo," research report for the World Bank, 2000. Accessed 21 April 2008 at http://wbln0018.worldbank.org/LAC /lacinfoclient.nsf/e9dd232c66d43b6b852567d2005ca3c5/9a4d6bea7b4b6ddb852568b 90075f48d/$FILE/Crime&Violence_Rio&SaoPaulo.pdf (no longer available).

23. On this issue, see William R. Reno, *Warlord Politics and African States* (Boulder, CO: Lynne Rienner Publishers, 1998).

24. Leongomez, *Una Democracia Asediada*, 181–82.

25. Diego Gambetta, *The Sicilian Mafia: The Business of Private Protection* (Cambridge, MA: Harvard University Press, 1993); Charles Tilly, "War Making and State Making as Organized Crime," in *Bringing the State Back*, ed. Peter Evans, Dietrich Reuschmeyer, and Theda Skocpol (Cambridge, MA: Harvard University Press, 1985), 169–91.

26. See Arias, *Drugs and Democracy in Rio de Janeiro*.

27. Luke Dowdney, *Children of the Drug Trade: A Case Study of Children in Organised Armed Violence in Rio de Janeiro* (Rio de Janeiro: 7Letras, 2003), 39–51.

28. See Michael Kenney, *From Pablo to Osama: Trafficking and Terrorist Networks, Government Bureaucracies, and Competitive Adaptation* (University Park: Pennsylvania State University Press, 2007), 27–36.

29. Francisco Thoumi, *Political Economy and Illegal Drugs in Colombia* (Boulder, CO: Lynne Rienner Publishers, 1995), 93–108.

30. Anthony Harriott, *Police and Crime Control in Jamaica: Problems of Reforming Ex-Colonial Constabularies* (Kingston: University of the West Indies Press, 2000).

31. Enrique Desmond Arias and Corrine Davis Rodrigues, "The Myth of Personal Security: Criminal Gangs, Dispute Resolution, and Identity in Rio de Janeiro's Favelas," *Latin American Politics and Society* 48:4 (2006): 53–81. See also, Bonaventura de Souza Santos, *Towards a New Common Sense: Law, Science, and Politics in the Paradigmatic Transition* (London: Routledge, 1995); Orin Starn, *Nightwatch: The Politics of Protest in the Andes* (Durham, NC: Duke University Press, 1999); and Daniel M. Goldstein, *The Spectacular City: Violence and Performance in Urban Bolivia* (Durham: Duke University Press, 2004).

32. Fernandes, *Private but Public*.

# 7 Authority outside the State

*Non-State Actors and New Institutions in the Middle East*

Anne Marie Baylouny

The Middle East appears rife with violent non-state actors operating outside domestic law and international norms. Through state incapacity, economic reforms, or war, increasing areas are untouched by state services or law. Territories are becoming effectively stateless even in the geographic heart of the nominal state itself. States considered strong (Tunisia) or rich (Saudi Arabia) are similarly affected. Yet unlike Hobbes's nightmare of all-out competition and violence, the areas are in fact governed. Instead of chaos in spaces where state sovereignty is sparse or absent, alternative authorities arise. New actors and institutions fulfill roles previously considered the preserve of the state. Gangs, militias, thugs, local men of influence, and religious political parties are the main contenders for authority. These actors and their authority are not traditional or longstanding; they are newly successful, self-made leaders. They establish authority through services to the community and legitimate it in terms of religion, identity, or violence.[1]

Who governs areas unregulated by the state, and how is their authority generated? What must an individual do to become an authority?[2] In most Western analyses of the Middle East, authorities are presumed to be preexisting, carried over from traditional allegiances such as tribes and longstanding wealthy or landowning families. Alternatively, non-state actors, whether armed or with political agendas, are assumed to either control the areas or be easily capable of doing so. Policymakers, journalists, and many scholars consider unregulated areas automatic prey to Islamists and other extremist ideologies.[3] The residents of the areas and their motivations for acknowledging one authority or another are typically missing from these descriptions.

States and the international community fear the potential insecurity produced by these areas and the likelihood that they will harbor terrorists and criminals and foment civil unrest and rebellion against state authorities. These fears are sometimes but not always well founded. These security outcomes are neither immediate nor direct but may be side effects of local rule based on alternative institutions and authority structures. Anti-state political organizing is not endemic to these areas but can arise when basic life concerns of residents are threatened. In many cases local institutions are weak and unable to reject troublemaking residents. In others, emerging actors and institutions with more legitimacy than the absentee state regard the government as a threat to their existence and bond easily with outlaws in common cause.

This chapter examines the constituent elements of authority in alternatively governed areas and finds that authority is tied to the provision of substantive services to the population.[4] Yet while the social welfare services of Islamists have received much attention, it is not these practices that are central to authority, but rather policing and conflict resolution. The relations among residents in informal and unregulated areas are often problematic, complicated by mundane neighborhood concerns. Those able to regulate and organize relations, minimize conflict, and create peaceful order among the inhabitants have influence. With investment in the community, this can become authority. Initially, influence can stem from market success, the threat of violence, or the organization of public space. If it is not utilized for conflict resolution, and if the power holder is not viewed as fair in his dealings with residents, however, he will not become an authority.[5]

Three variables govern the generation of authority in areas of the Middle East unregulated by the state: the initial basis for claiming influence, the method of legitimation, and the services that popularly validate the claim to authority. Through an examination of the types of authority and their roles in Middle Eastern communities, I delineate the common institutions organized by non-state authorities. These institutions indicate what practices and services furnish authority, and ultimately legitimacy, in unregulated contexts. Many posit that demands for public goods that the state does not provide— what Rodney Hall and Thomas Biersteker call "functional holes"—are integral to the rise of private authority. However, what specific goods and services confer authority to private non-state actors is not specified. I contribute to identifying the institutions and public goods that are at the heart of authority creation in relatively ungoverned, or unregulated, spaces.[6] Although the fulfillment of key functions leads to influence in the community and acquiescence to governance, this dynamic does not necessarily imply either legitimacy or approval. Notwithstanding the population's benefits from services and governance, non-state rule can be brutal, arbitrary, and oppressive, a fact not lost on the community.[7] Through an examination of the central roles empowering local leaders, this study seeks to uncover community priorities, the institutions considered necessary for daily life. An aspiring authority—unjust or not—who provides needed functions thus validates his prestige and leadership.

Few studies explore the substance of alternative authorities in the Middle East from the grassroots perspective. This study utilizes existing scholarship in addition to the author's fieldwork to arrive at a hypothesis regarding authority generation in these areas. Individuals become alternative authorities in large part by providing necessary and basic services. Alternative authorities provide services of infrastructure, policing and arbitration, mediation with the state, social services, and welfare. Their activities can further extend to economic connections and business aid. This chapter begins by first presenting the differing types of unregulated spaces and the various forms of authority in them. It then examines each of the institutions that are created to substantiate authority and finally the prevalent forms of legitimation for that authority—religious, identity, and violent. Data are primarily from Egypt, Algeria, Tunisia, the Palestinian territories, Lebanon, Syria, Jordan, and Iraq, supplemented with research on other countries in the region. Data for the militias come from Lebanon.

## Types of Authorities, Their Spaces, and Services

Many types of areas in the Middle East are outside state regulation. Most consist of a dynamic mix of new groups and socioeconomic classes, including the long-urbanized middle and lower classes and individuals with full-time formal jobs. Opposition to the state in its law-and-order functions is essential to securing a livelihood in many of these cases; in others, it is a by-product of organizing separate services and local governance and locating allies in these pursuits.[8] Contact with the state for residents of informal communities is necessarily adversarial because title to the land on which they live is not established. The majority of work in these areas also is informal.[9] Residents experience state authority as a threat to home and work, as police attempt to shut down or extract bribes from informal employment and periodically evict the residents of informal housing. Governments regard these extralegal communities as security threats that potentially hide criminals or terrorists and therefore bulldoze shanties and evict residents or arrest them in security sweeps.[10] In 1991, for instance, Algerians living in informal housing voted for the main opposition party in Algeria, the Islamic Salvation Front, because they viewed their interests as similar.[11] De facto authorities who are able to mediate with the state and keep police away accrue prestige in informal communities. The corruption of law enforcement often drives the populace to rely on intermediaries who are able to bribe and negotiate with officials of the state. Many local authorities invest heavily in cultivating a relationship with the state, and state authorities in turn informally rely upon these figures to mediate with residents of these unregulated spaces. The state has little direct relation with these citizens.[12]

The inhabitants of areas unregulated by the state create a variety of individual and collective arrangements to meet daily needs. Individual accommodations include tapping into existing utilities, such as water and power, off the meter and attempting to remain invisible to the state.[13] Some residents are wary about any collective organizing, preferring to act alone. For others, collective institutions of arbitration or policing and service provision are desirable. The latter can encompass basic public services such as electricity, water, sewage, and garbage disposal and can extend to the provision of day care or the organization of sports teams, tutoring, and personal loans. Policing includes arbitration of disputes and the regulation of social behavior in public spaces. In militia-controlled areas, services can be more elaborate, including the establishment of institutions for governance and justice. Leaders of lineage and village associations are expected to furnish welfare and employment networks. There is, however, less demand for arbitration for these groups when members' residences are not geographically concentrated.

The specific mix of institutions depends on capacity and need. Institutional capacity turns upon the existence of resources, potential leadership, and non-competition among power holders. The needs and desires of residents and the type of unregulated space constitute the second layer of variables determining institutional outcomes. Ungoverned spaces vary in the services they receive from the state; some lack basic sewage, while others have fundamental infrastructure but not social welfare. The extreme cases are found in squatter settlements and refugee camps, where state services and basic infrastructure are often nonexistent. Militias that contest and supplant the authority of the state likewise rule over areas with numerous needs. When they claim to substitute for the state, the call for absent services falls on them, although an adequate or any response is not necessarily forthcoming.

In general, after infrastructure, the priorities in collective institutions are the arbitration of disputes and policing of public spaces, and the provision of social services. Authorities can extend this into moral governance, a role most often performed by religious and political groups rather than individuals. While institutional creation in these areas can be quite dynamic, the generation of new accommodations to meet daily needs is not a given. Many areas have little to none of the services described here. Furthermore, even when services exist, the population is not necessarily equally served; the resulting institutions are often arbitrary and discriminatory.

Institutions for collective goods can be established only when a monopoly of power exists. Even in an area as small as an alleyway (*hara*), only one authority figure dominates. Residents of informal settlements are able to identify the exact geographical boundaries of each power holder—where one's influence ends and another's begins.[14] Competition constrains actors to struggle for dominance, forestalling the development of governance institutions. Militias in the Lebanese civil war that competed for control of territory, for instance, did not establish governance and service institutions. Even when the ideological bent of one of the approximately one hundred militias involved in that conflict promoted service and governance institutions, the group was unable to do so without a political monopoly and territorial control.

Alternative authorities generally start out as newcomers to the power game, concerned with obtaining a higher social status. They begin their claim to influence with either economic success or physical ability. These individuals made money and connections or obtained influence through the use of violence. In both cases, they must also have a reputation for fairness, honesty, and good works in the community. A reputation as a man of honor can be obtained through repeated interactions with constituents, but this takes time. Patronage of religious institutions, by contrast, is a fast but not mandatory method for demonstrating moral uprightness, and religion can serve as a shortcut to such a reputation. Militias can also impose their authority purely through force, but they usually also rely on political ideologies to justify their rule. Nevertheless, religion, political ideology, and reputation are not sufficient to cement a position of authority. To become an authority, one must furnish services and mediate with state authorities. Would-be authorities either intercede with state institutions on behalf of community members or replace the state entirely.

Authorities in unplanned or informal settlements are often successful merchants, real estate brokers, or contractors. They are known to residents and understood to deserve respect, deference, and admiration as men who have more power than those around them. Their status and influence are specific to a local area.[15] They are active in local organizations and charities and have personal connections with police and state authorities. They intercede for residents when necessary, obtain permits for weddings, and assure that the police stay away. The relationship is not one-sided; the authority has responsibilities to care for residents, pay the cost of reconciliation meetings, and aid those in need.

Violent authorities or specialists in violence obtain influence by forcibly ordering and policing unregulated spaces, often at the behest of residents. Militias order their territory by force; in some areas a militia and its accompanying political party is often the only game in town for residents. The validation of these groups' authority comes from their physical prowess and success in battles, yet this form of legitimization alone does not suffice. Militia wars must be viewed as necessary by the populace. The thugs enforcing street order must be perceived to be honest and fair to their constituent population.[16] The provision of an acceptable level of social welfare and public goods by violent authorities is an advertisement for the group's ability to rule and a consequence of their success in replacing the state. Political parties that rule refugee camps and militias that subjugate areas taken from the state assume a broad range of roles typically ascribed to the state, including infrastructure, policing, welfare, and moral governance.

In the same way, leadership by identity-based authorities such as hometown or kin associations accrues through their ability to provide aid, welfare, and employment contacts. Power is accorded to potential leaders well connected in business and job circles or those tightly linked to the state and able to secure influence there.[17] Affirmation of the identity's distinction from other social groups helps to solidify the unity of the organization.[18] Here the priority of community public goods is clear, as the leaders are voted in or out of office on the basis of their provision of economic aid and job networks rather than their identity.

## Dispute Settlement and Policing

Central to community cohesion are the policing of public space and fair arbitration of disagreements among residents. Both can extend into normative governance. Local dispute settlement is particularly important as rules and ownership in these ungoverned territories are informal. Various problems occur that need to be resolved for the parties to continue to live in the same neighborhood. This can include fights started by children in which adults, including women, become physically involved. Sides are taken, and the life of the community is disrupted. Even when the dispute is over, a reconciliation meeting (*musalaha*) is often held to "bury the hatchet" and soothe sore feelings. Candidates who ran in local and national elections on the platform of services to residents of informal neighborhoods won the wholehearted support of those residents, particularly when the candidates acted against criminals in the community.[19] Islamic activists garner influence in neighborhoods through mediating social and economic disputes.[20] Not all disputes can be resolved, however, and community mechanisms are often ill-equipped for many such conflicts; for instance, the community often cannot handle problems involving violent individuals and drugs. The police nevertheless will not be called because residents believe their typical response is likely to be wholesale arrests, including of the victims.

Local authorities also regulate social behavior in the street and public spaces. Responding to dangers for women in public areas is a common source of authority. In Algeria, where women faced problems with men when they went out in the streets, the local Islamists regulated male behavior in public, which spurred women to support the Islamists politically. The Islamist political party's platform incorporated concerns over threats in public spaces.[21] In areas of Tunisia, as a public space became unregulated by the state, it was taken over by drunk young men. Public drunkenness was a threat both to women and to their families' ability to use public spaces without being harassed. In the absence of state authority, female residents turned to religion, specifically the authority of the mosque, for help regulating the streets. The mosque took over the building where the drinking was taking place and enforced regulations for social behavior in public. While previously the mosque had had a marginal role in the quarter, it subsequently assumed the tasks of arbitrating right and wrong, proper and improper behavior, which gave its leaders a degree of civil authority within the community.[22]

Settlement of disputes is likewise a central role of militia institutions. The Lebanese Hizbullah, for example, take the lead in preventing intracommunal squabbles that threaten the social order. The organization established a judicial system of courts to prosecute crimes and mediation to deal with the problem of blood feuds. In the event mediation is unsuccessful, Hizbullah leaders will forcibly impose solutions on the parties to keep vendettas from escalating into tit-for-tat murders. The organization has mediated more than two hundred such feuds since its establishment in the early to mid-1980s, enacted reconciliation rituals involving both parties, and itself paid a handsome portion of the compensation to the aggrieved parties.[23]

Militias perform actual policing. The impetus for the development of policing institutions within militias stems from leaders' desire to prevent abuses of power among militia personnel themselves and thus maintain relations with the populace and preserve the militia hierarchy. The various militias of the Lebanese civil war established civil police bodies once their territory was secured. The earliest institutions of the Christian Lebanese Forces were set up to prevent crime and later evolved into a police force and military court system.[24] In the Druze or Progressive Socialist Party militia territory, the Civil Association of the Mountain instituted a police force to enact quick punishments, particularly for party members.[25] The Palestine Liberation Organization (PLO) used the Palestinian Armed Struggle Command as a police force and provided mediation and adjudication. It established a revolutionary court to prosecute violations by armed forces and serious crimes by the populace and to mediate factional disputes.[26] Today, by contrast, many Palestinian camps in Lebanon are without funding or support from the PLO, and no single faction is in control. Popular committees representing all the main factions run the camps, but there are no mechanisms of accountability or policing. Charities related to Hamas operate in some of the camps but are unable to provide law and order because none is dominant.[27]

## Public Services and Welfare

Public infrastructure and welfare are some of the main services typically performed by alternative authorities. From basic clean water, sewage, and utilities, these services can extend to the organization of sports teams, tutoring for students, the lending of money, and the establishment of economic development centers. As militias and political parties already are collectively and hierarchically organized, they have been the most efficient providers of public services. Residents of areas that lie outside the scope of state services take on a number of these tasks themselves. Identity groups build health clinics and provide job training in addition to periodic financial aid, loans, and welfare stipends.[28]

The militias that held consolidated territory in Lebanon invested in elaborate public services and welfare, but most began by providing basic infrastructure. The need for essential services such as clean water and electricity, for instance, spurred the formation of a public service administration for members of the Druze community. Apart from the health and educational aid that came from international bodies, the PLO was almost completely responsible for the Palestinian camp community, from roads to sewage. Hizbullah in its infancy in the mid-1980s provided electricity, drinking water, and garbage collection for the southern suburbs of Beirut where government services were absent, and still furnishes water and garbage services.

Others were more ambitious. The Lebanese Forces, a right-wing Christian coalition formed in the mid-1970s, furnished a wide array of services including security, infrastructure repairs, street cleaning, and garbage collection through its Popular Committees.[29] The Lebanese Forces' social service institution also furnished low-cost housing, health care, and schooling assistance, among other services.[30] Later, the coalition opened the Social Welfare Agency to help the needy by connecting them with those able to provide assistance. With thirty-five branch offices, the agency regularly aided twenty-five thousand families.[31] The PLO in the refugee camps in Lebanon provided services to orphans, refugees, and the wounded early in its tenure.[32] Other PLO institutions concentrated on education and child care, including extensive prenatal and postnatal care, and kindergartens. Educational programs included vocational and technical training, for women as well as men, summer camps, sports, and literacy drives. The organization provided medical and dental care, while prosthetic services were advanced to the degree that the devices were manufactured in the camps.[33] Health-care institutions for the Druze militia began with providing food for fighters,[34] and care for the dependents of militia fighters followed. Basic services and education expenditures came to constitute between 40 and 45 percent of the Druze group's budget. With the aid of international and national agencies, this militia built new schools, started economic ventures, and repaired homes and businesses.[35] It provided loans, monthly family support, grants, scholarships, and payments to thousands of families that had lost a bread-winner in the war.[36]

Hizbullah is well-known for its social services and management of the neglected southern areas of Beirut. The organization rebuilt almost eleven thousand institutions, homes, schools, shops, hospitals, infirmaries, mosques, agricultural cooperatives, and cultural centers and constructed seventy-eight new ones as of 2004. It provides health care at cheap, subsidized rates; financial aid for education; and low-cost loans.[37] Three-quarters of a million people were aided in its health centers in 2004.[38] The movement provides agricultural, irrigation, and veterinary services and has established a free transport system and a restaurant with free meals to the poor, in addition to low-price supermarkets, pharmacies, and clinics. Its participation in local government and provision of social services earned a United Nations best practices award for the municipality.[39] Currently the organization is engaged in wholesale reconstruction of homes and infrastructure in its area that were damaged or destroyed during the 2006 war.

## The Creation of Non-state Authority: Religion, Violence, and Identity as Mechanisms of Legitimating Power

All these services provided outside the purview of the state are backed up by ideological justifications for rule. Religion is a prominent source of legitimation, as it encompasses built-in morality, access to resources, a legacy of influence, and concerns for justice. Religion has established practical and normative systems that include leaders and authority networks and methods of communication to the community, as well as symbols and rituals linked to collective identity.[40] Public services are often organized through mosques, as they function as a substitute community center, a role common to religious institutions globally. Social services from child care to training programs take place at the mosque, and often sports clubs and educational classes as well.[41] Paired with charity and social welfare aid, as it frequently is, religion draws on the additional prestige of these socially rewarded tasks.

The centrality of morality and rectitude in religion is a boon to authority-seekers, for whom a reputation for fairness and honesty is another key attribute important in their local authority. Businesses utilize religious idioms to benefit from the honest reputation and social status accorded to the religious and also to distinguish themselves from other players in the economic field.

In this guise, Islam has been used to target markets by creating a consumer niche of goods with the Islamic label from Islamic vacations to Mecca Cola,[42] just as businesses in the United States promote themselves using the Christian fish symbol to indicate their religiosity. Various versions of Islam provide this religious distinction, not solely Salafi or strict Sunni Islam (most commonly referred to as fundamentalist). Mystic Sufi orders provide networks and legitimation, as do Shi'a groups and smaller sects. Indeed, religion as an alternative authority can also trump gender and age hierarchies. As young girls in Lebanon became experts in religious knowledge, their familial status changed as their parents deferred to this knowledge.[43] Similarly, young men with expertise in Islam increased their weight in the family and extended this influence to regulating the behavior and social relations of female family members.[44]

The legitimating power of religion works for both residents and the state, as both consider wealth and ownership to be justified when the individual has contributed significantly to charities and religious endowments. In one case, certain citizens whose status in the community was rising funded the construction of mosques, thereby insuring themselves against both raids by state police on their untitled homes and their neighbors' resentment.[45] The mosque is particularly central to the life of the community in unplanned areas without state amenities because social services are concentrated there. Religion and morality are also used to compel adherence to codes of social behavior. In cases of disputes over ownership or use of a building or the payment of rent, for example, local notables can invoke religious tenets to persuade disputants to settle their differences or comply with community norms.[46]

As prominent and pervasive as religious legitimation is, it is by no means the sole source of validation for the exercise of power. Violence that is perceived to be necessary to preserve a community against enemies is a source of legitimacy for thugs and militias, and the construction of such enemies justifies the violent regulation of public space. Militias use their representation of the fight against the adversary to justify their power in the community, which they typically back up with a political ideology that can be secular or religious. This sort of legitimacy was amply demonstrated in the positive opinions of Hizbullah by Lebanese across sectarian lines at the height of the 2006 war with Israel.[47]

Another form of violent authority rests on brute force or thuggishness, used in conjunction with good reputation or religiosity. The reputation of the thug for fairness and the value of his organizing skills justify his arrogation of power. Where no moral or civil authority exists, as in much of the Palestinian West Bank territories today, or where individuals do not acquiesce to the local authority, residents may resort to the services of thugs or specialists in violence.[48] Specialists in violence can be called on to organize taxi lines at checkpoints, for instance, to prevent cutting in line or "stealing" other people's business. In another example, masked youths in the Palestinian intifada enforced decrees by the political organizations and made sure retail shops stayed open.[49] These street-level authorities are often well disciplined, hierarchical, and orderly and can be composed of individuals from respectable professions who have formal jobs.

Common identity is a third source of legitimation. As with the other forms of justification for power, identity legitimation is effective only when it is invoked in conjunction with the kinds of services and institutions described above. Hometown and lineage groups and militias promote identities distinct from the rest of society or a specified enemy. While group identity rationalizes limiting leadership to those within the particular group, it does not indicate who in the group will lead. In hometown and kin groups, members elect and judge leaders on the basis of their ability to provide employment and their useful connections with state institutions.

Militias in control of territory often use education and the media in their attempts to establish legitimacy through ideological identity. The militias in Lebanon, for example, changed school textbooks, resurrected or outright created a particular version of history, and promoted new cultural rituals to consolidate their position as a legitimate authority. Dozens of television stations operated unofficially during the war, in addition to numerous new radio stations and newspapers operated by the various factions. The Lebanese Forces ran a weekly paper, a radio station, and the Lebanese Broadcasting Company, a television station that continued after the war as one of the top stations in Lebanon and the Arab world.[50]

Identity promotion did not stop there. The Lebanese Forces advanced a "Phoenician" ideology, asserting the essential differences of Lebanese Christians as non-Arabs and their constitution as a separate nation.[51] For the public schools under their jurisdiction, by contrast, the Druze revised existing textbooks and published history books of their own that played down this competing Phoenician history of the Lebanese Forces and expanded on Druze history and culture throughout Lebanon and neighboring countries. Druze education emphasized socialist values, sacrifice for the country, and scouting, while their cultural promotion extended to a new flag and the establishment of museums.[52]

The PLO for its part has promoted a new culture and distinct sense of nationhood through the arts, theater, and traditional crafts.[53] Holidays and celebrations focused on an abstract Palestinian nation, celebrating Land Day, important battles, and the fight with the Jordanian regime, and streets were renamed for political factions.[54] Hizbullah uses numerous rituals and symbols to promote both the uniqueness and validity of the Shi'a identity in Lebanon; the group has also transformed and tamed religious rituals, eliminated their excesses, and closely regulates events.[55] Festivals, parades, and cultural museums reinforce the separate identity of the inhabitants of the southern Beirut suburbs, whose spatial territory is clearly demarked by Hizbullah signs.[56]

## Conclusion

Authority creation and leadership in the Middle East are dynamic processes. In areas under the regulation of the state and outside it, new socioeconomic actors have arisen who offer essential services—policing or arbitration and social services—that garner them influence in the community. The legitimation of power holders' influence among the residents draws upon religion, identity, or violence. Newly successful individuals, whether financially prosperous or violently skilled, must demonstrate service, honesty, and fairness to the community before being accorded authority.

Residents and authorities in unregulated areas are not necessarily opposed to the state or a threat to it. For many residents, opposition to the state is a result of fearing state actions against their untitled housing and informal jobs. The state, with the potential to take away housing and fine or imprison residents, represents only a threat to these people. In most cases these fears are correct. Unable to differentiate among residents, state officials apply uniform punishments against all residents of these areas when they assert state authority. Areas have been leveled or residents rounded up by police. No benefits flow from the state, no services, policing, or infrastructure. Residents' apolitical desire to avoid the state can align with criminal and terrorist groups' own goals, and common cause can be made in the shared attempt to evade the state. Political stances opposed to the state can arise from this dynamic.

Lacking an alliance with groups that have political or criminal goals, residents and their leaders are willing to be co-opted by the state rather than compete with it. Local leaders serve as intermediaries for the state in connecting with residents and in return can satisfy their social status desires through elected or administrative positions. Indeed, even many political and violent actors have been incorporated into state institutions with the right incentive of decentralized autonomy for the region. States in the Middle East have not pressed their authority onto unregulated areas because of their lack of capacity economically and administratively. States have been unable to keep pace with rapid urbanization while at the same time shrinking their realm of service provision. The need to decrease state expenditure translates into withdrawing services and state administration from many areas, or not establishing them to begin with in new urban neighborhoods considered to be low priority. Social groups key to the state are unaffected: gated housing and private goods substitute for state services among the upper classes. In other areas, nongovernmental groups take up economic and infrastructure tasks. This corresponds both to an ideological turn to a small state with civil society taking up the slack and to the state's fiscal inability to furnish services itself. In still other cases, armed groups politically dispute the legitimacy of the state. Overt opposition to the state does not always translate into pitched battles for state overthrow, however; many rebel groups are happy to rule their small areas without expanding, and states unable to route them find a hands-off accommodation acceptable.

## Notes

The views expressed in this chapter are the author's alone and do not represent the Naval Postgraduate School, the U.S. government, or any other institutional affiliation.

1. This categorization differs from that used by Rodney Hall and Thomas Biersteker, who divide authority into market, moral, or illicit forms. Rodney Bruce Hall and Thomas J. Biersteker, eds., *The Emergence of Private Authority in Global Governance* (New York: Cambridge University Press, 2002). The present analysis distinguishes the initial basis for claiming influence, the methods of legitimation, and the services the individual or group provides for the populace that validate the claim to authority.

2. Authority in this context means the exercise of power that is considered legitimate or is willingly conceded by the population. Power holders use systems of meaning to bolster their claim to authority; however, they are not necessarily authorities.

3. Angel Rabasa and John E. Peters, "Comparative Analysis of Case Studies," in *Ungoverned Territories: Understanding and Reducing Terrorism Risks*, ed. Angel Rabasa, Steven Boraz, Peter Chalk, Kim Cragin, Theodore W. Karasik, Jennifer D. P. Moroney, Kevin A. O'Brien, and John E. Peters (Santa Monica, CA: Rand Corporation, 2007).

4. As William Reno noted, the distinction between collective and private interests in authority is a crucial one. William Reno, *Warlord Politics and African States* (Boulder, CO: Lynne Rienner, 1999).

5. In all the cases here, the authorities are male.

6. Thomas J. Biersteker and Rodney Bruce Hall, "Private Authority as Global Governance," in *The Emergence of Private Authority in Global Governance*, ed. Rodney Bruce Hall and Thomas J. Biersteker (New York: Cambridge University Press, 2002), 203–22.

7. This should not imply that state rule is less oppressive.

8. Asef Bayat, "From 'Dangerous Classes' to 'Quiet Rebels': Politics of the Urban Subaltern in the Global South," *International Sociology* 15, no. 3 (2000): 533–57; Asef Bayat, "Un-Civil Society: The Politics of the Informal People," *Third World Quarterly* 18, no. 1 (1997): 53–72.

9. Katarzyna Grabska, "Marginalization in Urban Spaces of the Global South: Urban Refugees in Cairo," *Journal of Refugee Studies* 19, no. 3 (2006): 287–307; Georg Stauth, "Gamaliyya: Informal Economy and Social Life in a Popular Quarter of Cairo," in *Informal Sector in Egypt*, ed. Nicholas Hopkins (Cairo: Cairo Papers in the Social Sciences, 1991); Salwa Ismail, *Political Life in Cairo's New Quarters: Encountering the Everyday State* (Minneapolis: University of Minnesota Press, 2006), xxi; Bayat, "Un-Civil Society"; Rebecca Miles Doan, "Class Differentiation and the Informal Sector in Amman, Jordan," *International Journal of Middle East Studies* 24, no. 1 (1992): 27–38.

10. Ninette Fahmy, "A Culture of Poverty or the Poverty of a Culture? Informal Settlements and the Debate over the State-Society Relationship in Egypt," *Middle East Journal* 58, no. 4 (2004): 1–115.

11. Salwa Ismail, *Rethinking Islamist Politics: Culture, the State, and Islamism* (New York: I. B. Tauris, 2003), 133.

12. Ismail, *Political Life*, ch. 2.

13. Bayat, "Un-Civil Society"; Asef Bayat, "Cairo's Poor: Dilemmas of Survival and Solidarity," *Middle East Report*, no. 202 (1996): 2–12.

14. Ismail, *Political Life*, 36.

15. Ibid.

16. There are numerous studies on the characteristics of the Mafioso or social bandit. See, for example, Diego Gambetta, *The Sicilian Mafia: The Business of Private Protection* (Cambridge, MA: Harvard University Press, 1993); E. J. Hobsbawn, *Primitive Rebels: Studies in Archaic Forms of Social Movement in the 19th and 20th Centuries* (New York: W. W. Norton, 1959); and Pino Arlacchi, "The Mafioso: From Man of Honour to Entrepreneur," *New Left Review*, no. 118 (1979): 53–72.

17. Anne Marie Baylouny, *Privatizing Welfare in the Middle East: Kin Mutual Aid Associations in Jordan and Lebanon* (Bloomington, Indiana University Press, 2010), ch. 6.

18. Tahire Erman, "Becoming 'Urban' or Remaining 'Rural': The Views of Turkish Rural-to-Urban Migrants on the 'Integration Question,'" *International Journal*

*of Middle East Studies* 30 (1998): 541–61; Sema Erder, "Where Do You Hail From? Localism and Networks in Istanbul," in *Istanbul: Between the Global and the Local,* ed. Çaglar Keydar (New York: Rowman & Littlefield, 1999).

19. Fahmy, "A Culture of Poverty or the Poverty of a Culture?"

20. Ismail, *Political Life,* 53.

21. Ismail, *Rethinking Islamist Politics,* 132.

22. Elizabeth Vasile, "Devotion as Distinction, Piety as Power: Religious Revival and the Transformation of Space in the Illegal Settlements of Tunis," in *Population, Poverty, and Politics in Middle East Cities,* ed. Michael E. Bonine (Gainesville: University Press of Florida, 1997).

23. Ahmad Nizar Hamzeh, *In the Path of Hizbullah* (Syracuse, NY: Syracuse University Press, 2004), 107–8.

24. Marie-Joëlle Zahar, "Fanatics, Mercenaries, Brigands . . . and Politicians: Militia Decision-Making and Civil Conflict Resolution," Ph.D. diss., McGill University, 1999, 117–8.

25. Judith P. Harik, "Change and Continuity among the Lebanese Druze Community: The Civil Administration of the Mountain, 1983–90," *Middle Eastern Studies* 29, no. 3 (1993): 377–98.

26. Julie Peteet, "Socio-Political Integration and Conflict Resolution in the Palestinian Camps in Lebanon," *Journal of Palestine Studies* 16, no. 2 (1987): 32, 39.

27. Rebecca Roberts, "Analysis of Governance in a Palestinian Refugee Camp," paper presented at the Political Science Workshop, University of York, York, England, 2001; Rebecca Roberts, "The Impact of Assistance on the Coping Mechanisms of Long-Term Refugees: The Case of Palestinian Refugees in Lebanon," Ph.D. diss., University of York, 2004.

28. Baylouny, *Privatizing Welfare*; Anne Marie Baylouny, "Creating Kin: New Family Associations as Welfare Providers in Liberalizing Jordan," *International Journal of Middle East Studies* 38, no. 3 (2006): 349–68.

29. Judith Harik, *The Public and Social Services of the Lebanese Militias,* ed. Centre for Lebanese Studies, Papers on Lebanon 14 (Oxford: Oxonian Rewley, 1994), 15–17 [Paper/Report]; Lewis W. Snider, "The Lebanese Forces: Their Origins and Role in Lebanon's Politics," *Middle East Journal* 38, no. 1 (1984): 27.

30. Zahar, "Fanatics, Mercenaries, Brigands," 72.

31. Harik, *The Public and Social Services of the Lebanese Militias,* 33.

32. Rashid Khalidi, "The Palestinians in Lebanon: Social Repercussions of Israel's Invasion," *Middle East Journal* 38, no. 2 (1984): 257.

33. Cheryl Rubenberg, *The Palestine Liberation Organization: Its Institutional Infrastructure,* Institute of Arab Studies Monograph Series, *Palestine Studies,* no. 1 (1983): 19–23.

34. Harik, *The Public and Social Services of the Lebanese Militias,* 17.

35. Harik, "Change and Continuity," 389–93.

36. Ibid., 384.

37. Hamzeh, *In the Path of Hizbullah,* 50–55.

38. Abbas al-Sabbagh, "20 Years since the Announced Launching of 'Hizb Allah'" [in Arabic], *al-Nahar*, 26 August 2005.

39. Mona Harb and Reinoud Leenders, "Know Thy Enemy: Hizbullah, 'Terrorism,' and the Politics of Perception," *Third World Quarterly* 26, no. 1 (2005): 173–97.

40. Christian Smith, ed., *Disruptive Religion: The Force of Faith in Social-Movement Activism* (New York: Routledge, 1996). On collective identity, see Francesca Polletta and James M. Jasper, "Collective Identity and Social Movements," *Annual Review of Sociology* 27 (2001): 283–305.

41. Vasile, "Devotion as Distinction."

42. M. Hakan Yavuz, "Opportunity Spaces, Identity, and Islamic Meaning in Turkey," in *Islamic Activism: A Social Movement Theory Approach*, ed. Quintan Wiktorowicz (Bloomington: Indiana University Press, 2004); M. Hakan Yavuz, *Islamic Political Identity in Turkey* (New York: Oxford University Press, 2003).

43. Lara Deeb, *An Enchanted Modern: Gender and Public Piety in Shi'i Lebanon* (Princeton, NJ: Princeton University Press, 2006).

44. Ismail, *Rethinking Islamist Politics*, 132.

45. Ibid., 122.

46. Vasile, "Devotion as Distinction."

47. See the opinion poll conducted by the Beirut Center for Research and Information, "Lebanese Public Opinion," *Mideast Monitor* 1, no. 3 (September–October 2006), available at http://www.mideastmonitor.org/issues/0609/0609_6.htm.

48. Rema Hammami, "On the Importance of Thugs: The Moral Economy of a Checkpoint," *Middle East Report*, no. 231 (2004): 26–34.

49. Adrien Katherine Wing, "The Intifada: The Emergence of Embryonic Legal Mechanisms for Palestinian Self-Determination," *Arab Studies Quarterly* 15, no. 4 (1993): 55–74.

50. Zahar, "Fanatics, Mercenaries, Brigands," 118, 33.

51. Asher Kaufman, *Reviving Phoenicia: In Search of Identity in Lebanon* (New York: I. B. Tauris, 2004), 238, 40.

52. Harik, "Change and Continuity," 391–92; Harik, *The Public and Social Services of the Lebanese Militias*, 47.

53. Peteet, "Socio-Political Integration."

54. Laleh Khalili, "Grass-Roots Commemorations: Remembering the Land in the Camps of Lebanon," *Journal of Palestine Studies* 34, no. 1 (2004): 6–22.

55. Lara Deeb, "Living Ashura in Lebanon: Mourning Transformed to Sacrifice," *Comparative Studies of South Asia, Africa and the Middle East* 25, no. 1 (2005): 122–37.

56. Mona Harb, "Deconstructing Hizballah and Its Suburb," *Middle East Report*, no. 242 (2007): 12–17; Helena Cobban, "Hizbullah's New Face: In Search of a Muslim Democracy," *Boston Review* 30, no. 2 (2005), available at http://bostonreview.net/BR 30.2/cobban.php.

# 8 Immigration and Subterranean Sovereignty in South African Cities

## Loren B. Landau and Tamlyn Monson

Border control—entry, exit, and movement within a territory—is inextricably tied to globally dominant definitions of spatial control and sovereignty. Under the Manichean rubric that informs much work on contemporary governance, where states are unable to systematically regulate movement into and within space, such spaces appear as only partially governed.[1] However, such designations are premised on a state-centric perspective of governance that ignores other critical forms of regulation and control that emerge when state power is inconsistent or when states act in "irregular" ways.[2] Through its "worm's-eye" view, this chapter argues that the various actors involved in regulating human mobility—states, citizens, and migrants themselves—act as catalysts for transforming the practice of sovereignty. Where public commitments to law are questionable and enforcement institutions weak, socially rooted regimes of control have emerged to regulate what might outwardly appear as South Africa's ungoverned spaces.

The chapter explores two different subnational regulatory regimes that have evolved around the regulation of human mobility. The first involves African immigrants who have developed and maintained subterranean economies and systems of privatized regulatory orders intended to undermine and frustrate state mechanisms of mobility control. While the state (and statist analysts) may see these as pushing toward anarchy, they contain within them informally and sometimes coercively systematized forms of control that generate important political subjectivities and interactions. Moreover, many of these mechanisms rely on state action and state agents for their sustenance. The second system of authority stems from citizens' anxieties over "illegal" immigration and the multiplying forms of corruption and illegal practice tied to it. The inability (or unwillingness) of state bodies to stem the perceived "human tsunami" of foreigners has given rise to alternative, popular systems of territorial control made visible by fragmented and localized vigilante entities. But these are not merely ad hoc reactionary forces; rather, they build on existing leadership structures that may both be illegal and draw on the power of state institutions and actors.

Beyond describing these overlapping and intersecting systems of non-state and quasi-state forms of regulation, the chapter speaks to their broader implications for the nature of the nation-state. It argues that these two non-state governance systems are helping to reify notions of the South African nation and a national territory among citizens, although the latter do not always see the state as rightfully maintaining a monopoly on power over this space. Working against the consolidation of a territorially bounded South African nation, noncitizens' desire to escape the systems of violence and values associated with citizens' territorial ambitions has helped entrench transnational practices and patterns of self-exclusion that are generating subnational and deterritorialized systems of regulation and power.

## Johannesburg: A Critical Case

At first glance, Johannesburg may seem an inappropriate place to witness migrants' catalytic influence and agency in transforming the exercise of state authority and regulation. Not only is the city uniquely prosperous and infrastructurally endowed by African standards, it is also the heart of the continent's strongest state by most conventional measures. It is for precisely these reasons that the city provides such a powerful illustration of migration's potential to transform state practice and generate heterogeneous systems of regulation and control.

Home to Johannesburg and Pretoria, Gauteng is the center of South Africa's trade and transport networks. The country's most densely populated and second most populous province, and responsible for close to 10 percent of sub-Saharan Africa's gross domestic product, it attracts business and people from around the country, the continent, and beyond. Data from the 2001 Census and the national 2007 Community Survey (both conducted by Statistics South

Africa) suggest that close to three-quarters (74 percent) of the province's population increase is due to "natural growth." However, because of its economically dominant position within both South Africa and southern Africa, Gauteng continues to attract substantial numbers of migrants. The net migration gain (that is, the difference between the arrivals and departures from the province) was 418,000 between October 2001 and February 2007. This translates into an annual gain of approximately 78,000 migrants. Although domestic migration accounts for the vast majority of these new arrivals, Gauteng is also a primary destination and transit point for international migrants. In 2007, Gauteng province hosted 46 percent of South Africa's population born outside South Africa. This is up from 42 percent in 2001 and is expected to increase during the years ahead. Marcello Balbo and Giovanna Marconi report that international migrants now represent 6.2 percent of Johannesburg's total population.[3] International migration is particularly prominent in certain municipalities and neighborhoods. For instance, Ted Leggett's survey in central Johannesburg found that almost 25 percent of residents were foreign-born,[4] and an unpublished 2007 survey by Kagiso Urban Management found that foreigners were the majority in a number of neighborhoods. For these and other reasons, Johannesburg, with its substantial migrant population, provides an apt laboratory for uncovering novel social forms in their early stages.[5]

A substantial portion of the information used here stems from migration-related research undertaken by the Forced Migration Studies Programme (FMSP) at the University of the Witwatersrand, Johannesburg, between 2002 and 2009. This includes a 2006 survey of 847 respondents in seven central Johannesburg neighborhoods, complemented by formal and informal interviews with migrants, service providers, advocates, and local government representatives. In some instances, we draw on data from the 2003 iteration of the survey, which asked a series of additional questions that are relevant here. We also reflect data from a 2007–2008 survey of 3,130 foreigners at refugee reception offices and nongovernmental organizations (NGOs) in Johannesburg, Pretoria, Durban, Cape Town, and Port Elizabeth; in-depth fieldwork on human smuggling across the South Africa–Zimbabwe border during 2007; and a series of interviews and focus groups conducted in 2008 and 2009 in eleven townships across South Africa. Though these data do not represent South Africa's "migrant stock" or Johannesburg's population as a whole, they nevertheless point to new forms of sociopolitical organization and categories of belonging.[6]

## Governance in Urban Africa

Since their colonial foundation, Africa's urban centers have been primary nodes of trade, transit, and political power. These tendencies have been enhanced and transformed by the declining importance of fixed assets (for example, factories and real estate) and unstable sociopolitical configurations, leading to new regulatory forms that place space, bodies, and institutions in novel and dynamic relations.[7] To survive and thrive in such environments, residents, however temporary, not only move through ostensibly state-regulated space, but they passively and actively transform it through strategies of accumulation and tactics intended to evade danger and regulation and, occasionally, eliminate perceived sources of competition.[8] Combined with state efforts to control these strategies or profit from them, and subsequent counterreactions from migrants and hosts, cities have become productive intersections where emergent forms of political and economic power meet. The remainder of this chapter explores ways in which sovereignty is being reshaped through "subterranean" practices that remain invisible in research that focuses solely on state actors, laws, and border control.

### Privatized Governmentality and the Immigrant Exception

South Africa's Refugees Act (1998) and Immigration Act (2002) outline the rights and obligations of various categories of immigrant and the procedural norms related to the management of these populations. Importantly, immigration also gives shape to the exception: the category of "illegal foreigner," whose rights are largely limited to administrative justice in detention and deportation. The constitutive "illegality" of such immigrants effectively leaves them in an extrajudicial space until such time as they are apprehended and removed from the territory through the state's system of immigration control. Needless to say, it is in the interests of an undocumented and hence "illegal" foreigner to extend the time spent in ungoverned space, primarily through the maintenance of invisibility to state systems. In the context of limited oversight and such immigrants' extralegal status, officials within the state's coercive apparatus have recognized in the demand for invisibility an emerging market that offers opportunities for private profit. The result has been the development of regularized networks of corruption and extortion in the issuing of documentation and the policing of immigration, which serve the interests of both parties while undermining the broader intentions of state territorial control as well as high-level government commitments to establishing the rule of law and a "human rights culture."

Building on the almost universalized principles of the modern state around controlling access to national territory, South Africa's immigration laws legitimize practices that are designed to aid in the control of illegal foreigners. Directed toward citizens, many of these would constitute an unconstitutional, discriminatory form of harassment reminiscent of the "pass laws" applied to black South Africans during the apartheid era. Foreigners are regularly arrested and detained on the basis of only their physical appearance, their inability to speak one of South Africa's nine official "African" languages, or simply their fitting an undocumented-migrant "profile."[9] Hence, in the 2006 FMSP survey, non–South Africans living or working in Johannesburg reported having been stopped by the police far more frequently (66.8 percent) than South Africans (33.9 percent), despite having generally lived in the city for shorter periods.[10]

While such measures superficially reflect the state's official migration policy, closer inspection reveals that what appears to be the exercise of the governmental disciplines of the state—in the checking of documents and just administration of "illegal" populations—is often a subterfuge obscuring extralegal transactions that work against state purposes.

Reports of demands for bribes in exchange for release or freedom from arrest are a commonplace in the literature on migration and xenophobia in South Africa,[11] and the practice is so routine that foreigners have been equated with "mobile ATMs."[12] This, and similar irregularities throughout the immigration control regime, which are outlined below, can be seen simply as victimization. This is clearly part of the story, especially where police confiscate, destroy, or refuse to recognize valid documents in order to justify an arrest for the purposes of extortion.[13] Yet such a reading fails to acknowledge the utility of this kind of financial exchange for illegal foreigners who would otherwise face deportation and the consequent destruction of their livelihoods in South Africa.

The black market for invisibility often begins at the border of the South African state. Fieldwork conducted in 2007 for a report on human smuggling across the South Africa–Zimbabwe border revealed that a limited number of police were involved in mutually beneficial arrangements with human smugglers—not only ad-hoc bribes, but also long-term, regular protection payments. Certain smugglers had acquired from contacts within state officialdom the border-patrol schedules, the keys to gates in the border fence, or both. In addition to this, some irregular migrants interviewed during the field visit reported paying police officers two hundred rand for direct passage through the Beitbridge border post that separates South Africa and Zimbabwe.[14]

Having entered the country through clandestine routes, in some cases negotiating access with the very state actors mandated to prevent it, undocumented migrants face the challenge of maintaining their invisibility. Close to one-fifth (18 percent) of undocumented non-nationals interviewed in a 2007–2008 survey of access to services among 3,130 respondents at NGOs and refugee reception offices across South Africa reported that they had paid a police officer or other government official in order to avoid arrest or escape detention. Among the documented respondents, a slightly lower proportion (16 percent) had bribed officials for the same reasons.[15]

These transactions may be bureaucratically invisible, but they are an inherent part of the bureaucratic political economy and are an open secret for South African citizens living alongside immigrants in townships and informal settlements. Interviews with local residents in areas affected by the xenophobic attacks of May 2008 revealed widespread anxieties about rent-seeking arrangements between police and foreign residents and traders, which many feel undermine the state's primary mission to protect South Africa's territorial integrity and South African livelihoods. In the township of Alexandra, in Johannesburg, these concerns were particularly prevalent. As one male focus group participant noted: "What they do is that when a foreigner is caught, they go around with him this whole area. You see this 4th street; they release him at 5th street. Before you know what happens he is now coming here through the passage. He raises cash and gives it to them and then is released." Another participant in the same focus group observed that such rents may be in cash or in kind: "You see this guy here who is a dressmaker; no police will arrest him. A police will pass here and say, 'How are you, man?' He will enter the house and come out with a liter of cold drink and give it to the police and the case is closed. What matters is money; police do not check too many things. They ask, 'How much do you have?'" What these systems reveal is not the absence of control over territory, but rather an illegal but systematized taxation regime that regulates rights to space and work on a pay-to-play basis. In the words of one Eritrean living in Johannesburg, "as foreign students we are not required to pay taxes to the government. But when we walk down these streets, we pay."

The costs for undocumented migrants to operate within South African communities has helped generate a further semiofficial subeconomy that allows migrants to escape the cycle of symbiotic extortion by obtaining South African identity documents through networks that penetrate the Department of Home Affairs. Although current anticorruption campaigns may break up these networks, officials continue to issue identity documents to foreigners for an unofficial "fee," by processing electronic marriages with or (usually) without the knowledge of a South African "spouse."[16] Although the process whereby documents are obtained is unclear to many locals, there are strong convictions that non-nationals "buy local surnames" or have valid identification documents because they "collaborate with . . . Home Affairs."[17] These networks have become so profitable that internal investigations have resulted in death threats and reassignment to other, less dangerous positions.

There is no evidence to suggest that the networks of corrupt exchange operating in these various domains of the immigration regime are integrated or centralized. Nevertheless, all feature the infiltration of ostensibly "state" governance structures by private interests; all generate illegal transactions between "state" actors and the populations they are tasked with administering. In doing so, they serve as a form of immigration regulation that is shaped but not bounded by immigration law and policy. Seen together, these activities constitute a subterranean governance system that uses the disciplines and organs of state coercion to circumvent official controls, transforming state sovereignty from below while maintaining particular forms of territorial control.

### Xenophobia and "Popular Justice"

Governance operates through aggregations of ideas, identities, individuals, and institutions. Where these are integrated into unified and balanced systems that incorporate key statist principles and practices, states can exercise sovereignty without the constant, visible application of force.[18] But where daily practices contradict state-centered principles, they threaten the maintenance or creation of officially governed spaces. This is the case in South Africa, where xenophobia often threatens fundamental principles of legalism and tolerance. Here, too, we see the state's hand at work: by demonizing and excluding foreigners in the interest of promoting political stability and unity, the state has created pockets of insecurity and alienation that threaten its efforts at national consolidation under a single constitutional order.

Anti-immigrant barriers are based in a strong, deeply rooted resentment of non-nationals on South Africa's ostensibly sovereign ground. A 2006 national survey conducted by the Southern African Migration Project revealed that 84 percent of South Africans believed that the country was admitting too many foreigners,[19] and a strong majority of respondents (64.8 percent) in the 2003 FMSP Johannesburg survey thought it would be good if most of them left.[20] Supported by a government that has done little to counter these sentiments—and has often hardened them through scapegoating—these attitudes have underwritten violent actions sometimes bordering on ethnic cleansing.

There have been a substantial number of large-scale, violent attacks on and/or evictions of non-nationals in South Africa.[21] Although often represented as "spontaneous" mob reactions to high-profile crimes, they typically reflect the illegal efforts of individuals or localized interest groups pursuing material and political benefits from non–state-centered forms of territorial control. One such example was that of Motherwell Township outside of Port Elizabeth, in the Eastern Cape Province,[22] where after an alleged robber was shot by a Somali shopkeeper on the afternoon of 12 February 2007, the store in question and then more than one hundred other Somali-run businesses were looted and plundered within just a few hours. It was only when the mob reached the Motherwell Centre, a small shopping mall containing larger South African–owned chain stores as well as some Somali-owned businesses, that the police dispersed the crowd.

Almost everyone interviewed spoke of a small group of motorists directing the mob from shop to shop and carrying away looted goods. Throughout, the police were said to have helped by taking shopkeepers into "protective custody" while doing nothing to protect their belongings, or, worse, taking goods themselves or transporting stolen property. Many people, both Somali and South African, reported hearing announcements from police vehicles demanding that the Somali residents vacate the township by eight the next morning for their own security. By the next day, the township had been "cleansed": more than four hundred Somalis had left, few with any belongings. Almost all of these were carrying official documents providing them with rights to live and work anywhere on South African territory. Through these actions, it was evident that local actors, together with the police, had established a form of control over "national" space that blurs the categories of private and public. The broad popularity and legitimacy of such actions further blurs the line between mobsterist criminality and law.

A similarly revealing incident occurred during March 2008 in the informal settlements of Sector 1, Atteridgeville, located west of Pretoria. At least seven people were killed when the voluntary leadership structures decided to turn on non-nationals living in the community.[23] Operating "parallel to

the government . . . like a government on their own,"[24] these structures involve three separate leaders of spatially defined parts of the sector, working
with some degree of cooperation from the Atteridgeville Civic Organization
(ACO). Elements of this structure are accused of charging protection fees and
levying fees to perform functions that government structures are mandated
to provide without charge.

Before the attacks, the ACO offices distributed pamphlets and put up no-
tices giving foreign residents two weeks' notice to leave the area.[25] When this
period expired without the departure of non-nationals, locals marched on
the police station. Some among the group were upset over the government's
plans to relocate residents to a formal settlement one hundred kilometers
from their workplaces. Others took part to express their frustrations over the
continued presence of foreigners. It was on the way back from this march that
attacks began.[26]

The actual violence was preceded by antiforeigner meetings held after
work hours during which the activities were apparently planned. The way in
which these meetings were called and the degree of organization suggest that
local leadership structures were intimately involved. The degree of precision
with which the attacks were conducted meant that houses owned by foreigners were burnt down while locally owned houses that were leased to foreigners
were merely looted.[27]

A high-ranking member of the Community Policing Forum (CPF)
claimed that police had been "tipped off" about a meeting to discuss foreigners and the date that attacks would take place but "didn't do anything about
the information." The same source reported that during the violence, police
"were telling people they must not kill the foreigners but must just take whatever they need" and took a specific attitude by escorting foreigners out of the
area without stopping the crime. Certain police officers, local leaders, and
civil servants were witnessed participating in the looting and eviction.[28]

Several of our informants identified the leader of one area (which now
bears his name—Jeffsville) as a primary instigator. His organization has benefited from the displacement of foreigners by charging non-nationals to rein-
tegrate into the community and levying protection fees.[29] Some area leaders
are also known to operate a racket in which they illegally sell stands in the
settlement to returning foreigners, who are later evicted and fined for illegal
occupation.[30] Although the precise details of the attacks remain unclear, there
is no doubt that community leaders did little to prevent them. As a number of

residents argue: "You can't do anything in the community without involving the leaders. . . . [Local leaders] are so influential such that even in criminal cases they can deal with you and the case does not go to the police. It is within their power to beat up a person who starts xenophobia and the case ends there, without even opening a case with the police."[31] Reflecting the degree to which these local authorities maintain a monopoly over the use of force, supra-local bodies have been effectively unable to investigate or charge those guilty of murder and wanton destruction of property. Soon after the attacks, a number of people were arrested, but the police soon released them under community pressure and an unwillingness of witnesses to identify guilty individuals.[32] The success in establishing a locally determined form of territorial control is evidenced by continued harassment of foreigners and the murder of one non-national who attempted to return two weeks after the attacks.[33]

### Outcomes of Non-State Systems of Governance: Reification and Self-Exclusion

For our purposes, the importance of all this lies in how, even as subterranean systems of governance challenge the sovereignty of the South African state and defy government immigration policy, they are legitimized by South African citizens' conceptions of nationality and rights to territory. In Atteridgeville, attackers asked non-nationals to produce identification documents in ways that mirrored state migration control procedures.[34] However, they retained the right to determine the validity of these documents without direct reference to law. Thus, while resembling the governmental disciplines of the state, and its imperative to regulate national space, the identification processes adopted by the local militia effectively collapsed the categories of legal and illegal entry so carefully demarcated by policy.

In Motherwell, the groups that ethnically cleansed the area of Somali shopkeepers made no pretense of enforcing law by checking documents. While drawing on the state's coercive power through collaboration with the police, they established their right to control space through reference to nationalist tropes. In an interview we conducted ten days after the Motherwell attacks, a young man told us: "The approach for the Somalis to come and just settle in our midst is a wrong one. Somalis should remain in their country. They shouldn't come here to multiply and increase our population and in future, we shall suffer. The more they come to South Africa to do business, the more the locals will continue killing them."[35] Through the actions associated with these sentiments, local groups—often involving officials—have denied the state the power to determine who has rights to space, and means by which rights to space are policed.

The micro-systems of symbiotic corruption of "state" officials on the one hand, and the mobilization of civilians against their foreign neighbors on the other, are interrelated. Popular forms of territorial control emerge in part because of local awareness that irregularities in the police and immigration bureaucracies are hobbling the state's monopoly on mobility into the South African territory.[36] And, as a respondent in Itireleng, another violence-affected community, observed, "If government is failing to stop them at the borders, we shall stop them in Itireleng."[37] In turn, these micro-systems give rise to contradictory effects: the reification of the idea of the nation-state, and the ghettoization of non-nationals in ways that threaten to further undermine sovereignty.

Along with coercion, governance depends on informal codes and categories that signify and define membership in a population and structure people's relationships: with the territory they occupy, with other groups, and with the institutions, agencies, and individuals charged with social welfare and security.[38] Ideally, these matrices are integrated into a single regime that extends uniformly across a country's territory. This regime fosters a unified population (the citizenry/nation) enmeshed in a codified set of values, measures of appropriateness, and norms of law and administrative responsibility.[39]

Models of immigrant/refugee integration often assume that foreigners' prior differences and external loyalties will be gradually supplemented and supplanted by forms of membership that link them to new national territory and institutions. But instead, Johannesburg's migrants are increasingly employing a rhetoric of self-exclusion that emotionally and socially distances them from the nationalist systems of control outlined in the previous pages.[40] Thus, rather than striving to integrate or assimilate, non-nationals reify differences and react to their extended interactions with South Africans by establishing a relationship with South African territory premised on transience and a system of values that undermines both state and citizens' rights to control space. The voice of a woman from Lesotho, resident in Johannesburg for four years, expresses a common sentiment among migrants, which has strengthened in the wake of the May 2008 violence: "I don't think any right-thinking person would want to be South African. . . . They are just so contaminated." The oft-cited sources of this "contamination" have generally included, among other things, low levels of education, South African (and especially female) promiscuity, the nation's tolerance of "deviance" (especially homosexuality), and citizens' lack of religious commitment. Because of these perceptions, few foreigners trust South Africans (see Table 8.1) or express a desire for close relationships with them, despite daily interactions with citizens. The evident inhumanity of locals during the May 2008 attacks has further undermined trust and has solidified anti–South African views. Instead of integrating into a South African nation, if such a thing exists, migrants avoid putting down roots by retaining loyalties to their origins and orientating themselves toward a future outside of South Africa (see Table 8.2). For migrants such as these, exclusion becomes its own form of being and belonging.

Regardless of their desire for distance, migrants have nevertheless had to develop a set of often contradictory rhetorical devices to justify their physi-

**TABLE 8.1** Percentage of Johannesburg respondents by nationality indicating whether they can generally trust South Africans

|  | Democratic Republic of Congo | Mozambique | Somalia | South African | Total[1] |
|---|---|---|---|---|---|
| Agree | 38.6 | 4.0 | 11.4 | 72.3 | 32.2 |
| Disagree | 46.6 | 75.6 | 85.9 | 20.7 | 56.0 |
| No opinion / don't know | 14.8 | 20.4 | 2.7 | 6.9 | 11.8 |
| N | 251 | 201 | 185 | 188 | 839 |

SOURCE: Survey conducted by Migrant Rights Monitoring Project, Forced Migration Studies Programme, University of the Witwatersrand, 2006.
1. The total includes other nationalities mistakenly included in the sample.

**TABLE 8.2** Percentage of Johannesburg respondents by nationality who believe it is better for South African society if immigrants maintain or do not maintain their customs

|  | South Africans | Non-nationals |
|---|---|---|
| Better if immigrants maintain their customs | 68.1 | 78.1 |
| Better if immigrants do not maintain their customs | 28.2 | 16.6 |
| Don't know / refuse to answer / other | 3.7 | 5.3 |
| Total (n = 832)[1] | 188 | 644 |

SOURCE: Survey conducted by Migrant Rights Monitoring Project, Forced Migration Studies Programme, University of the Witwatersrand, 2006.
1. Sample size reduced from 839 because of illegible responses.

cal presence despite political, legal, and social prohibitions. One of these is a neo–pan-Africanism partially intended to erode the barriers that separate foreigners from South Africans. By encouraging South Africans to realize connections to their continental kin, migrants promote an idea of belonging that makes space for a plurality of cultures and an openness to hybridity and multiple identities. When successful, such tactics undercut the dominance of South African nationalism and South African immigration policy.[41]

Elsewhere, migrant groups have used South Africa's relatively liberal, if irregularly applied, asylum laws to obtain rights of residence and work. In a number of instances, this means applying for asylum when applicants are well aware of their ineligibility. Given the long delays in processing claims and corruption within the system, this forms one quasi-legal way to penetrate South African territory. More commonly, however, even those who do not apply officially for asylum will nevertheless label themselves as refugees (economic, political, social, religious—any grounds imaginable). This rhetoric of the importunate "refugee" erodes the language and practices of exclusion through some kind of intrinsic claim to territorial access. While it may not convince South African citizens of their right to reside within the country, it nevertheless helps to generate an alternate, nonexclusionary ethos to which they subscribe.

Another set of discursive claims relies on norms of reciprocity: claiming territorial rights to South Africa on the basis of what countries of origin did to assist South Africans during the struggle against apartheid. Nigerians offer the university scholarships their country provided African National Congress activists during the 1970s and 1980s as their contribution. Mozambicans, Zimbabweans, and Namibians remember their suffering due to apartheid-era wars in their own countries. Others plausibly argue that because South African businesses derive so many profits from investments in their countries, both now and in the past, they have a reciprocal right to South Africa's territory and wealth. In this way, South Africa's own transnationalism, past and present, serves to justify immigrants' transcendence of national residential restrictions.

In addition, by drawing syncretically on European religious forms, African tradition, and almost any other rhetoric that is available, the ever-expanding pool of Nigerian and Congolese-run Pentecostal churches operating within Johannesburg's inner city is at once claiming space in South Africa and helping to situate people beyond national regulatory frameworks.[42] Indeed, in many cases, the churches orient members toward a life beyond any material nation while speaking on behalf of an authority far grander than the South African state. Part of this is accomplished by offering material and discursive links to Nigeria, Ghana, England, the Democratic Republic of Congo, and the United States, with the implicit promise that parishioners will one day live elsewhere. For pastors, South Africa is not so much a place to colonize and evangelize as a soapbox for influencing the lives of people across the continent and beyond. In the words of the Nigerian pastor at the Mountain of Fire and Miracles Church, "Africa is shaped like a pistol, and South Africa is the mouth from where you can shoot out the word of God."[43] It is no coincidence that the wording suggests an exercise of force beyond the agenda and boundaries of the state.

Much like the arbitrary and ad hoc applications of violence described in the previous section, these diverse tactics for claiming space without taking root do not (or do not yet) form a coherent or stable strategy. John Mang'ana and Jean Pierre Misago separately report, for example, that even people from the same country are careful to avoid the mutual obligations and politics that come from close association with other "exiles."[44] Although there are instances in which migrant groups assert a collective (usually national) identity, these are often based on instrumental and short-lived associations. Research on refugee associations throughout South Africa also finds an almost universal tendency toward repeated reconfiguration and fragmentation.[45] As Graeme Götz and AbdouMaliq Simone suggest, "these formations embody a broad range of tactical abilities aimed at maximizing economic opportunities through transversal engagements across territories and separate arrangements of powers."[46] Although many of the organizations' leaders have ambitions of power and influence, in practice there is far too much fluidity and freedom of association for a lasting and cohesive alternative form of governance to be established.

## Conclusions: Reconsidering Migration and Governance in Urban Africa

What does this kind of situation mean for governing space in other places or other times? For one, this chapter promotes a perspective on governance that considers the interactions and outcomes of formal and subterranean processes. Officials are not the only wielders of authority and are not necessarily where our analyses should begin. In areas with weak governing institutions, systems may emerge from the activities of migrants and citizens, all working in various capacities, that may collectively be more significant in governing space and the people within it than the centralized state. The impact may be felt through corruption of the existing official regulatory systems and illegal mechanisms for claiming and protecting space, as well as through counter-narratives of self-exclusion or nativism and varied conceptions of community and rights to space. These jostling emergent systems may allow migrants to elude the social pressures that bind people to territory and to behavioral norms, or to claim rights to space from which the state would prefer to exclude them. Alternatively, they may enable citizens to exclude migrants from areas to which many are legally entitled, through means that defy both the letter and the spirit of the law. In the social spaces where this occurs, forms of sovereignty emerge that may be criminal, deterritorialized, or both. At other times, illegal citizen action may coincide with and strengthen state strategies of territorial control.[47]

Although these micro-level mechanisms may not wield absolute authority, they clearly illustrate the need to situate the state among a pool of potentially equal governing "peers." At the very least, migrants' ability to exist on the sovereign territory of a foreign country elicits reactions that themselves reshape categories of belonging and state institutions.

We also recognize that through the creation of legal exceptions—such as the illegal foreigner—in instruments established to protect state sovereignty, space is made available for the emergence of forces that, to the contrary, undermine it. In such spaces, alternative forms of governance begin to consolidate that may quickly become a looking glass through which state actions intended to protect territory and peoples distort into economies of corruption and new political logics that ultimately erode the sovereignty they are intended to protect. This is not so much the instrumentalization of corruption many describe, but the creation of an alternative order that undermines state leaders' "power of law" and their "power to decide."[48]

Undoubtedly, many of our observations are specific to the history and position of South Africa, and in particular Johannesburg, in national, regional, and global configurations of trade and transit. Perhaps this is the most obvious and fundamental implication of this work: universal governance models can offer important analytical tools but are unlikely to produce accounts that accurately identify risks to human and institutional security and the factors that promote it. Their weakness comes from miscoding key factors or from overlooking critical actors that are insignificant elsewhere.

Our account also highlights the need to see gradations and multiple modes of governance. The absence of state-centered, stable regulatory regimes does not reflect an *ungoverned* space, but a space that is *alternatively* governed. Such alternatives may take any number of predictable and unexpected forms, where even the regulation and territorial control undertaken by state actors does not necessarily promote principled, state-centric systems of rules and regulation. In almost all cases, authority and power are shared among actors in dynamic ways that are not necessarily state centered, state authored, or informed by clearly articulated and unified strategies of control. Elsewhere in the literature, we are already seeing such discussions vis-à-vis international actors, other states, or occupying armies. The vision of governing regimes we suggest is one that implicitly includes the spatial conditioning effects of history and recognizes that sovereignty is something that is constantly negotiated through the interactions of actors with multiple intentions, resources, and strategies.[49] Certainly, the varied composition of the migrant community, their ambitions, their resources, and their interactions with the state bureaucracy are all unpredictable daily exercises that generate multiple, coexisting forms of regulation, governance, and sovereignty.

## Notes

1. See Catherine Dauvergne, "Challenges to Sovereignty: Migration Laws for the 21st Century," paper presented at the Thirteenth Commonwealth Law Conference in Melbourne, Australia, April 2003; and Hannah Arendt, *The Origins of Totalitarianism*, 2nd ed. (New York: Meridian Books, 1958).

2. See Stephen D. Krasner, "Sharing Sovereignty: New Institutions for Collapsed and Failing States," *International Security* 29, no. 2 (2004): 85–120; Robert O. Keohane, "Political Authority after Intervention: Gradations in Sovereignty," in *Humanitarian Intervention: Ethical, Legal, and Political Dilemmas*, ed. J. L. Holzgrefe and Robert O. Keohane (Cambridge: Cambridge University Press, 2003), 275–98; Brenda Chalfin, *Working the Border in Ghana: Technologies of Sovereignty and Its Others*, Occasional Paper 16, Institute for Advanced Study, Princeton University, 2003; Christian Joppke, "Immigration Challenges the Nation-State," in *Challenge to the Nation State: Immigration in Western Europe and the United States*, ed. Christian Joppke (Oxford: Oxford University Press, 1998), 5–48; and Gary P. Freeman, "The Decline of Sovereignty? Politics and Immigration Restriction in Liberal States," in Joppke, *Challenge to the Nation State*, 86–109.

3. Marcello Balbo and Giovanna Marconi, "Governing International Migration in the City of the South," *Global Migration Perspectives* 38, Global Commission for International Migration (2005): 3.

4. Ted Leggett, *Rainbow Tenement: Crime and Policing in Inner Johannesburg*, Monograph 78, Institute for Security Studies, Pretoria, 2003.

5. See Achille Mbembe and Sarah Nuttall, "Writing the World from an African Metropolis," *Public Culture* 16, no. 3 (2004): 347–72; AbdouMaliq Simone, *For the City Yet to Come: Changing African Life in Four Cities* (Durham: Duke University Press, 2004).

6. These FMSP surveys include those conducted as part of the "New African Cities" Project in Johannesburg (2003, 2006), Maputo (2006), Lumbumbashi (2006), and Nairobi (2006). Each of these surveys interviewed between six hundred and eight hundred people, including non-nationals and citizens. The study also draws on data from a 2008/2009 survey at South Africa's five Refugee Reception Offices (n = 3130) and qualitative research conducted in eleven South African townships in the wake of the 2008 "xenophobic attacks." Data from these surveys are available upon request from the authors. Published reports drawing on these surveys are available at FSMP, Reports, http://www.migration.org.za/research-outputs/reports, and include Roni Amit, Tamlyn Monson, Darshan Vigneswaran, and George Mukundi Wachira, "National Survey of the Refugee Reception and Status Determination System in South Africa," MRMP Research Report (Johannesburg: 2009); Jean Pierre Misago with Loren B. Landau and Tamlyn Monson, *Towards Tolerance, Law, and Dignity: Addressing Violence against Foreign Nationals in South Africa* (Johannesburg: International Organization for Migration [IOM], Regional Office for Southern Africa, 2009); and Loren B. Landau and Aurelia Wa Kabwe-Segatti, *Project No. 5: Immigration, Transit and Urban Transformation: A Comparative Study of Post-Apartheid Migration and Urbanisation in Lubumbashi, Maputo and Johannesburg* (Johannesburg: 2008).

7. Simone, *For the City Yet to Come*, 2; also Achille Mbembe, "Aesthetics of Superfluity," *Public Culture* 16, no. 3 (2004): 373–405; Manuel Castells, *The Power of Identity* (London: Blackwell, 2004); and Zygmunt Bauman, *Globalization: The Human Consequences* (New York: Columbia University Press, 2000), 78.

8. Peter Arnade, Martha C. Howell, and Walter Simons, "Fertile Spaces: The Productivity of Urban Space in Northern Europe," *Journal of Interdisciplinary History* 32 (2002): 515–48.

9. Emma Algotsson, *Lindela: At the Crossroads for Detention and Repatriation* (Johannesburg: South African Human Rights Commission, 2000); Stephen Lubkemann, "The Transformation of Transnationality among Mozambican Migrants in South Africa," *Canadian Journal of African Studies* 34, no. 1 (2000): 41–63; and Morten L. Madsen, "Living for Home: Policing Immorality among Undocumented Migrants in Johannesburg," *African Studies* 63, no. 2 (2004): 173–92.

10. Statistics drawn from the 2006 "New African City" survey conducted by FMSP in central Johannesburg.

11. Loren B. Landau, "Urbanisation, Nativism, and the Rule of Law in South Africa's 'Forbidden' Cities," *Third World Quarterly* 26, no. 7 (2005): 1115–34.

12. "Open hearings on Xenophobia and problems related to it," South African Human Rights Commission, 2004, http://www.sahrc.org.za/sahrc_cms/downloads

/Xenophobia%20Report.pdf; P. Zvomunya, "From Terror to Misery," *Mail and Guardian*, 25 August 2005, and Alameen Templeton and Solly Maphumulo, "Immigrants Get Raw Deal," *Star*, 20 June 2005, A1–A2. In the latter article, the authors quote a police officer referring to refugees as "mobile ATMs."

13. Ingrid Palmary, Janine Rauch, and Graeme Simpson, "Violent Crime in Johannesburg," in *Emerging Johannesburg: Perspectives on the Postapartheid City*, ed. Richard Tomlinson, Robert Beauregard, Lindsay Bremner, and Xolela Mangcu (London: Routledge 2003).

14. Tesfalem Araia, "Report on Human Smuggling across the South Africa/Zimbabwe Border (Johannesburg: Forced Migration Studies Programme, 2009).

15. Survey conducted by Migrant Rights Monitoring Project, Access to Social Services Survey, Forced Migration Studies Programme, University of the Witwatersrand, 2007–2008.

16. Lauren Mannering, "Woman Told to Divorce Man She Never Married," *Star*, 26 July 2004, 5; Lyse Comins, "Fake Marriage Racket Bust," *Mercury*, 28 February 2007.

17. Cited here are a Zulu female respondent at Nobuhle hostel, Alexandra; and a Zulu male participant in the male focus group in Alexandra.

18. Michel Foucault, "Governmentality," in *The Foucault Effect: Studies in Governmentality*, ed. Graham Burchell, Colin Gordon, and Peter Miller (Chicago: University of Chicago Press, 1991), 87–104; Mitchell Dean, "Foucault, Government, and the Enfolding of Authority," in *Foucault and Political Reason: Liberalism, Neo-Liberalism, and Rationalities of Government*, ed. Andrew Barry, Thomas Osborne, and Nikolas Rose (Chicago: University of Chicago Press 1996), 209–29.

19. Southern African Migration Project, "The Perfect Storm: The Realities of Xenophobia in Contemporary South Africa," ed. Jonathan Crush (Cape Town: IDASA, 2008), 2.

20. Statistics drawn from the 2003 "New African City" survey conducted by FMSP in central Johannesburg.

21. Thabo Mohlala, "Xenophobic Thugs Roam Zandspruit," *Mail and Guardian*, 4 October 2000, 15; Jonathan Crush, "The Dark Side of Democracy: Migration, Xenophobia and Human Rights in South Africa," *International Migration* 38, no. 6 (2000): 103–33; interviews conducted by Tara Polzer and Loren Landau with South Africans and non-nationals in Choba for the Centre for Development and Enterprise, Johannesburg.

22. The account of violence in the Eastern Cape draws heavily from Loren B. Landau and Hakima Haithar, "Somalis Are Easy Prey," *Mail and Guardian*, 2 March 2007, 15.

23. Forced Migration Studies Programme Database on Xenophobic Attacks in South Africa, 2006–2009, ed. Tamlyn Monson, Ver 1: 9 January 2009. These data were generated during interviews conducted by the FMSP in the wake of 2008 attacks that killed at least sixty-two people and displaced more than one hundred thousand. Because of the sensitive and incriminating nature of the data, access to the interview transcripts is available only on approval of a formal written request.

24. Quoting a high-ranking member of the community policing forum, Atteridgeville.

25. Interview with South African male resident in Atteridgeville for eighteen years; interview with Mozambican male displaced from Atteridgeville.

26. ACO disciplinary committee member; Zulu male respondent resident in Atteridgeville for fifteen years; non-national male respondent resident in Atteridgeville for two years; Mozambican female respondent resident in Atteridgeville for ten years.

27. Zimbabwean male respondent displaced from Atteridgeville to Malas refugee camp.

28. Zulu male respondent resident in Atteridgeville for fifteen years; two Zimbabwean males displaced from Atteridgeville to Malas refugee camp.

29. High-ranking member of Atteridgeville CPF; ACO disciplinary committee member; Zimbabwean male displaced from Atteridgeville to Malas refugee camp.

30. High-ranking member of ACO in Atteridgeville.

31. High-ranking member of Atteridgeville CPF; Zimbabwean male displaced from Atteridgeville to Malas refugee camp.

32. Zulu male respondent resident in Atteridgeville for fifteen years.

33. High-ranking member of Atteridgeville CPF.

34. Zimbabwean male respondent displaced from Atteridgeville to Malas refugee camp.

35. Interview by authors.

36. A substantial number of interview transcripts across a variety of sites confirm an awareness of corruption in border control, policing, and the issuing of documents by the Department of Home Affairs.

37. Pedi male respondent resident in Itireleng for nine years.

38. Roger Friedland and Robert R. Alford, "Bringing Society Back In: Symbols, Practices, and Institutional Contradictions," in *The New Institutionalism in Organizational Analysis*, ed. Walter W. Powell and Paul J. DiMaggio (Chicago: University of Chicago Press, 1991), 232–66; Clifford Geertz, *Negara: The Theatre State in Nineteenth Century Bali* (Princeton, NJ: Princeton University Press 1980).

39. See Peter G. Mandaville, "Territory and Translocality: Discrepant Idioms of Political Identity," *Millennium: Journal of International Studies* 28, no. 3 (1999): 653–73; John Agnew, "Mapping Political Power beyond State Boundaries: Territory, Identity, and Movement in World Politics," *Millennium: Journal of International Studies* 28, no. 3 (1999): 499–522; and Foucault, "Governmentality." For a more general discussion, see Bauman, *Globalization*.

40. This idea is reflected in Edward Said, *Reflections on Exile and Other Essays* (Cambridge, MA: Harvard University Press, 2001), 183; see also, Georg Simmel's discussion of the stranger in *The Sociology of Georg Simmel*, trans. Kurt Wolff (New York: Free Press, 1964).

41. See Ulf Hannerz, "Cosmopolitans and Locals in World Culture," in *Global Culture: Nationalism, Globalization and Modernity*, ed. Mike Featherstone (London: Sage 1990), 237–51.

42. The account of Johannesburg's migrant churches draws heavily on discussions with Lawrence Chamba Petkou and his unpublished work.

43. Interview conducted by Laurence Chamba, Johannesburg, February 2007, as part of a project on migration and religion supported by the Social Science Research Council.

44. John M. Mang'ana, "The Effects of Migration on Human Rights Consciousness among Congolese Refugees in Johannesburg," master's thesis, University of the Witwatersrand, Johannesburg, 2004; Jean Pierre Misago, "The Impact of Refugee–Host Community Interactions on Refugees' National and Ethnic Identities: The Case of Burundian Refugees in Johannesburg," master's thesis, University of the Witwatersrand, Johannesburg, 2005.

45. Baruti Amisi and Richard Ballard, "In the Absence of Citizenship: Congolese Refugee Struggle and Organisation in South Africa," Forced Migration Working Paper 16, University of the Witwatersrand, Johannesburg, April 2005, http://www.migration.org.za/research-outputs/working-papers?page=2.

46. Graeme Götz and AbdouMaliq Simone, "On Belonging and Becoming in African Cities," in *Emerging Johannesburg*, 123–47.

47. See John C. Torpey, *The Invention of the Passport: Surveillance, Citizenship and the State* (Cambridge: Cambridge University Press, 2000), 30.

48. See Patrick Chabal and Jean-Pascal Daloz, *Africa Works: Disorder as Political Instrument* (Oxford: James Currey, 1999); and Jean-Francois Bayart, Stephen Ellis, and Beatrice Hibou, "From Kleptocracy to the Felonious State?" in *The Criminalization of the State in Africa: African Issues*, ed. Jean-Francois Bayart, Stephen Ellis, and Beatrice Hibou (Oxford: James Currey, 1999), 1–31.

49. See Stephen Krasner, "Sharing Sovereignty: New Institutions for Collapsed and Failing States," *International Security* 29, no. 2 (2004): 85–120; Catherine Boone, *Political Topographies of the African State: Territorial Authority and Institutional Choice* (Cambridge: Cambridge University Press, 2003); Agnew, "Mapping Political Power"; Timothy Mitchell, "The Limits of the State: Beyond Statist Approaches and Their Critics," *American Political Science Quarterly* 85 (1991): 77–96.

PART IV
   ALTERNATIVE ECONOMIES
   IN THE SHADOW OF THE STATE

# 9 Rules and Regulations in Ungoverned Spaces

*Illicit Economies, Criminals, and Belligerents*

Vanda Felbab-Brown

This chapter explores the "lack of governance," or more precisely, the lack of "official or recognized governance," in the domain of illicit economies. The emergence of illicit economies is an expression of the limits of state capacity or state will to enforce domestic or international regulations. Not only is the intensity of resources required by states to eliminate illicit economies frequently very high and beyond the capacity of the state, but the high rents it garners from illegality may well tempt the state to tolerate the illicit economy. The state, especially if weak, may choose to co-opt the illicit economy or even deliberately set one up (see Chapter 1). This chapter examines the nexus of conflict and illicit economies and argues against the common assumption that state efforts at suppressing illicit economies, such as the eradication of illegal drug crops, inevitably weaken belligerents. Inherently difficult, such policies frequently fail in their goal of substantially reducing the belligerents' financial income, while they often have the greatly damaging effect of losing the hearts and minds of the population.

## How Illicit Economies Emerge

Illicit economies encompass economic transactions and commodities of which the production and marketing are either completely prohibited by governments and/or international regimes or partially proscribed unless their production and provision comply with special licenses, certification, taxation, and other economic and political regulations. Illicit economies thus include, for example, the cultivation of banned crops and production of illegal drugs, illicit logging, the smuggling of wildlife, money laundering, and systematic insurance fraud.[1] Illegal economies differ from ordinary crime by their sustainability, the repeated nature of the transactions, and their complexity. They frequently involve a multitude of actors who engage in sustained economic exchange on a repeated basis. At minimum, these actors include suppliers and consumers, but they can also involve layers of intermediaries, subcontractors, and specialized service providers. A one-time mugging at gunpoint on the streets of Nairobi or a bank robbery in Los Angeles represent crime, but they do not quite amount to an illicit economy. A systematic protection racket enforced by violence, as conducted by the Mungiki in Nairobi's slums, for example, or a contract market for hit men, such as the *sicarios* of Medellín, however, do constitute illicit markets and economies.

I use the term "illicit economies" instead of "black markets" because the former better captures the scope and extent of many illicit economies. Many encompass economic and political arrangements that go beyond the market exchange component of the illegal trade, including layers of production chains, patronage networks of access to land and labor, and complex transshipment and insurance schemes. At the same time, illicit economies also occasionally lack the market exchange component altogether and are simply for subsistence: for example, some of the illicit logging in the Amazon Basin is not meant to generate hardwoods for sale but takes place to clear land for farming. A sizable component of illicit exploitation of wildlife and other non-timber forest products in the indigent hill areas of Burma today is not for illicit trade to China but for foraging for personal consumption.

Illicit economies arise because of, and are shaped by, a multitude of factors. At the most basic level, the existence of an illicit economy is caused by lack of governance. The lack of state presence or attention permits, and sometimes necessitates, economic activity outside of the legal realm. The very existence of an *illicit* economy, however, requires some kind of *preexisting regulation*—state or international—that prohibits certain economic transactions from taking place. The impetus for the emergence of a particular illicit economy can be the criminalization of certain behavior, such as the consumption and production of banned substances, or the imposition of some limitation on economic activity, such as the requirement that all trade with legal goods be subject to taxation. In fact, any form of government regulation sets up the first required, though not in itself sufficient, condition for the emergence of an illicit economy. Without such regulation, in the true absence of state and international governance, in the truly ungoverned space, the emergent economic activities may be irregular or informal, but they would not be illicit. This distinction is far from merely definitional: as will be explained below, it has crucial implications for the ability of belligerent actors to exploit such economies and defines the range of states' policy options for dealing with such economies.

Second, the emergence of an illicit economy also critically depends on the inability or unwillingness of the state or international regime to fully enforce its prohibition.[2] In other words, the existence of an illicit economy is an expression of the limits of the regulating entity's *official governance capacity*. The stress is on *official* capacity because the existence of an illicit economy despite government or international prohibition frequently leads to and is predicated on the corruption of the regulators and enforcers who are tempted by the large profits from the illicit economy. The ungoverned space of the illicit economy is frequently neither ungoverned nor without the participation of official representatives of the state. In fact, often the actors best positioned to profit from an illicit economy and manage it are the official state enforcers.[3]

A third crucial condition for the emergence of an illicit economy is some level of *demand for the commodity or service* (even though existing supply may have precipitated that demand). The existence of such demand despite criminalization is what leads to the very high profits that illicit economies generate. Criminalization and enforcement do have a direct effect on demand, discouraging some consumers from consuming the product or service by the threat of punishment and by the psychological discomfort of violating a social norm. But without a concerted and complex effort to address demand directly, criminalization and enforcement by themselves tend to be insufficient to stamp out all existing demand. Sometimes, criminalization or regulation even generates new demand by making a product look "cool" or by creating the expectation of an upcoming shortage of supply—hence the arguments that some young people are drawn to marijuana precisely because it is in defiance of parental and state regulation, and the paradoxical effect that placing a species on the endangered species list can result in its greater slaughter.[4]

These three elemental conditions for the existence of illicit economies—extant regulation, limits to state capacity, and demand—are of course ever-present. Hence, illicit economies exist virtually everywhere: in rich and poor

countries, in the context of violent conflict and in the midst of peace, right
outside the police station of a city's capital and in remote periphery jungles.
Even in developed countries with very strong law enforcement capacity, the
state—be it the Stalinist Soviet Union or the United States—faces crucial
limits to its reach. The state does not have to be failing for it to have an extensive illicit economy. The differing abilities of states to provide legally for the
economic and security needs of their populations, however, largely determine
the importance of the illicit economy for those populations. These varying
capacities also greatly alter the security and political implications for the state
of suppressing an illicit economy. In a poor country where most of the legal
economy has collapsed and an illicit economy is the only game in town, the
state's effort to destroy it is naturally resented and opposed by a large segment of the population who depend on the illicit economy for basic livelihood. Violent protests by Bolivia's *cocaleros* against the state's forced coca
eradication campaign during the 1990s are one example. Moreover, given the
importance of the illicit economy for the livelihood of the large segment of
the population, the corruption of government representatives easily becomes
widespread. It should not be surprising or shocking, for example, that corruption related to the drug trade is endemic in Afghanistan, given that the illicit
economy generates between one-third and one-half of the country's gross domestic product (around US$3.1 billion a year) while foreign aid generates the
bulk of the rest.[5] On the other hand, in a rich country with plentiful sources
of legal livelihood and economic advancement, the state's crackdown against
an illicit economy may well be welcomed by the population, whose economic
well-being allows it to place higher importance on the need to uphold regulation and moral restrictions.

Even in poor countries, there are, to be sure, great differences in the size
and kinds of illicit economies. Coca, for example, can be grown equally well
in Ecuador and Colombia, yet Ecuador has so far experienced only very little
coca cultivation while Colombia has supplied most of the world's cocaine
since the mid-1990s. Whatever the comparative "advantage" that centers coca
cultivation in Colombia and not in Ecuador, once a large-scale illicit economy
takes hold in an area, its existence frequently provides a favorable environment for spawning other illicit economies. The suppression of an illicit economy in a particular locale thus frequently leads only to its transformation
into a different kind of illicit economy. The development of a *technology of
illegality*—smuggling networks, the corruption of officials, crime and pro-

tection rackets, and the rise of powerful actors with vested interests in the preservation of the illicit economy—creates extremely auspicious conditions for the perpetuation of illicit economic activity. Though no doubt helped by the suppression of coca cultivation in Peru during the mid-1990s, the emergence of the coca-cocaine economy in Colombia, for example, grew organically from decades of smuggling of various ilk, including cigarettes and licit tariffed household goods.

## What Makes Illicit Economies Function Smoothly?

Although illicit economies thrive in ungoverned spaces where the official regulating entity's means of suppression are limited, they nonetheless frequently require some level of internal regulation. At a minimum, just like licit economies, the illicit ones greatly benefit from and frequently depend on some degree of predictability and the assurance of property rights. The "wild" space is rarely fully wild; in the case of illicit economies, it is only differently governed. In his classic study of the Sicilian Mafia, Diego Gambetta demonstrated that the key activity of the Mafia is not its provision of illegal and otherwise-absent goods, such as drugs, but its provision of protection and enforcement of contracts. In poorly administered regions, such as Sicily, the threat of untrustworthy and dangerous business competitors and corrupt government officials, as well as thieves and robbers, is so acute that the residents of these regions require extralegal physical protection as well as contract enforcement guarantees so that basic economic transactions can take place. Gambetta's central claim is that "the main market for mafia services is to be found in unstable transactions in which trust is scarce and fragile."[6] In other words, in the absence of social trust, even basic economic transactions—whether licit, illicit, or informal—require the provision of regulation and enforcement.[7] Total chaos and complete removal of the governing authority pose critical threats to the survival of the illicit (and licit) economies and threaten the interests of traffickers as well as the wider population. In fact, such a profound lack of governance can even hamper terrorist activity, as Ken Menkhaus and Jacob Shapiro effectively show in Chapter 4.

Just as in licit economies (arguably even more so since authority is frequently subject to fierce contestation in ungoverned spaces), in illicit economies the ability to assure property rights and enforce contracts critically depends on the effective use or threats of violence. What kinds of actors are available in illicit economies to provide security and assure property rights, and have military means at their disposal? By defining the economy as illicit, the state (or international regime) is officially removing itself from the menu of actors available to assure the functioning of that economy. Here is where the distinction between illicit and informal becomes critical: if the state (or international regime) had defined the economy merely as informal, it would be capable of officially inserting itself into the economy and taking over its regulation, with all the traditional benefits of deriving financial profits through taxation and capturing the top positions in the economy so as to establish political control. By defining the economy as illegal, however, the state is officially committing itself to suppressing the economy, not to facilitating its function. Hence, other actors willing to use violence fill the lacuna of governance necessary to provide the minimum protection and regulatory functions that the economy needs to function smoothly. Common examples include well-armed criminal groups, such as the Mafia; warlords; insurgents and terrorists; paramilitaries; and corrupt government representatives, such as military and police officials. The ability of such actors to successfully spread through a particular ungoverned space is inextricably linked to their ability to succeed (and outcompete others) in the provision of the services necessary for the illicit economy to thrive.

Afghanistan and Somalia provide two examples. Before the emergence of the Taliban in late 1994, Afghanistan deteriorated into numerous violent fiefdoms controlled by tribally based warlords and their militias. As a result of the 1984 Soviet invasion and the subsequent civil war, the legal economy came close to a complete halt. Two illicit markets dominated economic activity in the country and provided for the majority of the population: the expanding cultivation of the opium poppy and illicit smuggling with licit goods. Estimated at $2.5 billion a year,[8] the smuggling of goods was nonetheless critically hampered by predatory warlords who complicated the life of the smuggling mafia. Charging increasingly higher and higher tolls and sometimes even stealing the contraband, the warlords threatened not only to severely jeopardize profits for the smuggling mafia, but also to paralyze the trade itself.

The emergence of the Taliban presented the traffickers with a regulatory force that could assure that transaction costs were significantly lowered and business was carried out in a more predictable fashion. Purported to be long incensed with the excesses of the predatory warlords on the highways and by their arbitrary extortion, Taliban leader Mullah Omar willingly provided protection to the illicit smuggling enterprise. Already in the fall of 1994, just as the Taliban was first emerging around Kandahar, it cleared the chains from the roads, set up a one-toll system for trucks entering Afghanistan at Spin Baldak, and patrolled and protected the highways against the warlords. Crucially, the Taliban also declared that it would not allow goods bound for Afghanistan to be carried by Pakistani trucks, thus satisfying a key demand of the Afghan transport mafia.[9] The interests of the transport mafia were satisfied, and from the beginning the traffickers and the Taliban developed very good relations. As a result, the traffickers paid the Taliban handsomely and did not interfere with the Taliban's military expansion. This relationship held throughout the Taliban tenure as the government of Afghanistan. In fact, not only did the reduction in transaction costs satisfy the needs of the traffickers, but it also greatly pleased the general population, who also found it much easier to move their products to markets.

Similarly in Somalia, a key element in the successful rise of the now deposed Islamists and their umbrella organization, the Islamic Courts Union (ICU), during 2005 and 2006 was their ability to provide the minimum security to permit various licit and illicit economies to take off. The larger population benefited from greater security and stability, as did the tribally based business elite, which saw its transaction costs fall drastically.[10] These elites then tolerated and at times facilitated the expansion of the Islamists' control. Ironically, it was the religiously motivated effort by the ICU to suppress smuggling of the narcotic qat, which threatened key economic interests of the tribal business elites in Somalia and their qat suppliers in Kenya, that alienated these influential elites from the ICU.[11]

Belligerents such as warlords, insurgents, and terrorists do not, however, perform regulatory and protection functions only for the illicit business elite. Critically, they perform a similar protection and regulatory function for the producers of the illicit product, such as the cultivators of illicit crops. These producers are vulnerable to predation by the traffickers they depend on and who frequently pay them meager wages and otherwise abuse them. The belligerents hence have the opportunity to fill the role of a protection and regulation agent, bargaining on behalf of the producers for better wages and limiting the physical abuse by the traffickers. During the 1980s in Peru, for example, the insurgent group Sendero Luminoso (Shining Path) curtailed abuse of the *coca-leros* by the traffickers and several times negotiated better prices for the farmers from the traffickers. In 1985, for example, U.S.-Peruvian interdiction efforts under Operation Condor succeeded in disrupting processing and traffic. The subsequent overproduction of unprocessible coca leaves led to a precipitous decline in the price of coca leaf, slashing it by half.[12] Sendero Luminoso's reaction was to force the traffickers to pay the peasants above the market price. It repeated this practice in April 1990 and used it to recover political legitimacy with the rural population involved in the illicit economy.

The dual audiences of the belligerents operating in illicit economies point to the complicated relationship between the belligerents and the criminal entrepreneurs, one that is frequently full of friction. To the extent that the state is cracking down on them, the criminals and the belligerents may well cooperate. But at the same time, the criminal entrepreneurs and the belligerents have some key diverging objectives and frequently end up fighting each other. Instead of representing permanent alliances or the merger into one agglomerate actor with common goals, the relationship is fraught with problems and falls apart just as easily as it comes together.

## Threats That Illicit Economies Pose to States

Although themselves precipitated by the lack of official governance, illicit economies further perpetuate and even enlarge the scope of ungoverned spaces within states. Moreover, they also enable the production of alternatively governed spaces, with the "alternative authority" frequently antagonistic to the state. These ungoverned or alternatively governed spaces in turn generate a variety of threats to states (see Chapter 2 for more on the capacity gap).

- They *threaten the state politically* by providing an avenue for criminal organizations and corrupt politicians to enter the political space, undermining the democratic process. As such actors are able to secure official positions of power or wield influence from behind the scenes, the legitimacy of the political process is subverted.

- Large-scale illicit economies *create international political costs* for the state by generating a reputation for it of weakness, incompetence, and illegitimacy. Influential international actors, such as powerful states, international organizations, and multinational corporations, may react to the perception of weakness and corruption by rescinding membership in economic or security organizations, withholding critical loans and grants, restricting trade and investment, or otherwise marginalizing the offending state.

- Large illicit economies with powerful traffickers *threaten the judicial system* of the country. First, as the size of an illicit economy grows, the investigative capacity of the law enforcement and judicial systems diminishes. Impunity for criminal activity also increases, undermining the credibility and deterrence capacity of the judicial system and the authority of the government. Second, powerful traffickers frequently turn to disruptive, often violent means to deter and avoid prosecution, killing or bribing prosecutors, judges, and witnesses.[13]

- Illicit economies *have large economic effects*. For example, drug cultivation and processing on one hand generate employment for the poor rural population, numbering frequently in the hundreds of thousands. Not only does the drug economy allow the impoverished poor to make ends meet, it also facilitates upward mobility for many participants. On the other hand, the presence of a large-scale illicit economy contributes to inflation and can hence harm legitimate, export-oriented, import-substituting industries. It encourages real estate speculation and a rapid rise in real estate prices, and undermines currency stability. It also displaces legitimate production, complicating efforts of the state to develop legitimate economic activity.[14]

- Certain illicit economies *create environmental threats* to the state. The smuggling of wildlife in Burma and Indonesia, for example, depletes biodiversity and contributes to the demise of endangered species. Illicit logging in Afghanistan leads to further soil erosion and desertification, making land inhospitable for agriculture. Coca cultivation in Latin America results in deforestation, and the processing of coca leaves into cocaine leaks highly toxic materials, such as kerosene, into the waterways of some of the richest ecosystems in the world. Illicit smuggling of toxic waste into Africa generates critical health problems and ecological catastrophes, such as happened in the Côte d'Ivoire port of Abidjan in August 2006.[15]

- Finally, the presence of a large-scale illicit economy in the context of violent conflict greatly *exacerbates security threats* to the state. Belligerent groups that embrace illicit economies, such as the Taliban in Afghanistan, the Sendero Luminoso in Peru, and the Revolutionary Armed Forces of Colombia (FARC) and the paramilitaries in Colombia, derive a multitude of benefits from such illicit economies. With the large profits they accumulate, belligerents improve the physical resources they have to fight the state: they can hire more combatants, pay them better salaries, and equip them with better weapons. In fact, the increase in the belligerents' physical resources is frequently immense; in the case of FARC and the officially demobilized paramilitaries in Colombia, for example, the financial profits from drugs are on average estimated at about US$100 million a year, or between 50 and 70 percent of the groups' incomes.[16]

Better procurement and logistics also enhance what can be called "the freedom of action" of belligerents, that is, the scope of tactical options available to them and their ability to optimize both tactics and their grand strategy. Before penetrating illicit economies, belligerents frequently have to deplete much time and energy on activities that do little to advance their causes, such as robbing banks and armories to obtain money and weapons or extorting the local population for food supplies. Once their participation in an illicit economy, such as the drug trade, solves the belligerents' logistics and procurement needs, they become free to concentrate on high-value, high-impact targets.

Critically, participation in illicit economies greatly increases the belligerents' political capital—that is, the extent to which the population welcomes and tolerates the presence of the belligerents. Large-scale illicit economies frequently provide a basic livelihood for the population in a conflict zone, and by sponsoring the illicit economy, belligerents are able to distribute real-time economic benefits to the population. Moreover, as already indicated above, belligerents also supply protection and regulation services to the illicit economy and its producers against, for instance, brutal and unreliable traffickers. With large financial profits from the illicit economy, belligerents often deliver a variety of otherwise-absent social services—such as clinics, roads, and schools—as did Peru's Sendero Luminoso during the 1980s.[17]

Four factors have a decisive influence on the extent to which belligerent groups derive political capital from their sponsorship of illicit economies: the state of the overall economy in the country or region; the character of the illicit economy; the presence or absence of independent traffickers; and the government's response to the illicit economy.

- The *state of the overall economy* determines the extent to which the local population depends on the illicit economy for basic livelihood and any chance of social advancement. On one hand, the poorer the country and the smaller the size and accessibility of the licit economy, the greater is the dependence of the population on the illicit one and the greater is the political capital that accrues to belligerents for sponsoring the illicit economy. On the other hand, in a rich developed country with a plentitude of legal economic opportunities, the larger population may well object to the illicit economy, and the belligerents' participation in it can discredit them. Hence, in Afghanistan today, the Taliban derives substantial political capital from its protection of the poppy fields. This political capital is all the more vital for the movement because its brutality has antagonized the population. By contrast, the Catholics in Northern Ireland, where legal economic opportunities were far greater than in Afghanistan, objected to the participation of the Provisional Irish Republican Army in drug distribution. The resulting loss of legitimacy ultimately led the group to abandon its participation in the drug trade.[18]

- The *character of the illicit economy* determines the extent to which it provides employment for the population. Labor-intensive illicit activities, such as the cultivation of banned crops, easily employ hundreds of thousands to millions of people in a particular locale. The smuggling of drugs or other contraband, by contrast, is a labor-nonintensive illicit activity that frequently employs only hundreds of people. Belligerents' sponsorship of labor-intensive illicit economies thus brings them much greater and more widespread political capital than their sponsorship of labor-nonintensive ones. The Taliban's regulation of the labor-nonintensive illicit smuggling of licit goods bought it the favor of Afghanistan's trafficking groups in the early 1990s, but it was only in late 1995 when it came to tolerate and regulate the labor-intensive opium economy that it obtained political capital from the larger population.

- The *presence or absence of independent traffickers* determines the extent to which belligerents can provide protection and regulation for the population against the traffickers. To the extent that independent traffickers are present and abuse the population, the belligerents can insert themselves into the relationship and act as protection and regulation agents, thus increasing the well-being of the population and their own political capital. If traffickers are not present, perhaps because the belligerents eliminated them, belligerents cannot provide the same scope of protection and regulation services to the producers, and hence their political capital decreases. During the 1980s and early 1990s, for example, FARC bargained on behalf of farmers for better prices from the traffickers and limited the abuses by the traffickers against the population. Its actions were met with widespread approval from the *cocaleros*.[19] During the late 1990s, however, FARC displaced independent traffickers from the territories it controlled, demanded a monopoly on the sale of coca leaf, and set a ceiling on the price paid to the *cocaleros*. Consequently, its political capital plummeted substantially, further contributing to the deterioration of its legitimacy, which already was in decline as a result of its brutality and failure to protect the population from the paramilitaries' massacres. In fact, some *cocaleros*, such as those in the Nariño region, have complained that they would prefer that FARC were absent because it interferes with their drug cultivation and profits by demanding a monopoly on sales of coca leaf and paste.[20]

- Finally, *government response to the illicit economy* critically influences the extent of the political capital belligerents can derive from it. The government's response can range from suppression—eradication and interdiction—to laissez-faire, to some form of official sanction, such as legalizing the illicit economy. Although political considerations make legalization difficult to imagine in the case of illicit drugs, such legalization or licensing could be feasible in the case of other contraband, such as gems or tariff goods; the Kimberly certification of diamonds from Africa is an example. The more the government attempts to suppress the illicit economy, the more it boosts demand for the belligerents' protection and regulation services, and the more dependent both the criminal business elites and the wider population are on the belligerents for the preservation of the illicit economy. Government suppression policies, such as the effort to eradicate illicit crops, thus frequently have the inadvertent effect of strengthening the belligerents politically by undermining the willingness of the population to provide intelligence on them to the government. Accurate and actionable human intelligence is of course essential for successful counterterrorism and counterinsurgency operations.

Although they frequently alienate the population, government efforts to crack down on illicit economies rarely result in a substantial curtailing of the belligerents' financial income. For example, drug eradication policies so far have not bankrupted or seriously weakened any belligerent group.[21] They tend to fail because belligerents and producers of the illicit products and services have a variety of adaptive methods at their disposal: relocating production to new areas, altering production methods to avoid detection or survive suppression, or even switching to other illegal activities. Going after the belligerents' finances, including those derived from illicit economies, is inherently difficult and rarely limits their physical resources. But in the case of labor-intensive illicit economies in poor countries, such suppression efforts, especially those that affect the larger population, can greatly increase the belligerents' political capital and hamper the government's intelligence acquisition, and hence the overall counterinsurgency and counterterrorism efforts.

## State Co-option of Illicit Economies

Although illicit economies threaten states in a multitude of ways, and although they frequently thrive in ungoverned spaces, criminal actors with vested interests in the illicit economy frequently do not desire a complete collapse of the state. Once again, Chapter 4 echoes how a lack of effective national or at least regional governance made even Al-Qa'ida's operations in Somalia very costly and difficult. This is especially the case if there are no belligerents ready to provide the governing function and the crime entrepreneurs themselves are unable or unwilling to provide it. Nor do the criminal business elites necessarily desire a weak state, as long as the state is not antagonistic to the illicit economy. In fact, if the state is at minimum not attempting to suppress the illicit economy or is in fact favorably disposed to its existence, traffickers and producers may even support the state and oppose the belligerents. When eradication policies were suspended in Peru in 1989, for example, both the traffickers and the larger population were willing to provide critical information on the Sendero Luminoso to the military, so that the military was able to deliver fatal blows to the insurgents in the Upper Huallaga Valley.[22] Rather than criminal elites always existing in a fully antagonistic relationship with the state, criminal organizations and the governing elites sometimes develop a mutually beneficial accommodation.[23] Such an accommodation is not optimal from the perspective of society and certainly undermines the rule of law and democracy, but it may well result in a sustainable internal modus operandi, at least to the extent that external actors do not threaten such an accommodation by insisting on the destruction of the illicit economy.

Similarly, despite the simplistic assumption that large illicit economies always contribute to state failure, the state is not always eviscerated, or even undermined, by their presence. A democratic, accountable regime will of course be threatened in the multiple ways indicated above by the presence of a large-scale illicit economy, but the survival of a weak or unaccountable state may well be enhanced by its ability to capture or profit from illicit economies. For example, the regimes in Burma, North Korea, Afghanistan, and Haiti during the 1990s survived precisely because they were able to capitalize on several illicit economies.

Moreover, the elimination of an illicit economy, whether inadvertent or systematically carried out by the state or an international actor, may actually cause the full unraveling of the state and the emergence of new threats in a governance vacuum. There is nothing inevitable about legal economic enterprises emerging in the wake of the destruction of an illicit economy. The consequent economic void and the resulting political instability can sometimes generate greater threats to the international system and neighboring states than state co-option of an illicit economy and the perpetuation of a corrupt authoritarian government in power. The total governing and economic collapse following the destruction of an illicit economy, without the systematic and directed buildup of a legal economy to take its place, is also likely to be considerably more damaging to the basic interests of the population than the continuation of a large-scale illicit economy with its corrupt governing elites. For example, the suppression of marijuana and poppy cultivation in the Bekka Valley in Lebanon during the 1990s was not accompanied by an increase in legitimate economic activity, but further impoverished the local population and made it more susceptible to the influence of Hizbullah.[24] Although Lebanon's overall legal economy experienced spectacular growth between the early 1990s and 2006, the Bekka Valley population was largely unable to participate in the boom, and its dependence on Hizbullah was only strengthened. But even in the case of legitimate governments that nonetheless are unable to exercise effective control over large portions of their territory, such as in Peru's Monzón Valley since the late 1990s, government efforts to suppress an illicit economy that provides the only available livelihood to tens of thousands of people can further weaken and reduce the reach of the state.[25]

## Conclusion

The presence of a large-scale illicit economy frequently undermines official governance and enables what is effectively alternative governance by groups that may be antagonistic to the state. Illicit economies thus generate a multitude of threats to the state, including threats to the political structure, government accountability, and rule of law; the economy and natural environment; and most critically, state security. The ability of belligerent groups that oppose the government or threaten other states to sponsor and participate in illicit economies provides them not only with large financial profits, but also frequently with critical political capital. This is especially the case when belligerents protect and regulate labor-intensive illicit economies in poor countries, where the population faces a severe lack of legal economic alternatives and depends on the illicit economy for their basic livelihood.

Despite the multitude and sometimes magnitude of threats that illicit economies pose to states, the policy implication is not that states always and by all means should attempt to suppress the illicit economy. Such suppression efforts frequently fail to reduce belligerents' resources, because they can adapt their financing strategies in a variety of ways. But in the absence of a strong legal economy, such suppression efforts can have devastating economic effects on the larger population and hence lose the government's competition for hearts and minds. In other words, ill-conceived measures against illicit economies can in fact aggravate the problem of ungoverned spaces.

Moreover, if the goal of the policy is to prevent state collapse and the unraveling of what minimal governance and economic activity exists, no matter how corrupt and authoritarian, the suppression of illicit economies may well critically undermine such a goal. Policies against illicit economies, while unquestionably desirable and important, thus need to be carefully weighed with respect to the goal they are supposed to accomplish as well as their secondary, but important, effects. They also need to be carefully calibrated with systematic and directed efforts to build up a legal economy that can reduce the economic and social importance of the illegal one for the population. The provision of security and the growth of the legal economy are as essential for conflict limitation as they are for reducing the size of illicit economies. But even once security has been achieved, legal economies will not simply naturally emerge. Before the state and the international community decide to tear out illicit economies in a country that recently achieved peace and stability, they need to make a well-resourced commitment to help build up a legal economy and the state more broadly in the country, lest they risk squandering the dividends of peace and social stability itself.

## Notes

1. For an overview of the variety of illicit economies, see R. T. Naylor, *Wages of Crime: Black Markets, Illegal Finance, and the Underworld Economy* (Ithaca, NY: Cornell University Press, 2002).

2. See H. Richard Friman and Peter Andreas, "Introduction: International Relations and the Illicit Global Economy," in *The Illicit Global Economy and State Power*, ed. H. Richard Friman and Peter Andreas (Lanham, MD: Rowman and Littlefield, 1999), 1–23.

3. Every country that has dealt with the problem of large illicit economies has abundant stories of official corruption, such as entire police units in Mexico that function as drug traffickers' hit men; the Blue Cartel in Colombia; the permeation of the state by drug traffickers in Burma; or friendly relations between Al Capone and the police in Chicago.

4. See Philippe Rivalan, Virginie Delmas, Elena Angulo, Leigh S. Bull, Richard J. Hall, Franck Courchamp, Alison M. Rosser, and Nigel Leader-Williams, "Can Bans Stimulate Wildlife Trade?" *Nature* 477:7144 (May 31, 2007): 529–30. Neither Rivalan nor I argues against environmental protection or awarding special protection to certain species. But the issue of environmental regulation for species protection once again highlights the need to have the necessary enforcement ready to uphold the regulation before it is issued or otherwise risk setting up large-scale and pernicious illicit economies.

5. United Nations Office on Drugs and Crime, *2007 World Drug Report*, http://www.unodc.org/pdf/research/wdr07/WDR_2007.pdf, accessed July 15, 2007.

6. Diego Gambetta, *The Sicilian Mafia: The Business of Private Protection* (Cambridge, MA: Harvard University Press, 1993), 17.

7. For more discussion about the role of trust and social capital, see Robert D. Putnam, "The Prosperous Community: Social Capital and Public Life," *American Prospect* 4:13 (March 1993), http://www.prospect.org/cs/articles?article=the_prosperous_community.

8. Frederik Balfour, "Dark Days for a Black Market: Afghanistan and Pakistan Rely Heavily on Smuggling," *Business Week*, 15 October 2001, http://businessweek.com/magazine/content/01_42/b3753016.htm.

9. Ahmed Rashid, *Taliban* (New Haven, CT: Yale University Press, 2001), 29.

10. Extremists in the ICU also provided safe haven to Al-Qa'ida members and sought to impose a strict sharia code on the country. For the nature of Somalia's extralegal economies, both illicit and informal, and their political implications, see Khalid Medani, "Financing Terrorism or Survival in Somalia? Informal Finance, State Collapse and the US War on Terrorism," *Middle East Report*, no. 223 (Summer 2002): 2–9; and Kenneth J. Menkhaus, "Constraints and Opportunities in Ungoverned Spaces," in *Denial of Sanctuary: Understanding Terrorist Safehavens*, ed. Michael Innes (Westport, CT: Praeger, 2007), 67–82.

11. Sunguta West, "Qat Ban in Somalia Exposes Cracks in ICU Leadership," *Terrorism Focus* III, no. 46 (28 November 2006): 3.

12. See, for example, Richard Craig, "Illicit Drug Traffic: Implications for South American Source Countries," *Journal of Interamerican Studies and World Affairs* 29:2 (Summer 1987): 21.

13. Mónica Serrano and María Celia Toro, "From Drug Trafficking to Trans-

national Organized Crime in Latin America," in *Transnational Organized Crime and International Security: Business as Usual?* ed. Mats Berdal and Monica Serrano (Boulder, CO: Lynne Rienner, 2002), 141–54; and Mauricio Rubio, "Violence, Organized Crime, and the Criminal Justice System in Colombia," *Journal of Economic Issues* 32 (2): 605–10.

14. See, for example, Francisco E. Thoumi, *Illegal Drugs, Economy, and Society in the Andes* (Baltimore, MD: John Hopkins University Press, 2004); and Mauricio Reina, "Drug Trafficking and the National Economy," in *Violence in Colombia 1990–2000: Waging War and Negotiating Peace*, ed. Charles Bergquist, Ricardo Peñaranda, and Gonzalo Sánchez G. (Wilmington, DE: Scholarly Resources, 2001), 75–94.

15. A tanker carrying five hundred metric tons of European industrial waste illegally dumped its cargo in the port, killing or sickening thousands and overwhelming the state's infrastructure. See International Centre for Trade and Sustainable Development, "Abidjan Toxic Waste Poisoning Raises Questions of Responsibility," *Bridges Trade BioRes* 6:15 (8 September 2006), accessed at http://ictsd.net /i/news/biores/9057/.

16. Author's interviews in Colombia, fall 2005.

17. See, for example, Cynthia McClintock, *Revolutionary Movements in Latin America: El Salvador's FMLN & Peru's Shining Path* (Washington, DC: U.S. Institute of Peace Press, 1998); and Cynthia McClintock, "The War on Drugs: The Peruvian Case," *Journal of Interamerican Studies and World Affairs* 30:2 and 3 (Summer/Fall 1988): 127–42.

18. Andrew Silke, "Drink, Drugs, and Rock 'n' Roll: Financing Loyalist Terrorism in Northern Ireland—Part Two," *Studies in Conflict and Terrorism* 23:2 (April–June 2000): 107–27.

19. See, for example, Nazih Richani, *Systems of Violence: The Political Economy of War and Peace in Colombia* (Albany: State University of New York Press, 2002); and Francisco Gutiérrez Sanín, "Criminal Rebels? A Discussion of Civil War and Criminality from the Colombian Experience," *Politics and Society* 32:2 (June 2004): 257–85.

20. Author's interviews with Colombian and U.S. government officials, Bogotá, Colombia, November 2005, and Washington, D.C., spring and summer 2007.

21. A 2007 classified White House study estimated that FARC's drug income fell between 2003 and 2005 by one-third and it was now between $60 million and $115 million a year. Author's interviews with U.S. government officials, Washington, D.C., spring 2007. See Juan Forero, "Colombia's Low-Tech Coca Assault," *Washington Post*, 7 July 2007: A01. Even disregarding the notorious difficulties in estimating profits from illicit economies, the estimates betray the extraordinary challenge of trying to bankrupt belligerent groups by eradication. If six years of the largest aerial spraying campaign ever—Plan Colombia—managed to reduce FARC's income only to a still extraordinarily high $60 million a year (the lower bound of the estimate), the prospects are not good that such efforts will be successful elsewhere. Indeed, bankrupting belligerents via the eradication of illicit crops from which they profit has yet to work anywhere.

22. José E. Gonzales, "Guerrillas and Coca in the Upper Huallaga Valley," in *Shining Path of Peru*, ed. David Scott Palmer (New York: St. Martin's Press, 1994), 123–44.

23. Bertil Lintner, "Drugs and Economic Growth: Ethnicity and Exports," *Burma: Prospect for a Democratic Future*, ed. Robert I. Rotberg (Washington, DC: Brookings Institution Press, 1998), 165–84.

24. Christopher Hack, "Lebanon's Growing Drug Worries," BBC Online Network, 11 October 1998, http://news.bbc.co.uk/1/hi/world/middle_east/191154.stm.

25. See Vanda Felbab-Brown, "Trouble Ahead: The *Cocaleros* of Peru," *Current History* 105:688 (February 2006): 79–83.

# 10 Nuclear Trafficking in Ungoverned Spaces and Failed States

Lyudmila Zaitseva

The problem of trafficking in nuclear and other radioactive material is a global one. Since 1990 it has affected many dozens of countries, ranging from highly industrialized ones, such as Germany and France, to failed states, such as Afghanistan and the Democratic Republic of Congo. Ungoverned spaces and failed states can serve both as excellent conduits for the acquisition and trafficking of radioactive and dual-use materials or an actual device, and as relatively convenient locations for the assembly of a device. As the analysis below shows, this problem has already manifested in several such states and areas that have the necessary preconditions to facilitate the diversion, theft, or trafficking of nuclear and other radioactive materials through their territories. Low standards of living, high unemployment rates, weak and demoralized law enforcement, poorly controlled borders, and rampant corruption all contribute to an environment conducive to illegal activities, whether it is drug trafficking or nuclear material smuggling. Not all ungoverned spaces and failed states, however, are equally affected by nuclear trafficking. Those that either have nuclear and radioactive materials of their own or are geographically located between potential supplier and end-user states are much more likely to find themselves drawn into this problem than others.

Compared with other types of smuggling activities, the scope of nuclear trafficking is, fortunately, small in scale. The International Atomic Energy Agency (IAEA), which collects government-confirmed cases of illicit trafficking (such as theft, smuggling, and illegal sale) and other unauthorized activities (such as loss, discovery, and disposal) involving nuclear and other radioactive material, has recorded about 1,500 such incidents between January 1993 and December 2008.[1] The Database on Nuclear Smuggling, Theft, and Orphan Radiation Sources (DSTO), which in addition to government-confirmed cases also collects unconfirmed open-source reports, has recorded 2,230 such cases within the same time frame and an additional 80 cases for the years 1991 and 1992.[2] The actual number of cases in which radioactive material was lost, stolen, found, and confiscated is higher still, for a number of reasons. First, many countries do not participate in the IAEA Illicit Trafficking Database (ITDB) program, created to promote an information exchange between members, and therefore do not report their incidents. As of December 2008, 104 states are part of the program.[3] Second, there is an issue of underreporting among the participating states. For example, according to Chinese experts, about 300 cases of theft and loss of radioactive sources were recorded in China between 1988 and 1998, none of which the country's authorities reported to the IAEA ITDB.[4] Thus, a lack of officially reported data from certain countries, not to mention ungoverned spaces, does not necessarily mean a lack of occurrences. Third, the international press and mass media, which are a good and often the only source of information in countries where official confirmation is hard to obtain, may not pick up all the incidents. For example, in the United States, only about 10 percent of incidents of theft and loss of radioactive sources reported to the U.S. Nuclear Regulatory Commission by licensees are highlighted by the national news agencies.[5]

With this in mind, it is clear that obtaining accurate and objective open-source information on the situation inside failed states, and particularly ungoverned spaces, presents a significant challenge. The local press may be either nonexistent or heavily influenced by the ruling factions or non-state actors in charge. Some ungoverned spaces may be impenetrable to outside observers and reporters. If they are allowed in, this is likely to be on the condition that only preapproved visits, meetings, and interviews take place. Even intelligence agencies find it extremely difficult to penetrate some ungoverned spaces, as demonstrated by the fact that Osama bin Laden has successfully managed to evade capture for more than six years, hiding in the uncontrolled areas inside Pakistan and Afghanistan. Such isolation from the rest of the world makes ungoverned spaces very attractive to both terrorist and criminal networks. The lack of effective controls in these areas, as well as the existing trafficking routes and associated infrastructures in many of them, also provides an ideal setting for the smuggling, storage, and handling of radioactive material.

This chapter explores whether and to what extent illicit trafficking and other unauthorized activities involving radioactive material have affected ungoverned spaces. It also provides a brief overview of the situation in the states that have been identified as failed in the "Failed States Index 2008" of the Fund for Peace and Carnegie Endowment for International Peace.[6] This analysis will be based mostly on the DSTO, a collection of some twenty-three hundred nuclear trafficking and orphan source incidents reported globally since 1991.

## Exploring Nuclear Trafficking in Ungoverned Spaces

As noted above, assessing the nuclear trafficking situation inside ungoverned spaces is a difficult task because of the lack of reliable, or often any, data from such areas. Therefore, this section concentrates only on those ungoverned spaces where nuclear smuggling activities have been reported. These include Chechnya, Abkhazia, South Ossetia, Nagorno-Karabakh, and Transdniester, all of them located in the Newly Independent States of the former Soviet Union, where the large presence of poorly guarded nuclear and other radio-active material brought about the problem of theft and smuggling since the fall of communism in the early 1990s. These areas have become involved in nuclear trafficking activities because of their favorable geographical location between the suppliers and potential end users, the existing trafficking routes for licit and illicit goods, the presence of radioactive substances on their own territories, and the presence of non-state actors interested in acquiring or using such substances for terrorist purposes.

### Chechnya

The Chechen Republic is located in the North Caucasus region of southern Russia. After the collapse of the Soviet Union in 1991, Chechnya tried to secede from the Russian Federation. A long struggle for independence followed, which resulted in two wars with the Russian Federal Army in the 1990s that left tens of thousands dead. Although the situation in Chechnya has stabilized in the past several years, the country was largely an ungoverned space throughout the 1990s.

Chechnya has probably been associated with more nuclear terrorist threats and trafficking activities than all the other ungoverned spaces combined.[7]

Chechen militants are known to have threatened Russia with nuclear and radiological terrorism on numerous occasions, ranging from detonating a "dirty bomb" and stealing a nuclear weapon to attacking a Russian nuclear facility and seizing a nuclear submarine. In November 1995, a Chechen field commander, Shamil Basayev, arranged the burial of a canister containing cesium-137 in Moscow's Izmailovsky Park and then informed a national television channel of its location in an attempt to gain publicity. He claimed that four more radioactive sources had been smuggled into Moscow, of which two were connected to explosives. Only the one source buried in the park, however, was found by the Russian authorities.[8] Although this incident caused neither significant contamination nor harm to public health, it demonstrated the resolve of these terrorists to carry out a radiological attack, as well as their ability to obtain radioactive material.

A vast pool of evidence indicates that such material could be and indeed was acquired by the fighters in Chechnya during the 1990s. For example, about half of the nine hundred cubic meters of radioactive waste stored at the radon waste repository near Tolstoy Yurt went missing after the first military campaign in 1995–1996.[9] Authorities suspected that the radioactive material was either pilfered and sold to the Chechen militants by demoralized Russian soldiers or recovered by the rebels themselves for use in acts of terrorism and sabotage. Thus, two two-hundred-liter barrels containing cesium-137, buried in the repository in 1983 and found in the region of Gudermes in 1999, were believed to have been intended for such acts.[10]

Other radioactive substances discovered in Grozny, the Chechen capital, after the end of the military conflict may also have originated from the radon facility, which was taken over by Russian federal troops in January 2000. Two sources, for example, were removed from a school courtyard by local rescue forces in April 2001. The area had to be decontaminated because of an apparent breach of the container shielding, which protects the radioactive material inside and makes a source safe to handle. This fact may indicate that somebody tried purposefully to extract the material. Russian authorities believed that these sources were a legacy of Chechen militants who, before the start of the second Chechen war, had "established a workshop for the production of mortars and grenade cup discharges" belonging to Shamil Basayev. According to Russian intelligence, the separatists tried to produce explosive devices filled with radioactive material for greater effect.[11] An apparent act of radiological sabotage was prevented by the Chechen Security Service in December 1998, when a container filled with radioactive substances was found attached to a mine near a railway line outside the town of Argun.[12] The mine was successfully defused, but Chechen officials worried that more such acts would follow given the abundance of radioactive material in the republic.[13]

It was not just from the radon facility, however, that radioactive material could be obtained by the militants in Chechnya. Several research institutions and industrial plants operating on the territory of the republic had used radioactive sources, which were not adequately protected and were subject to theft. For instance, in September 1999 several criminals broke into a chemical factory in Grozny, which had stored twenty-eight strong radiation sources in its underground vault, and removed two hundred grams of cobalt-60 rods from the protective container in an attempted theft. Three of the suspects died of radiation exposure shortly after they handled the material, and three more sought medical treatment.[14] According to Russian press reports, some of the stolen rods were never recovered.

Concerned about the safety and security implications of the unused radioactive sources, the Russian authorities sent special teams to industrial sites in Chechnya to locate and recover them. In July 2000, the Ministry of Emergency Situations recovered twenty-four radiation sources in Grozny, mostly on the premises of the above-mentioned chemical plant. Some of the sources emitted such high dose rates that special robots had to be used to secure them.[15] Eighteen other sources were removed from the premises of a cement plant in Chechnya's Chiri-Yurt in November 2001.[16] Ten more radiation sources—five of them containing cesium-137 and used for industrial applications—were discovered on the grounds of a warehouse in Grozny in April 2002.[17] According to a statement by the director of the Grozny chemical plant made in April 2003, a total of eighty radioactive sources had been collected in Chechnya since 2000, and twelve more remained missing.[18]

In addition to using the locally available radioactive material, Chechen militants have been implicated in the trafficking of nuclear material stolen elsewhere. For example, some Georgian security service officials believed that the kilogram of low-enriched uranium seized in Batumi in September 1999 might have come to Georgia via Russia and Chechnya, since two of the three suspects arrested in the case previously had been held prisoner by Chechen fighters.[19] The material was reportedly on its way to Iran. Two more cases are known in which Chechnya was used as a transshipment route for smuggled nuclear material of foreign origin. In November 1992, Azerbaijani nationals were arrested in Grozny trying to purchase an unspecified amount of low-enriched uranium for subsequent resale to Iran. The uranium had been diverted by conspiring employees from the Chepetsk plant, a nuclear fuel production facility in Udmurtia, Russia.[20] The six-kilogram batch of uranium seized by law-enforcement authorities in Turkey in March 1993 was reportedly smuggled via Chechnya as well. The material had allegedly followed a long route from Uzbekistan to Grozny, to Georgia, and to the Azerbaijani exclave of Nakhichevan before finally arriving in Istanbul.[21]

Even Al-Qa'ida apparently considered resorting to the Chechen fighters in its quest for radioactive material. According to an Al-Qa'ida insider named Abu Walid al-Misri, Osama bin Laden was once pressured by his network affiliates to purchase radiological material through contacts in Chechnya.[22] It is uncertain, though, whether this resulted in an actual transfer. There are also indications that Chechen nationals might have participated in sophisticated trafficking schemes and provided their services as brokers to some states interested in the illegal acquisition of nuclear and dual-use materials. For example, Russian press reports claimed that in late 1992, the Chechen government had purchased 148 tons of zirconium tubing from the above-mentioned Chepetsk plant and then resold it to Pakistan in a secret deal.[23] Again, the accuracy of this claim is difficult to verify.

Chechnya represents a prime example of how an ungoverned space can be affected by the various facets of nuclear trafficking and radiological terrorism, from losing control over its own radioactive material, which may end up in the hands of criminals and terrorists, to serving as a transshipment point and a middle party for material smuggled in from outside, and, possibly, supplying material to terrorist networks and proliferating states upon specific orders.

### South Ossetia

The region of the South Caucasus, which includes Armenia, Azerbaijan, and Georgia, is an extremely sensitive geopolitical area located between Europe, Asia, and the Middle East. Since 1990 it has established itself as a major drug-trafficking route from Asia and Afghanistan into Russia and Europe. This highly lucrative business, bringing large profits to those involved, has further corrupted and criminalized the region, which had already been known for its "shadow" economies during Soviet times. According to the "2008 Corruption Perceptions Index," compiled by the private German organization Transparency International, Azerbaijan and Armenia are among the most corrupt countries. With scores of 1.9 and 2.9, respectively—10 being "least corrupt"—they rank 158th and 109th out of 180 countries. Georgia, with a score of 3.9, ranks 67th.[24] Official corruption, organized crime, weak law enforcement, porous borders, and continuing economic turmoil facilitate the use of the region as a transit route not only for conventional forms of trafficking, but also for the smuggling of nuclear material from Russia and Kazakhstan to Turkey and the Middle East.[25] The situation in the South Caucasus is aggravated by the presence of three conflict regions.

South Ossetia, which had been striving for its independence from Georgia since the late 1980s, is one such region. An armed conflict erupted in the province in 1992 after the government of the newly independent Georgia canceled its autonomous status and tried to suppress resistance among the local Ossetian population. The hostilities left an estimated two thousand to four thousand dead and displaced tens of thousands of people.[26] The conflict remained frozen until August 2008, when the Georgian government tried to take control of the province using its military power. After this attempt failed because of interference by the Russian Army, the Russian Federation formally recognized the independence of South Ossetia. Officially, Georgia still considers the province to be an integral part of its territory, although it does not exercise any control over its territory.

Georgian officials and experts often raised concerns about the trafficking of radioactive material through the uncontrolled territories in Georgia.[27] To date, no actual thefts or seizures of radioactive material have been registered in South Ossetia; however, one significant case, intercepted in Georgia's capital Tbilisi, suggests that South Ossetia has been implicated in nuclear smuggling schemes, although it was not used for actual transport of material. In early 2006, Georgian authorities, who were tipped off by their informers in South Ossetia, apprehended a Russian citizen and his three Georgian accomplices in an attempted sale of highly enriched uranium (HEU).[28] According to the IAEA, the criminals possessed 79.5 grams of uranium enriched to 89 percent, which is just 1 percent below the enrichment level considered to be weapons-grade (90 percent).[29] The main culprit, Oleg Khintsagov, was a resident of the adjacent North Ossetia, a part of the Russian Federation. He and his accomplices had originally wanted to meet with undercover agents in the capital of South Ossetia, Tskhinvali, but were persuaded to go to Tbilisi instead. As a result, Khintsagov entered Georgia through the Kazbegi border checkpoint, which is an alternative to South Ossetia as a route from Russia.[30]

Although the suspect did not pass through South Ossetia on his way to Tbilisi, the case nevertheless fueled concerns about the border security of the breakaway regions. The Georgian Ministry of Foreign Affairs asserted that the case emphasized the need to install international monitors along the Russian border with both South Ossetia and Abkhazia, claiming that trafficking of illicit goods through these territories was rampant.[31] Interestingly, along with nuclear trafficking offenses, Khintsagov was also charged with a drug-related offense, although its specific nature was not indicated.[32] It is therefore possible that he may also have been a drug courier traveling to and from South Ossetia, which does not require visas from residents of adjacent North Ossetia—a loophole many traffickers and document forgers use.[33] Two of Khintsagov's accomplices had also been engaged in small-time drug peddling before they ventured into nuclear material.[34] Thus, the feared connection between drug-trafficking networks and nuclear smuggling in the Caucasus is already a reality, although its magnitude is hardly possible to assess. To use the words of a U.S. expert on Russian organized crime, Louise Shelley, "a viable smuggling route remains a viable smuggling route," irrespective of what type of contraband it is used for.[35]

### Abkhazia

Abkhazia is another breakaway province, located in the northwest of Georgia and sharing a border with Russia. In the early 1990s, Abkhazia sought its independence from Georgia, which led to a military conflict in October 1992, resulting in about ten thousand people killed and another two hundred thousand displaced.[36] Since the end of hostilities in 1993, Abkhazia has remained outside of the Georgian government's control. Its independence from Georgia was recognized by the Russian government in August 2008 after the military campaign in South Ossetia.

Georgian officials have referred to Abkhazia as a "region of lawlessness, highly popular among international terrorists, drug smugglers and weapons dealers."[37] The geographical location of this breakaway province, with difficult mountain passes and access to the sea, allows criminals to transport their contraband by land, sea, and air. It is reasonable to assume that these same routes may be used to move nuclear contraband across Abkhazia, although no evidence of such nuclear transit has been found so far.

Two thefts of radioactive material were recorded in Abkhazia, however. One of them is particularly worrisome because it involved uranium enriched to higher than 90 percent, which could be used to build a nuclear explosive device. According to conflicting reports, between 650 grams and 2 kilograms of HEU disappeared from the I. N. Vekua Physics and Technology Institute, a research facility in the capital Sukhumi.[38] The material went missing sometime between the last inventory conducted in 1992 and 1997 when a team of Russian nuclear specialists was finally allowed access for the first time since the start of the armed conflict.[39] To date, this material has not been located, making this incident the only known theft of weapons-usable nuclear material that did not result in its subsequent recovery. Considering Abkhazia's geographical position and troubled history, the missing HEU is equally likely to have ended up in the hands of criminals, terrorists, or one of the proliferating states in the Middle East. Another theft registered in Sukhumi involved a medical radioactive source, containing seven capsules of cesium-137, stolen from a research institution in May 2002. The culprits, who had only wanted the lead shielding for melting into bullets, discarded the extracted cesium powder in a garage. All three of them received high doses of radiation and had to undergo special treatment.[40]

## Nagorno-Karabakh

Nagorno-Karabakh, the third disputed territory in the South Caucasus, had been part of Azerbaijan since 1924. Inspired by Mikhail Gorbachev's perestroika, the region, populated mostly by ethnic Armenians, tried to reunite with Armenia in 1988. This resulted in a long and violent ethnic conflict between native Armenians and Azerbaijanis, which devolved into a civil war between the two countries after they had gained independence in 1991. By the end of the hostilities in 1994, thirty thousand people on both sides had been killed and close to a million displaced from the disputed areas.[41] Since then, the two countries have formally remained at war over this territorial dispute. Nagorno-Karabakh still remains outside of international control regimes. According to Azerbaijani officials, the areas controlled by the Karabakh Army, with the support of Armenia, constitute 20 percent of Azerbaijan's territory. As a result, 132 kilometers of the border with Iran are not controlled by Azerbaijan, which raises concerns about possible trafficking activities along this segment.

No nuclear trafficking incidents in Nagorno-Karabakh or its adjacent territories are known to date. This is hardly surprising, considering that the region is closed off to the rest of the world. Nevertheless, one cannot exclude the possibility that the disputed territories have been used as a corridor for the illicit transit of nuclear materials or technologies. Its unique geographical location on the crossroads of Europe, Asia, and the Middle East, and between the potential supplier and end-user states, makes this a highly attractive transit route. If one adds the lack of border controls, the presence of transnational organized crime, and the high number of nuclear smuggling cases registered in adjacent Armenia, Azerbaijan, Georgia, and Turkey, it is hard to imagine why nuclear trafficking networks would not take advantage of such a unique opportunity to avoid detection on this route.[42]

Azerbaijani officials have claimed on numerous occasions that the Russia-Armenia-Iran route is used as a corridor for illicit nuclear commerce. Accusations of secret nuclear trade with Iran have also been leveled specifically against Nagorno-Karabakh. For example, in 2002, the delegation of Azerbaijan to the Council of Europe Parliamentary Assembly submitted a draft resolution to the Secretariat which stated that several Armenian companies— Razdanmash, Armavir, Akopyan, JacMacMetals, and Vartaniol—had used Nagorno-Karabakh to resell nuclear technologies to Iran and Iraq. The document also accused Armenia of disposing of the spent fuel from its Metzamor nuclear power plant inside the disputed territories, which apparently led to large-scale contamination of agricultural land and forests. Furthermore, Azerbaijani officials expressed a serious concern about the threat of radiological terrorism from Nagorno-Karabakh, claiming that the separatist regime had accumulated enough highly radioactive spent fuel for a number of large-scale terrorist acts.[43] Because of the lack of knowledge about the situation inside the uncontrolled territories, it is hard to judge whether any of these accusations and concerns are justified. Until these frozen conflicts are resolved on a political level, the fears and mistrust—and danger—will likely remain.

## Transdniester

Transdniester, also known as Pridnestrovye, is a narrow stretch of land along the Dniester River between Moldova and Ukraine. Fearing that Moldova might reunite with Romania, the region, populated largely by ethnic Russians, broke away from Moldova in 1990, which led to a short war in 1992. Since then, the self-proclaimed Transdniester Republic continues to hold out for independence from Moldova and integration into Russia. Like many other ungoverned spaces, it has the reputation of being a smuggling paradise, used for drug trafficking, illegal weapons sales, and money laundering.

The first radiological incident registered in the region occurred in March 1992 during the military hostilities when a container with cesium-137 was stolen from a police base in Transdniester. The thieves threatened to detonate the container in the city of Dubossary if the fighting did not stop.[44] Despite frequent claims to the contrary, no other nuclear trafficking cases have been recorded in Transdniester. The absence of evidence, however, does not mean that these activities are not happening. Neighboring Ukraine prevented several attempts to smuggle radioactive material on its border with Moldova, the other side of which is controlled by the separatist regime.[45] This suggests that the territory of Transdniester may in fact be used for the transit of radioactive material from Ukraine.

Moldova itself, weakened by this conflict and a continuing economic crisis, has developed a serious and complex organized crime problem. Considering the number of trafficking cases involving Moldova or its nationals, the country has also been a significant player in the nuclear black market. A total of six thefts and seizures involving radioactive sources were registered in Moldova between 1992 and 2008. Seventeen other cases have been identified in which materials were either confiscated from Moldovan nationals abroad or smuggled to, from, or through Moldova. Nine of them were registered in Ukraine, seven in Romania, and one in France.[46] In this context, it is important to note that Moldova played a significant role in two trafficking cases involving almost identical samples of HEU: one at the Romanian-Bulgarian border in May 1999, and the other in Paris in July 2001. In the first, a Turkish national, who was apprehended with the first sample by Bulgarian border guards, was heading to Moldova. The suspect admitted that he had been instructed to sell the HEU in Turkey, but when the potential buyers did not show up, he decided to take it back to Moldova. The incident appears be linked, at least indirectly, to Transdniester, since the courier had lived in its capital Tiraspol. Besides, he claimed to have received the material from a Ukrainian acquaintance, which prompts a guess that the HEU might have been smuggled into Moldova from Ukraine through the breakaway region.[47]

The other sample—2.5 grams of uranium enriched to slightly more than 72 percent—was seized by the police in Paris from a French man and two Cameroonian nationals.[48] Just as in the previous case, the material, also stored in a glass vial inside a lead container, was determined to be of Russian origin and had transited via Moldova. The seized HEU, which had been analyzed by the U.S. Lawrence Livermore National Laboratory in the Bulgarian case and the French Nuclear Commission in the Parisian case, was found to be practically identical in its enrichment and physical and chemical properties. Besides this, the investigation led by the Bulgarian authorities revealed the same links to

Moldova and Romania, through which both samples were smuggled to their destinations. According to an assessment by a Europol official, the smuggling network behind the Paris seizure "appeared to be well-organized and functioned for possibly several years."[49] Considering the commonalities between the two cases, it can be assumed that the same network was behind the Bulgarian seizure as well. Since the material was of Russian origin, it is possible that players from Moldova, or even Transdniester itself, were the ones supplying the HEU using their old connections in Russia.

## Overview of Nuclear Trafficking in Failed States

It is not just non-state actors in ungoverned spaces that raise concerns regarding nuclear trafficking, but failed, or failing, states as well. Failed states can engage in, and indeed have engaged in, the illicit acquisition and supply of both nuclear material and technologies. The prime example was the discovery of a clandestine network that was selling the equipment and material needed to produce nuclear weapons to Iran, Libya, and North Korea. The network operated out of Pakistan, a nation among the ten with the highest risk of failure, according to the "Failed States Index 2008."[50] The Democratic Republic of Congo, a uranium-rich African country ranking sixth on the list of failed states, was allegedly visited by North Korean and other foreign nationals who investigated the possibilities of exporting uranium from a closed mine in Katanga Province.[51]

Table 10.1 provides an overview of the situation regarding nuclear trafficking in the sixty states ranked as most at risk of failure in the "Failed States Index 2008." The highest possible total score, signifying complete failure, is 120 points. An analysis of the DSTO shows that half of the listed states—thirty—have registered at least one case of illicit trafficking or other unauthorized activities involving nuclear material and radioactive sources. The fact that no such activities have been recorded in the other thirty states may be, at least partially, due to the lack of knowledge of what goes on in these countries. The situation in Lebanon provides a good example of how much difference in detecting trafficking cases can be made, for instance, through the installation of radiation monitoring systems at a few entry points. Until recently, Lebanon was not present on the map of nuclear trafficking like many other countries: only one nuclear smuggling case was interdicted there by the intelligence agency in 1999. However, with the installation of radiation detectors at just two of its ports—Beirut and Tripoli—the number of detected cases has increased dramatically, from one before 2005 to fifty-three since then.[52] Although all of these cases appear to have involved unintentional cross-border movement of radioactive material or contaminated scrap metal rather than intentional nuclear smuggling, they still emphasize the importance of using radiation detection equipment for both interdicting and deterring nuclear trafficking. The example of Lebanon begs the question of how many other failing states with no or few recorded smuggling incidents do not know about what happens at their borders because of the lack of radiation detectors. On the other hand, some of these states may be tracking illicit trafficking and other unauthorized activities involving radioactive substances but keep the information to themselves. As can be seen from Table 10.1, only twenty-five of the sixty listed states report their cases to the international authorities by participating in the IAEA ITDB.

The failed states listed in Table 10.1 have been involved in nuclear trafficking activities as countries of material origin (for example, Iraq and Democratic Republic of Congo) and transit (for example, Bangladesh and Nepal); as nations seeking to illegally acquire nuclear material (for example, Pakistan, Iran, and North Korea); as nations not able to control their radioactive sources, which have gone missing or been stolen as a result (for example, Nigeria, Uganda, Bolivia, and the Philippines); as nations affected by the inadvertent movement of radioactive scrap metal across their borders (for example, Lebanon, Sri Lanka, Syria, and Indonesia); or as nations with most of the above (for example, Georgia and Tajikistan). This shows that the problem of nuclear trafficking and the security of radioactive material in failed states— albeit like in more successful states as well—is a complex one, demanding a comprehensive analysis.

## Conclusion

Ungoverned spaces and failed states are vulnerable to the proliferation of crime, lawlessness, and corruption and therefore are also well suited for illicit trafficking in nuclear and other radioactive material. However, little hard evidence has been found so far to be able to ascertain with full conviction that they are indeed major conduits for nuclear trafficking. Of course, a large portion of smuggling activities remain under the radar because far from all trafficking cases are detected by law-enforcement authorities, especially in

**TABLE 10.1** Nuclear trafficking incidents in failed states based on the DSTO, 1991–2008

| Rank | Score | Country | Incidents recorded | Participates in IAEA ITDB |
|------|-------|---------|--------------------|---------------------------|
| 1 | 114.2 | Somalia | — | |
| 2 | 113.0 | Sudan | 1 | |
| 3 | 112.5 | Zimbabwe | 2 | × |
| 4 | 110.9 | Chad | — | |
| 5 | 110.6 | Iraq | 6 | × |
| 6 | 106.7 | Democratic Republic of the Congo | 3 | |
| 7 | 105.4 | Afghanistan | 3 | |
| 8 | 104.6 | Ivory Coast | — | |
| 9 | 103.8 | Pakistan | 3 | × |
| 10 | 103.7 | Central African Republic | — | × |
| 11 | 101.8 | Guinea | — | |
| 12 | 100.3 | Bangladesh | 2 | × |
| 12 | 100.3 | Burma | — | |
| 14 | 99.3 | Haiti | — | |
| 15 | 97.7 | North Korea | 1 | |
| 16 | 96.1 | Ethiopia | — | × |
| 16 | 96.1 | Uganda | 4 | |
| 18 | 95.7 | Lebanon | 54 | × |
| 18 | 95.7 | Nigeria | 7 | × |
| 20 | 95.6 | Sri Lanka | 4 | × |
| 21 | 95.4 | Yemen | — | × |
| 22 | 94.5 | Niger | — | × |
| 23 | 94.2 | Nepal | 1 | |
| 24 | 94.1 | Burundi | — | |
| 25 | 93.8 | East Timor | — | |
| 26 | 93.4 | Republic of the Congo | — | |
| 26 | 93.4 | Kenya | 9 | |
| 26 | 93.4 | Uzbekistan | 7 | × |
| 29 | 92.9 | Malawi | — | × |
| 30 | 92.4 | Solomon Islands | — | |
| 31 | 92.3 | Sierre Leone | — | × |
| 32 | 91.3 | Guinea-Bissau | — | |

| Rank | Score | Country | Incidents recorded | Participates in IAEA ITDB |
|------|-------|---------|--------------------|---------------------------|
| 33 | 91.2 | Cameroon | — | |
| 34 | 91.0 | Liberia | — | |
| 35 | 90.1 | Syria | 4 | |
| 36 | 89.9 | Burkina Faso | — | |
| 37 | 89.0 | Colombia | 15 | × |
| 38 | 88.9 | Tajikistan | 29 | × |
| 39 | 88.8 | Kyrgyzstan | 9 | × |
| 40 | 88.7 | Egypt | 4 | |
| 40 | 88.7 | Laos | — | |
| 42 | 88.0 | Equatorial Guinea | — | |
| 42 | 88.0 | Rwanda | — | |
| 44 | 87.4 | Eritrea | — | |
| 45 | 86.8 | Togo | — | |
| 46 | 86.2 | Turkmenistan | — | |
| 47 | 86.1 | Mauritania | — | × |
| 48 | 85.8 | Cambodia | — | |
| 49 | 85.7 | Iran | 7 | × |
| 49 | 85.7 | Moldova | 7 | |
| 51 | 85.4 | Bhutan | — | |
| 52 | 84.6 | Papua New Guinea | — | |
| 53 | 84.4 | Belarus | 34 | × |
| 54 | 84.3 | Bosnia | 2 | |
| 55 | 84.2 | Bolivia | 2 | × |
| 56 | 83.8 | Angola | 1 | |
| 56 | 83.8 | Georgia | 73 | × |
| 58 | 83.6 | Israel/West Bank | 4 | × |
| 59 | 83.4 | Philippines | 12 | × |
| 60 | 83.3 | Indonesia | 13 | × |

SOURCE: "ITDB Quarterly Report: 1 October–31 December 2008," IAEA Office of Nuclear Security, Vienna 2009 (restricted). As of 31 December 2008, only the countries marked with "×" participated in the Illicit Trafficking Database (ITDB) of the International Atomic Energy Agency (IAEA). DSTO indicates Database on Nuclear Smuggling, Theft, and Orphan Radiation Sources.

the areas and countries where law and order are at best questionable. Ungoverned spaces and failed states—and all states for that matter—either in possession of radioactive material or located next to potential nuclear suppliers or end-user states have a higher probability of being affected by the problem of nuclear trafficking. Thus, ungoverned spaces in the former Soviet Union, which meet both of the above criteria, have shown more signs of nuclear trafficking activities since 1990 than similar territories in other parts of the world. These activities ranged from losing control over radioactive material, to providing transit and middle-party services for material smuggled from outside, to delivering material to clients in other countries upon specific orders. Although nuclear security and border control in Russia and other Newly Independent States have significantly improved since the early 1990s because of international assistance and the countries' own efforts, as has been reflected in the decreased number of serious nuclear smuggling cases registered in these countries in the past few years, some real risks remain. Besides this, the threat of radiological terrorism persists as well. Therefore, the issue of nuclear trafficking is unlikely to disappear in the near future and will continue to cause concerns with regard to the situation in ungoverned spaces and failed states.

## Notes

1. International Atomic Energy Agency, "IAEA Illicit Trafficking Database (ITDB)," Fact Sheet, Vienna, September 2008. According to the fact sheet, the ITDB contained 1,340 confirmed incidents as of 31 December 2007. About 180 more cases were reported to the IAEA in 2008. See ITDB Quarterly Reports, IAEA Office of Nuclear Security, Vienna, 2008 (restricted).

2. Friedrich Steinhäusler and Lyudmila Zaitseva, *Database on Nuclear Smuggling, Theft, and Orphan Radiation Sources*, University of Salzburg, Austria. For a recent analysis of the DSTO data, see "Illicit Trafficking in Radioactive Materials," in *Nuclear Black Markets: Pakistan, A. Q. Khah and the Rise of Proliferation Networks*, International Institute for Strategic Studies, Strategic Dossier, London, 2007: 119–38.

3. ITDB Quarterly Report, 1 October 2008–31 December 2008, IAEA Office of Nuclear Security, Vienna, 2008 (restricted).

4. Hua Liu et al., "Supervision of Radioactive Source Safety in China," paper presented at the International Conference on the Safety and Security of Radioactive Sources, Bordeaux, France, 27 June to 1 July 2005: 243.

5. Roy Lindley, Joseph Adduci, Robert Johnson, and Dave LePoire, "Perspectives on International Radiological Trafficking," paper presented at the NATO Advanced

Research Workshop "Prevention, Detection and Response to Nuclear and Radiological Threat" (PDR-2007), Yerevan, Armenia, 3–6 May 2007.

6. "Failed States Index 2008," Fund for Peace and the Carnegie Endowment for International Peace, *Foreign Policy* 167 (July/August 2008), http://www.foreignpolicy.com/story/cms.php?story_id=4350.

7. Jeffrey M. Bale, "The Chechen Resistance and Radiological Terrorism," *Issue Brief,* Center for Nonproliferation Studies, Monterey Institute of International Studies, April 2004, http://www.nti.org/e_research/e3_47a.html.

8. Rensselaer W. Lee III, *Smuggling Armageddon: The Nuclear Black Market in the Former Soviet Union and Europe* (New York: St. Martin's Griffin, 1999), 135–36.

9. "Russian Nuclear Cache 'Lost,'" *Sunday Times,* 10 November 1996.

10. "There Are No Collections of Substances on the Territory of Chechnya, Whose Leakage May Lead to Ecological Disaster, Says Head of the Ministry of Defense's Radiation Safety Department", *RosBusinessConsulting,* 15 December 1999 (in DSTO).

11. "Radioactive Legacy of Basaev," *Vremya Novostei,* 2 April 2001 (in DSTO).

12. "Container with Radioactive Substances Found in Chechnya," ITAR-TASS, 29 December 1998 (Center for Nonproliferation Studies: NIS Nuclear Trafficking Database), http://www.nti.org/db/nistraff/index.html. Hereafter CNS: NIS database.

13. "Radioactive Container with Bomb Found in Chechnya," Agence France-Presse, 29 December 1999 (in CNS: NIS database).

14. "Criminal Dies Stealing Radioactive Material," ITAR-TASS, 14 September 1999 (in CNS: NIS database).

15. "24 Radiation Sources Found in Grozny," *Vesti,* 7 July 2000 (in DSTO).

16. "Disposal of Radiation Sources Goes On at Cement Plant in Chechnya's Chiri-Yurt," Interfax, 15 November 2001 (in DSTO).

17. "Ten Sources of Ionizing Radiation Rendered Harmless in Grozny," ITAR-TASS, 8 April 2002 (in DSTO).

18. Yuri Bagrov, "Cache of Unprotected Radioactive Material Found in Chechnya," Associated Press, 16 April 2003; see also "Radioactive Material Found in Grozny," Associated Press, *Moscow Times,* No. 2661, 17 April 2003: 3 (both in DSTO).

19. "Georgian Customs Foil Attempt to Export Uranium," RIA Novosti, 21 September 1999.

20. "Planned Sales in Poland Thwarted," *JPRS-Proliferation Issues,* 7 January 1993; see also "Nuclear Materials Reportedly Smuggled to Middle East," *Moskovskie Novosti,* 23 May 1993 (both in CNS: NIS database).

21. "Overview of Reported Nuclear Trafficking Incidents Involving Turkey: 1993–1999 (Abstracts)," Center for Nonproliferation Studies, 2000, http://http://cns.miis.edu/wmdme/flow/turkey/index.htm. See also Phil Williams and Paul Woessner, "The Real Threat of Nuclear Smuggling," *Scientific American* (January 1996): 40–44.

22. "Al-Qaeda's WMD Activities," Center for Nonproliferation Studies, Weapons of Mass Destruction Terrorism Research Program, 13 May 2005, http://cns.miis.edu/pubs/other/sjm_cht.htm.

23. Lee, *Smuggling Armageddon*, 120, 132–35. Zirconium tubing is used in the guide tubes for a nuclear fuel assembly.

24. Transparency International, "2008 Corruption Perceptions Index," 2008, http://www.transparency.org/news_room/in_focus/2008/cpi2008/cpi_2008_table.

25. Lyudmila Zaitseva, "Illicit Trafficking in the Southern Tier and Turkey since 1999: A Shift from Europe?" *Nonproliferation Review* (Fall–Winter 2002): 168–76.

26. Jim Nichol, "Armenia, Azerbaijan, and Georgia: Security Issues and Implications for U.S. Interests," CRS Report for Congress, updated 1 February 2007: 11, http://fpc.state.gov/documents/organization/81353.pdf.

27. See, for example, Alexander Kupatadze, "Radiological Smuggling and Uncontrolled Territories: The Case of Georgia," *Global Crime* 8, 1 (February 2007): 40–57.

28. Lawrence Scott Sheets and William J. Broad, "Smuggler's Plot Highlights Fear over Uranium," *New York Times*, 25 January 2007.

29. "Preliminary 2006 Report from IAEA Illicit Trafficking Database," IAEA Staff Report, 1 February 2007, http://www.iaea.org/NewsCenter/News/2007/itdb_update .html#.

30. Michael Bronner, "100 Grams (and Counting): Notes from the Nuclear Underworld," Project on Managing the Atom, Harvard University, Cambridge, MA, June 2008.

31. Molly Corso, "Georgia: Uranium Smuggling Highlights Border Security Concerns," *Eurasia Insight* (1 March 2007), http://www.eurasianet.org/departments /insight/articles/eav030107a.shtml.

32. The news source mentioned Paragraph 1 of Article 260 of Georgia's Criminal Code on "Illegal manufacturing, production, acquisition, storage, transport, and sale of narcotics, their analogues, and precursors." See "Georgia: Russia Interested in Its Own Image, Not Nuclear Security" (in Russian), Regions.ru, 31 January 2007, http:// www.regions.ru/news/2049635/.

33. Daniil Kobyakov, Elina Kirichenko, and Alla Azkova, "'Gray Zones' of Proliferation in the South Caucasus," *Yadernyi Kontrol*, No. 4 (74), Vol. 10 (2004) (in Russian): 66.

34. Bronner, "100 Grams (and Counting)," 5–6.

35. Ibid.

36. Nichol, "Armenia, Azerbaijan, and Georgia."

37. For more details, see Kobyakov et al., "Gray Zones," 64.

38. Tom Parfitt, "The Nuclear Nightmare," *London Times*, 3 March 2004: 7.

39. William C. Potter, "A US NGO Perspective on US-Russian MPC&A Cooperation," paper presented at the 39th Annual Meeting of the Institute for Nuclear Materials Management, Naples, Florida, 26 July 1998.

40. "Loot Injures Thieves," Prima News Agency, 29 October 2002 (in CNS: NIS database).

41. Kobyakov et al., "Gray Zones," 66.

42. Zaitseva, "Illicit Trafficking in the Southern Tier," 171–76.

43. N. Aliev and I. Yusifoglu, "One More Threat: Armenian NPP Supplies Kara-bakh Separatists with 'Material' for Terrorist Acts," *Ekho* (Baku) 133 (17 July 2002).

44. "Radioactive material reportedly stolen from Moldovan police base," BBC Summary of World Broadcasts, 20 March 1992 (in DSTO).

45. Lyudmila Zaitseva and Friedrich Steinhaeusler, DSTO, July 2007.

46. Ibid.

47. Mariya Nikolaeva, "Bulgarian Weekly Reports on US Investigation into Ura-nium Route," *168 Chasa* (Sofia), 8 December 2000 (in CNS: NIS database).

48. "French Arrest 3 for Nuclear Trafficking," Reuters, 22 July 2001.

49. Michal Otrebski, "A Perspective on Supporting an Investigation by Europol," paper presented at the Fourth International Conference on Export Controls, War-saw, Poland, 30 September–3 October 2002, http://www.exportcontrol.org/library/conferences/1379/1003-07-Otrebski.pdf.

50. "Failed States Index 2008," http://www.foreignpolicy.com/story/cms.php?story_id=4350.

51. "Congo Wants Help at Uranium Mine," BBC News, 25 March 2004. See also "IAEA Concern as BBC World Service Reveals Illegal Mining at 'Closed' DRC Ura-nium Mine," BBC Press Office, 26 March 2004.

52. ITDB Quarterly Reports, 1 January 2005 to 31 December 2008, IAEA Office of Nuclear Security, Vienna, 2005–2009 (restricted).

PART V
CONTESTING GOVERNANCE
IN VIRTUAL SPACES

# 11 From Anti–Money Laundering to . . . What?

*Formal Sovereignty and Feudalism in Offshore Financial Services*

Bill Maurer

There is no contradiction between the formal enhancement of state sovereignty and ungoverned space. Indeed, the former may bolster the latter, not just passively, by drawing boundaries and leaving the spaces between as no-man's lands, or epistemologically, by defining the sovereign space of governance negatively against spaces of sovereignty's exceptional absence. State sovereignty may more actively support ungoverned spaces. The two may also achieve a kind of coexistence within the same space: not necessarily in a causal relationship but simply coexistent and coterminous. This chapter argues that the latter kind of coexistence has been achieved in the space of flows of offshore finance (see Chapter 2). It examines the discursive and practical shift from anti–money laundering to "information sharing" in the global effort to regulate offshore finance and considers the implications of multilateral efforts to control offshore finance through soft law—norms, standards of practice, and peer review—rather than through the traditional tools of sovereign states such as direct sanction, treaty, and legislation (not to mention military force). It finds that in the aftermath of the 1996–2006 campaign of the Organization for Economic Co-operation and Development (OECD) against "harmful tax competition," the formal sovereignty of offshore centers increased despite multilateral efforts to curtail it and that at the same time the ungoverned space of flows through offshore centers continued relatively unabated. The task of this chapter is to explain how and why this happened and what it might mean for understanding ungoverned spaces. It suggests that a kind of neofeudalism exists at the heart of global finance and that an adequate response to it might require an equally neofeudal mindset.

Although this chapter is mainly limited to a consideration of the period from 1996 to 2006, the issues it takes up have received renewed attention since the U.S. presidential campaign of 2007, the subsequent election of President Barack Obama in 2008, and the global financial crisis that began around the same time. During the campaign, Obama and his running mate Joseph Biden of Delaware made ending tax haven abuses one plank of their platform. Biden especially railed against the revenues lost to offshore finance centers while his opponent, Sarah Palin, derided what she saw as his support for Americans paying more taxes. In the summer of 2007, the U.S. Senate Finance Committee held a hearing on the use and abuse of offshore tax havens, lending momentum to a regathering of forces against the offshore that had weakened under the administration of George W. Bush. And, after the election, President Obama attended his first G20 summit, where the release of a new OECD report on tax havens caused not a little diplomatic dispute among the delegates, notably smoothed over by President Obama himself. As *New York Times* columnist Gail Collins wryly noted: "'Look,' the G20-ers must have been telling each other, 'he can resolve the controversy over the use of the Organization for Economic Cooperation and Development's list of tax havens, and he knows the difference between Australia and Austria. Surely, this is a new kind of American leader.'"[1]

The Obama administration's new focus on offshore finance is connected to the global financial crisis and the revenue challenges facing the United States and other northern powers. At the time of this writing (summer 2009), the United States is actively pursuing the repatriation of funds held in Swiss bank accounts and a change in the tax deferral rules for corporations' foreign-earned profits (which are often deemed "foreign" because they are recorded as the profits of offshore subsidiaries rather than the parent company); and the OECD is composing new "black," "gray," and "white" lists of jurisdictions based on their compliance with international norms of taxation, discussed further below. The motivation seems to be both to provide new revenue streams to fund social welfare programs—especially, in the United States, health-care reform—and to hold more bargaining chips for use in negotiation with pharmaceutical companies and business groups as the effect of the financial crisis on revenue becomes more pressing.[2]

From the point of view of the offshore jurisdictions, however, this new attention smacks of neocolonialism. As British Virgin Islands Premier R. T. O'Neal, at the time of the G20 summit in April 2009, remarked to the Associated Press: "Why is it that we now in the colonies, because we are still a colony, can't have a financial center? If you are doing something and you are saying I can't do it, are you saying that I am inferior?"[3] And the *BVI Beacon* newspaper, in a report on that territory's conclusion of an eleventh Tax Information Exchange Agreement—conducted in order to comply with new OECD recommendations—implicitly mocked the color-coding scheme used since the mid-1990s by the OECD and multilateral agencies concerned with tax haven abuses. "Almost 'white,'" the newspaper declared.[4] The global politics of rank and race are painfully evident. They are the starting point for my consideration of neofeudalism in the debate over global revenue regimes, anti–money laundering, and tax information exchange.

This invocation of feudalism may be jarring. It is motivated by two related concerns. First, as discussed by Phil Williams (Chapter 2) and others in this volume, many contemporary ungoverned spaces seem to be organized along medieval lines, with politics of rank and bondage doing the work of social and economic organization rather than the bureaucracies, police, and markets of conventional territorial nation-states. International finance seen from the perspective of the offshore has some of the same characteristics: many offshore financial service centers are located in feudal and colonial microstates (principalities like Monaco and colonies like the British Virgin Islands), and much of the wealth being "protected" offshore is inherited and disguised through non–market-oriented vehicles like charitable trusts. Second, the OECD's effort to curtail harmful tax competition invoked the rhetoric of obligation but was thwarted by a rhetoric of "fairness." This emphasis on fairness obscures our view of the other strong normative component to the harmful tax competition debate. This is the norm obviating payment as a solution to the tax haven problem.

"Payment" is used here in an anthropological sense and in contrast to the notion of exchange. Payments are monetary transactions such as fees, fines, penalties, and gifts for which nothing is directly received in return.[5] Payments are morally and epistemologically problematic in societies in which money is supposed to index price and the value of goods marked to each other by free exchange in the market. Where money was not commensurate with all goods, payments were less awkward. Tribute, for example, often conveyed the sense of giving wealth to a higher cosmological order. One did not pay tribute to the king in return for protection or grace, even if such was often the result, but simply because he was king. Payments to the state become morally ambiguous when rulers lose their cosmological or divine status: when a state is of the people rather than of the gods, then the rule of law must replace the whim of humans lest payments to the state come to appear to be a protection racket, bribery, or extortion.[6]

The thesis here is that this same sense of the moral ambiguity of payments both sustains offshore finance in the first place and prevents one practical solution to the problem of harmful tax practices. People seek to avoid taxes in part because of the whiff of feudal bondage about them, even if their own wealth evinces the politics of rank rather than the economics of market relationships. This same normative commitment against payments prevents an obvious solution to the problem of global tax competition: to buy off the tax havens and to insist on a redistribution of wealth from individuals of rank to the leveling of the market. In other words, our own commitment to not being medieval hinders our policy responses to the feudalism at the heart of finance.

The chapter proceeds as follows. First, it reviews the OECD's effort to curtail harmful tax competition, along with the related efforts of the Financial Action Tax Force (FATF) and the Financial Stability Forum (FSF). Then, it explores how the OECD's emphasis on consultation and peer review as governance mechanisms to achieve compliance led to a shift in rhetoric from harmful tax competition to tax cooperation and fairness. Next, it reviews the erosion of the onshore/offshore distinction in the wake of compliance. Finally, the chapter returns to the question of the relationship between sovereignty, neomedievalism, and ungoverned spaces in the effort to achieve global tax regulation.

## Governance through Blacklisting

"Harmful tax competition" became a hot issue in the late 1990s as a number of international actors began to worry about the consequences of neoliberal restructuring that characterized the period of the 1980s when Ronald Reagan was president of the United States and Margaret Thatcher was prime minister of the United Kingdom. A political philosophy that emphasized the free movement of money and the rolling back of the state sector raised the specter of a global race to the bottom, as governments scaled back revenue collection in order to attract foreign capital.[7] Although part of an increasingly unquestioned neoliberal ideology, "tax competition" had the potential, if taken too far, to eviscerate the ability of states to provide needed services to their citizens. Nongovernmental organizations (NGOs) such as Oxfam worried about social welfare provision; but state-level defense actors had reason to be concerned as well. Bleeding the state dry in the interest of the free movement of money might also mean the erosion of state support for the military and the privatization of defense itself. Even the World Bank, which had imposed structural adjustment loan conditions on developing countries throughout the 1980s, began to sound warning bells about the effect of neoliberal reform on revenue collection, as well as on the control and interdiction of financial crime and money laundering.

These concerns crystallized in an effort initiated by the OECD, which in 1998 began publishing "blacklists" of countries engaging in what it termed "unfair tax competition." The OECD is an international organization made up of representatives from thirty countries "sharing a commitment to democratic government and the market economy"; it promulgates agreements and recommendations and operates through "dialogue, consensus, peer review and pressure."[8] The OECD's effort against tax havens was directed at countries that assessed minimal corporate and income taxes, as well as countries that provided safe havens for corporate and personal wealth with minimum regulatory scrutiny. In the world of freely mobile money, wealthy agents could, and still do, shop around for the lowest tax jurisdiction in which to place and thereby "protect" their assets. Of course, protecting private assets simultaneously drains wealth from the public assets that states finance through taxes. And this was precisely the OECD's point. It maintained that some states' lenient tax codes were undermining other states' tax systems, creating a global race to the bottom that would jeopardize the public financing of government functions. It argued that "harmful tax practices affect the location of financial and other service activities, erode the tax bases of other countries, distort trade and investment patterns and undermine the fairness, neutrality and broad social acceptance of tax systems generally. Such harmful tax competition diminishes global welfare and undermines taxpayer confidence in the integrity of tax systems." "Harmful preferential tax regimes" not only "distorted" financial flows, but had the potential to transform "confidence" and "acceptance" and to diminish perceptions of "fairness."[9] As we shall see, the invocation of fairness represented the introduction of a cornerstone liberal norm in international affairs that ultimately undid the OECD's effort.

Major powers took varied positions on the OECD's initiative. For the most part, European countries supported it (key exceptions being those countries such as Switzerland with histories of banking secrecy), but the United States' position fluctuated with the change of administration from Bill Clinton to George W. Bush in 2001, and again to Barack Obama in 2008. Despite the intensified awareness of the dangers of ungoverned financial flows in the wake of the terrorist attacks of September 11, 2001, the Bush administration argued that the OECD was engaged in precisely the kind of multilateral global governance project it had opposed in other domains, from the Kyoto protocols to the United Nations' effort to conduct weapons inspections in Iraq. The effort to "name and shame" tax havens, as it became known, was, to the Bush administration, an affront to the sovereignty of jurisdictions and a form of regulatory "overreach," with dire implications, it was claimed, for the principle of sovereignty itself. As former Treasury Secretary Paul O'Neill put it, the Bush administration was "troubled by the underlying premise that low tax rates are somehow suspect and by the notion that any country, or group of countries, should interfere in any other country's decision about how to structure its own tax system." Furthermore, the United States, O'Neill stated, "would not participate in any initiative to harmonize world tax systems."[10]

The main parties opposed to the OECD were the Society for Trust and Estate Practitioners, a professional association of tax planners; the Center for Freedom and Prosperity (CFP), a think tank in Washington, D.C.; and the International Tax and Investment Organization (later renamed the International Trade and Investment Organization, ITIO), a multilateral body of tax haven countries that was established with the assistance of the Commonwealth Secretariat, explicitly modeled on the OECD itself as a consultative body made up of representatives from its own member states as well as entities with observer status.[11]

The CFP was founded specifically to challenge the initiative. It argued that tax competition should in fact be encouraged as "an important check on excessive government."[12] It claimed that the OECD initiative was an "attack" on taxpayers, free trade, sovereignty, and privacy. It charged the OECD with "empire-building,"[13] and it spearheaded the formation of the Coalition for Tax Competition, which includes the Heritage Foundation, the Cato Institute, the American Enterprise Institute, and a number of other right-wing, libertarian, and Christian organizations (such as the Discovery Institute, which promotes creationism in U.S. public schools).

This multilateral effort brushed up against U.S. racial politics, as well. The generally left-leaning Congressional Black Caucus joined the Bush administration in opposing the OECD initiative. In a letter signed by notable progressive congressional representatives such as Maxine Waters, Barbara Lee, and Charles Rangel (archived by CFP), the Congressional Black Caucus expressed the concern that the OECD initiative would "impose economic harm on developing nations" and promoted the virtues of "the free flow of capital" in "improving economic conditions in poorer nations" by providing governments with "funds that are critically needed to provide education, health care, and social services."[14] Statements from CFP, the Congressional Black Caucus, and the Bush administration resonated with similar rhetoric from Caribbean leaders that the initiative was "nothing less than a determined attempt to bend other countries to [the OECD's] will . . . a form of neo-colonialism in which the OECD is attempting to dictate the tax, economic systems and structures of other nations for the benefit of the OECD's member states" (according to Ronald Sanders, senior ambassador from Antigua to the United Kingdom).[15] Caribbean leaders accused the OECD of "bullying" (Julian Francis, Bahamas Central Bank) and called its actions a threat to the islands' "economic sovereignty" (Ambrose George, Dominica Finance Minister).[16]

Yet partisans on the opposite side invoked sovereignty as well. NGOs like Oxfam and Christian Aid demonstrated how tax competition eroded the sovereignty of developing nations by hindering their efforts to provide for their citizens' welfare. Seiichi Kondo, OECD deputy-secretary, put it this way in a speech in 2002:

> The OECD's project on counteracting harmful tax practices is part of a wider initiative to promote good governance in a globalised economy. Globalisation has enormous potential to improve living standards around the world. But it also brings risks, including the risk of abuses of the free market system. The activities of tax havens distort the free flow of capital and undermine the ability of governments to finance the legitimate expectations of their citizens for publicly provided goods and services. By providing a framework within which all countries—developed and developing—can work together to fight harmful tax practices, the OECD seeks to encourage transparent and fair tax competition.[17]

In its first report on the matter, "Harmful Tax Competition: An Emerging Global Issue," the OECD identified two types of harmful activity offshore:

classic tax havens, with no or only nominal tax on business entities, and what it called "harmful preferential tax regimes," characterized by "ring fencing," which separates nonresident corporate people from domestic economies and taxes and denies to resident corporate people the same privileges as foreign ones. The report also challenged the "lack of transparency" in the jurisdictions where these activities occur.[18]

In the years that followed the initial 1998 report, a number of agencies published other blacklists of tax haven jurisdictions, as well. By 2004, most of these jurisdictions had managed to get themselves off those lists.[19] Mark Hampton and John Christensen note that the different initiatives stemmed from slightly different factors and forces.[20] The OECD effort has been aimed at tax competition, while the FATF of the G7 nations has focused on money laundering. The European Union has several projects on tax harmonization, which have troubled officials in member states such as Austria that offer certain financial services, as well as nonmember states traditionally invested in bank secrecy such as Liechtenstein. The G7's FSF has examined the role of offshore finance in precipitating or sustaining financial crises. Susan Roberts, and Hampton and Christensen, also document the outpouring of concern from various sectors of civil society, represented, for their purposes, by international NGOs and the mass media.[21] The various civil society organizations and NGOs that got involved in the tax competition debate also had varied reasons for doing so. Christian Aid emphasized economic development; Transparency International focused on the potential forms of corruption opened up by tax competition.

Many commentators have pointed out the obviously political character of the changing composition of the blacklists over time. Initially, the focus was on jurisdictions commonly understood to be tax havens or offshore financial service centers—the Cayman Islands, the British Virgin Islands, the Isle of Man, and so forth—but it shifted between 1998 and 2004 to jurisdictions in Africa and Southeast Asia not conventionally lumped with these microstates but of concern to major powers because of what the contributors to this volume would recognize as their ungovernability and even potential for "ferality." The lists have also shifted from politically dependent or otherwise anomalous jurisdictions—remnants of British imperialism, on one hand, or fragments from the world of feudal monarchies, on the other—to fully politically independent republics. In part, the shift is an effect of the different objectives of the OECD and the FATF, the former oriented toward tax regimes and the latter toward financial crime and money laundering. The changing patterns of concern over time suggest that these lists are the product of the intersecting politics of north-south relations, colonial clientage, and geopolitics, as well as the OECD's soft-law governance strategy and the ITIO's effort to counter it.

## "Participating Partners" and the Level Playing Field

Tax haven countries saw the OECD initiative as heavy-handed, imperial, and unfair. Being blacklisted evoked old colonial forms of domination, surveillance, and control. Countries so targeted felt sidelined and caught off guard. OECD members with histories of bank secrecy such as Switzerland and Luxembourg vociferously opposed the initiative. But the possible damage to the reputations of offshore jurisdictions by being blacklisted led them quickly to seek to minimize the damage. Most sought to get themselves off the blacklists by adopting best practices proposed by the OECD and FATF or by issuing press releases committing themselves to compliance. Jason Sharman, Gregory Rawlings, and others have amply documented this process.[22] All the while, a discursive war raged over the OECD's concepts and definitions.

The OECD's modus operandi demanded that the ITIO be incorporated into its process of consultation as a participating partner. The result was the creation of the Global Forum on Taxation, which would meet every two years under the auspices of the OECD. The Global Forum consisted of OECD and non-OECD members, including the ITIO membership. The discourse of harmful tax competition very quickly shifted to "principles of transparency and effective exchange of information for tax purposes."[23] Furthermore, "The focus of the meeting was on how to achieve a global level playing field and how to improve further the process by which this initiative can be taken forward based on the widely accepted principles of equity and shared responsibility."[24] The ITIO quickly issued its own press release, headlined, "It's Official: OECD Tax Project Depends on Level Playing Field." The chief outcome of the first Global Forum meeting was the creation of a "Level Playing Field Joint Working Group." The "level playing field" slogan has by now made its way into the title of nearly every major report by the OECD and other parties to the tax competition debate, including the title of the OECD's own report on the 2005 Global Forum meeting and a 2007 report by the Commonwealth Secretariat titled *Assessing the Playing Field*.[25]

The effect of the inclusion of the ITIO into the Global Forum has been a kind of politics by press release.[26] ITIO press releases frame the issue in terms of weak versus strong states and call into question the universality of rules and practices devised by the few and the powerful. This is a profoundly postcolonial rhetoric as well, drawing on legacies of imperial rule and touting the principles of liberty, equality, and fairness. It also draws on the postcolonial network of expertise embodied in the Commonwealth Secretariat (which, earlier, had issued another volume in support of small states' "fiscal sovereignty").[27]

Viewed one way, the international effort against "harmful tax competition" at the turn of the twenty-first century can be seen as a story of the limits of "soft law" peer pressure, social governance, or multilateral regulation of the financial sphere. Spearheaded by the OECD, the effort to curb tax competition relied on consultation and peer review, which allowed other actors such as estate planning practitioners and representatives from tax haven countries to shape the normative deliberations of the OECD and ultimately to shift the discourse on tax competition itself. In striving to achieve a kind of epistemic governance based on persuasion rather than force,[28] the OECD of necessity had to invite "society"—here, in the form of NGOs and international organizations formed specifically to counter the OECD's initiatives—to the table. Once they became a part of the consultative process, they were able to use the power of words to transform it. The tax havens and their advocates were able to turn the language of the OECD against it, calling into question its "reputation for impartial expertise."[29] Relatively weak, small states like the British Virgin Islands and Cayman Islands were able to trump the concerted efforts of the powerful OECD countries by using the very tools of organizations like the OECD: peer pressure and the deployment of rhetoric about reputation and fairness in the context of new social networks that were created through the consultative process. Jason Sharman ends his compelling account of the global effort to coordinate tax regulation by noting the unpredictability of regulation through rhetoric. Given the double-edged nature of the tax havens' relative victory in this affair—small states won, but tax havens still operate, continuing those states' dependence on the capricious perceptions of tax and estate planners—Sharman concludes that "there is no reason to think that a more social view of politics and economics entails a world of greater harmony or justice."[30]

## Onshore and Offshore: What's the Difference?

The deployment of the level playing field had another effect as well: it spotlighted OECD member states' own tax practices, many of which would not have been deemed in compliance with the OECD and FATF's norms. This fact underscored the "fairness" discourse that buttressed the opponents of the OECD initiative. And this rhetoric of fairness and the level playing field, in turn, drowned out all other competing approaches to tax competition. The larger issue of global tax regulation took a back seat to matters such as the procedures for facilitating information exchange among OECD and non-OECD countries—should they be automatic or on demand?—and timetables for the expiration of exemptions for information exchange regimes from four recalcitrant OECD members (Austria, Belgium, Luxembourg, and Switzerland, which are exempted until 2010).

Meanwhile, tax havens in compliance with OECD and FATF recommendations set up corporate registers, Know Your Customer, and due diligence procedures, which only served further to highlight the lack of such procedures in many onshore jurisdictions, again bolstering the "fairness" rhetoric. While the British Virgin Islands and almost all other tax havens have either outlawed or immobilized bearer shares, for example, Nevada and Wyoming still permit them. Current U.S. Vice President Biden's home state of Delaware permits anonymous beneficial corporate ownership; most offshore centers in compliance with OECD and FATF recommendations do not.[31] The International Monetary Fund even concluded in 2004, "Compliance levels for offshore financial centres are, on average, more favourable than those for other jurisdictions assessed by the Fund."[32] The U.S. Government Accountability Office reported much the same in its 2006 survey of corporate ownership information ("Most states do not require ownership information at the time a company is formed").[33]

Ronen Palan argues that the result has been a shift from curbing tax haven abuses to ensuring that tax havens "play by the rules of the advanced industrial countries that by and large represent—let us have no illusions—business interests,"[34] and that this is essentially a story of the triumph of those interests. Indeed, Palan notes, the liberalization of onshore regulatory regimes demonstrates more than ever the importance of the offshore to contemporary global political economy, because the offshore and onshore are always defined in relation to one another and because offshore has historically been central to the imagination and practical construction of onshore sovereign regimes.

## Avoiding Payments All Around

In its effort to curtail offshore finance, the OECD used its signature method of epistemic governance—bringing parties together to discuss and to review each others' standards and practices—in order to foster a new common sense and thereby to create and disseminate new financial norms. Despite compliance, however, most proponents and critics of the initiative concur by now that the exercise has been futile: small states initially targeted have issued letters of commitment, but nearly all make as a condition of that commitment the compliance of OECD member states. They demanded a level playing field, in other words. As discussed above, the ITIO introduced this concept into the OECD deliberations, and the concept quickly spread.[35] The ITIO, not the OECD, appears to have been the more successful in creating a new episteme. While the idea of a level playing field echoes classically liberal concerns with fairness and equality of opportunity to compete, its effect has been to permit the continued use of offshore financial services by wealthy individuals and corporate persons seeking to minimize their exposure to risks, including national revenue collectors.

The outcome of the OECD initiative thus begs the question of which spaces are ungoverned: onshore or offshore? When considering the vast flows of money from the world's wealthiest natural and corporate persons, who often use the tools of debt and charity to mask their relationships of exchange and evade their obligations to states, what are the dimensions and characteristics of the ungoverned space of the market? Indeed, given the nonmarket relationships through which high-net-worth individuals can shunt their funds, using entities like offshore charitable trusts, for example, is this ungoverned space even best characterized as a "market" at all? This chapter argues that policy initiatives seeking to curtail offshore finance and the dangerous space of flows they may represent paradoxically work to increase the ungovernability of the world's superwealthy elites who rely on offshore finance to protect their assets. Wealthy nomads flourish in the current global political economy.[36] Meanwhile, the consensus that the OECD initiative has failed misses the fact that failure took the form of "compliance": all of the world's tax havens agreed to comply with the new international norms against harmful tax competition when and if—crucially—the world's most powerful states would do the same. In the meantime, they embarked on a number of information-sharing and double-taxation treaties, making use of the standard tool kit of international law and thereby making a claim to their formal status in international law as sovereign actors.[37]

The discourse of fairness set in motion by the level playing field concept is a liberal discourse associated with market efficiencies.[38] In a world to be governed by the rational self-interests of individual free men rather than the whim of kings, Hobbes's "force and fraud" had to be banished lest markets become distorted and men's interests thereby obscured.[39] With the invention of modern accounting, furthermore, a fair price, arrived at without fraud or force, came to be taken as a "true" price, reflecting the real value of a thing, and fairness and truth were thereby conflated.[40] There are also, of course, strong undertones in this set of understandings of notions of justice as equity, which cannot be treated fully in this short chapter. My point here is simply that the tax competition debate tapped into the rich associations among these concepts in Western jurisprudence, religion, and political economy.

Taxes, by contrast, have long been associated with tyranny and, especially in the United States, their avoidance with liberty and sovereignty. The CFP directly referenced these historical connections. Hence the double bind in which Treasury Secretary O'Neill was stuck: "troubled by the underlying premise that low tax rates are somehow suspect and by the notion that any country, or group of countries, should interfere in any other country's decision about how to structure its own tax system," yet called upon by the OECD to address tax competition. Adam Smith himself argued that a just tax could be possible only in a political system in which the courts of justice served a dual role as revenue collection agencies, in order to ensure the fairness and the certainty of taxation.[41] At issue in modern, Western tax discourse is thus a set of understandings about just rule and sovereign government.

The focus on fairness in the harmful tax competition debate highlighted these associations about sovereignty and justice together with market-talk about competitive deregulation and the rules of the game in a globalized world, in which states emphasize the comparative advantage of a market in sovereignty.[42] The market-talk, in turn, obviated other ways of thinking about taxes and their avoidance, and ways to address that avoidance: a discourse on payment without expectation of return, much like the language game of tribute in feudal societies. But because payment without return is morally suspect in market societies, the OECD, with its harmful tax competition initiative, cannot bring itself directly to target high-net-worth individuals and others seeking tax planning to "protect" their assets from state revenue collectors, who are avoiding what they see as unfair payments. That same reticence is evident in the norm against buying off the tax havens. In other words, both a demand-side and a supply-side attack on tax havens would first have to resolve the ambivalence toward the logic of payment. And this is a much bigger problem than tax competition or information sharing.

Jason Sharman, an expert on efforts to achieve global tax regulation, argues that the best way to get rid of harmful tax competition, while avoiding charges of imperialism and respecting the sovereignty of small states yet also curbing tax evasion, is simply to buy the havens off. He write that "there is no one who contests the fact that tax havens receive much less revenue . . . than higher taxing countries lose."[43] The countries listed on the OECD's 2000 blacklist reported a *combined* government revenue of less than $13 billion. The U.S. Internal Revenue Service estimates that Caribbean tax havens alone cost the United States $70 billion per year in lost income tax revenue.[44] Pay thirteen, save fifty-seven. Yet, Sharman writes, "despite the huge disparities in tax revenue lost to OECD countries versus the very meager revenue and employment benefits to tax havens . . . no such deal [of buying out the havens] looks likely in the near future."[45] Such a deal is not likely because buying the havens off would smack of extortion and would tap into the same normative commitment against payment that leads the wealthy offshore in the first place.

In invoking payments thus, this analysis offers a conceptual and political challenge. Where Williams (Chapter 2) sees a kind of creeping neomedievalism in many of the more exotic ungoverned spaces that historically have occupied military and intelligence analysts, run by resurgent tribal leaders or warlords demanding allegiance and exacting tribute, this chapter reveals a New Middle Ages at the heart of the global financial system. It also suggests an equally feudal solution to the problem of tax competition. If the rich insist on the global flow of wealth upward to themselves, then the corresponding part of the moral relationship linking lord and serf should be invoked: redistribute the tribute!

## Notes

I thank Tom Boellstorff and Gregory Rawlings for their helpful comments on earlier drafts of this chapter. All errors remain my responsibility alone. Research on Caribbean offshore financial services and the OECD initiative has been supported by the National Science Foundation (SES-0516861). Any opinions, findings, and conclusions or recommendations expressed in this chapter are those of the author and do not necessarily reflect the views of the National Science Foundation.

1. Gail Collins, "Barack's Continental Coolness," *New York Times*, 3 April 2009, A17.

2. On the "bargaining chip" idea, see Robert Reich, "Why Obama Is Taking On Corporate Tax Havens," Salon.com, 5 May 2009, available at http://www.salon.com /opinion/feature/2009/05/05/tax_havens/index.html.

3. Ben Fox, "Islands Resent Crackdown of Tax Havens by G-20," Associated Press, April 3, 2009, available at http://www.ap.org/.

4. Dan O'Connor, "VI Edges Closer to 'White List,'" *BVI Beacon*, 11 June 2009, 1.

5. Jane Guyer, *Marginal Gains: Monetary Transactions in Atlantic Africa* (Chicago: University of Chicago Press, 2004).

6. Pierre Bourdieu, "Rethinking the State: Genesis and Structure of the Bureaucratic Field," in *Practical Reason*, ed. P. Bourdieu (Cambridge: Polity, 1998), 43.

7. Although not all of the jurisdictions targeted by these efforts are politically independent nation-states (many are dependent territories, like the British Virgin Islands), the term "state" or "country" is used throughout this chapter for convenience. And although the term "tax haven" is a highly charged one for those counties so labeled, it appears here in place of more convoluted locutions (such as "countries or territories deemed not in compliance with the FATF's forty recommendations"), also for convenience. See J. C. Sharman, *Havens in a Storm: The Struggle for Global Tax Regulation* (Ithaca, NY: Cornell University Press, 2006), 165, n.1. To read this history in more detail, see Bill Maurer, "Due Diligence and 'Reasonable Man,' Offshore," *Cultural Anthropology* 20:4 (2005): 474–505; and Maurer, "Re-regulating Offshore Finance?" *Geography Compass* 2:1 (2005): 155–75.

8. "About OECD," Organization for Economic Co-operation and Development, http://www.oecd.org/pages/0,3417,en_36734052_36734103_1_1_1_1_1,00.html.

9. "Harmful Tax Competition: An Emerging Global Issue," OECD report, Paris, 1998: 8.

10. Paul O'Neill, "Treasury Secretary O'Neill Statement on OECD Tax Havens," U.S. Department of Treasury, Office of Public Affairs, PO-366, 10 May 2001.

11. The members of the ITIO are Anguilla, Antigua and Barbuda, the Bahamas, Barbados, Belize, the British Virgin Islands, the Cayman Islands, St. Kitts and Nevis, St. Lucia, St. Vincent and the Grenadines, the Turks and Caicos Islands, Panama, the Cook Islands, Samoa, and Vanuatu. The observers are the Commonwealth Secretariat, the CARICOM Secretariat, the Caribbean Development Bank, the Eastern Caribbean Central Bank, and the Pacific Islands Forum Secretariat.

12. Center for Freedom and Prosperity, "CF&P At-A-Glance," available at http:// www.freedomandprosperity.org/Glance/glance.shtml#coalition.

13. Robert Goulder, "New Coalition Strikes Back at OECD Tax Haven Campaign," Center for Freedom and Prosperity (2 December 2000), available at http:// www.freedomandprosperity.org/Articles/tni12-02-00/tni12-02-00.shtml.

14. Letter from the Congressional Black Caucus to The Honorable Paul O'Neill,

14 March 2001, at http://www.freedomandprosperity.org/ltr/cbc/cbc.shtml, accessed 9 June 2008.

15. Ronald M. Sanders, "The OECD's 'Harmful Tax Competition' Scheme: The Implications for Antigua and Barbuda," speech to the Antigua and Barbuda Chamber of Commerce and Industry, St. John's, Antigua, 27 March 2001.

16. Catherine Kelly, "Don't Count on Friends in the New Global Economy," *Punch* (Nassau, Bahamas), 17 July 2000; "Stabilization, Consolidation and Diversified Growth—Foundations for a Sustainable Recovery," budget speech 2000/2001, Government of Dominica, Roseau, Dominica. See Vaughan E. James, "Twenty-first Century Pirates of the Caribbean: How the Organization for Economic Cooperation and Development Robbed Fourteen CARICOM Countries of Their Tax and Economic Policy Sovereignty," *University of Miami Inter-American Law Review* 34:1 (2002): 1–62.

17. Seiichi Kondo, "Ending Tax Haven Abuse," Organization for Economic Cooperation and Development, 18 April 2002. Copy in author's possession.

18. Switzerland and Luxembourg, both OECD member states, appended lists of concerns about the report. Luxembourg challenged the report's assumption "that bank secrecy is necessarily a source of harmful tax competition"; see OECD, "Harmful Tax Competition," 74. Switzerland defended the value of bank secrecy, noting that the report conflicted with Swiss secrecy laws. Alongside sovereignty as a state's autonomous right to author law and a state's obligation to the public weal, Switzerland and Luxembourg thus introduced a third kind of sovereignty: the sovereign proprietor of one's own affairs and personal data.

19. See Maurer, "Re-regulating Offshore Finance," for a review of the relationship between the OECD, FATF, and FSF blacklisting exercises; also, Sharman, *Havens in a Storm.*

20. Mark P. Hampton and John Christensen, "Offshore Pariahs? Small Island Economies, Tax Havens, and the Re-configuration of Global Finance," *World Development* 39:9 (2002): 1657–73.

21. Susan M. Roberts, "Offshore Financial Centers and Moral Geographies," paper presented at the 102nd Annual Meeting of the American Anthropological Association, Chicago, 19–23 November 2003; Hampton and Christensen, "Offshore Pariahs?"

22. In addition to Sharman, *Havens in a Storm,* and Maurer, "Due Diligence," see Gregory Rawlings, "Mobile People, Mobile Capital, and Tax Neutrality: Sustaining a Market for Offshore Finance Centres," *Accounting Forum* 29:3 (2005): 289–310; M. C. Webb, "Defining the Boundaries of Legitimate State Practice: Norms, Transnational Actors, and the OECD's Project on Harmful Tax Competition," *Review of International Political Economy* 11:4 (2004): 787–827; and R. Woodward, "Offshore Strategies in the Global Political Economy: Small Islands and the Case of the EU and OECD Harmful Tax Competition Initiatives," *Cambridge Review of International Affairs,* 19:4 (2006): 685–99.

23. Global Forum on Taxation, Closing Statement by the Co-Chairs, OECD, Ottawa, 14–15 October 2003; http://www.oecd.org/document/0/0,3343,en_2649_33745_16643264_1_1_1_1,00.html.

24. Ibid.

25. C. Stoll-Davey, *Assessing the Playing Field: International Cooperation in Tax Information Exchange* (London: Commonwealth Secretariat, 2007).

26. After Rawlings's phrase, "compliance by press release"; see Gregory Rawlings, "Taxes and Transnational Treaties: Responsive Regulation and the Reassertion of Offshore Sovereignty," *Law and Policy*, 29:1 (2007): 51–66, esp. 59.

27. R. Biswas, ed., *International Tax Competition: Globalisation and Fiscal Sovereignty* (London: Commonwealth Secretariat, 2002).

28. Martin Marcussen, "OECD Governance through Soft Law," in *Soft Law in Governance and Regulation: An Interdisciplinary Analysis*, ed. Ulrika Mörth (Cheltenham, UK: Edward Elgar, 2004), 103–27.

29. Sharman, *Havens in a Storm*, 161.

30. Ibid.

31. R. J. Hay, "OECD Level Playing Field Report Released: Consensus or Conflict?" *Tax Planning International Review* (June 2006): 1–8; "Tax Cooperation: Towards a Level Playing Field," OECD report, Paris, 2006.

32. "Offshore Financial Centers: The Assessment Program: An Update," International Monetary Fund (2004): 7, available at http://www.imf.org/external/np/mfd/2004/eng/031204.htm.

33. Ibid.

34. Ronen Palan, *The Offshore World: Sovereign Markets, Virtual Places, and Nomad Millionaires* (Ithaca, NY: Cornell University Press, 2003), xvi.

35. "Tax Cooperation," OECD report.

36. The term "nomad" is Palan's.

37. Rawlings, "Taxes and Transnational Treaties."

38. See Webb, "Defining the Boundaries."

39. I have intentionally chosen the male pronoun here.

40. Gregory Rawlings, "Cultural Narratives of Taxation and Citizenship: Fairness, Groups, and Globalization," *Australian Journal of Social Issues* 38:3 (August 2003): 269–305, esp. 297.

41. Ann Mumford, *Taxing Culture: Toward a Theory of Tax Collection* (London: Ashgate, 2002), 81.

42. Palan, *The Offshore World*.

43. Sharman, *Havens in a Storm*, 154.

44. Ibid., 152–53.

45. J. C. Sharman, "South Pacific Tax Havens: From Leaders in the Race to the Bottom to Laggards in the Race to the Top? *Accounting Forum* 29:3 (2005): 311–23, esp. 321.

# 12 Negotiating Internet Governance

## Security Implications of Multilateral Approaches

### J. P. Singh

Networking is highly interactive. The analyst's challenge lies in accounting for governance and security issues that arise from interactions in and about virtual and hyperreal spaces. John Perry Barlow's 1996 statement describing the Internet as a new frontier epitomized the thinking that governance as usual had come to an end. To the "Governments of the Industrial World," Barlow declared, "You have no sovereignty where we gather."[1] In this sense, the Internet frontier was the ultimate ungoverned space. As Ronald Deibert and Rafal Rohozinski's chapter in this volume suggests (Chapter 13), the Burkean suspicion among political scientists that global governance of the Internet is not so revolutionary and that governments will eventually dominate it lingers. However, so does the contrary notion; namely, that Internet governance in the long run will diminish the centrality of the nation-state in global politics.[2] According to the introduction to this volume, the Internet remains a contested space featuring various worldviews among multiple stakeholders. Sociologists accord persuasion, creation of meaning, and socialization to human interactions, whether they take place in "real space" or in "cyberspace." The contested nature of Internet governance highlighted in this chapter thus features a plurality of global actors, but also, more importantly, rival collective meanings regarding the appropriate form of governance and security.

The Internet continues the interconnections among spaces and populations that in the nineteenth century were fostered by telegraphs and ships. Such interconnections underscored the need for multilateral governance, and it is not a coincidence that one of the oldest surviving multilateral organizations is the International Telecommunications Union (ITU), which came into being in 1865. The concept of multilateralism has been around at least since the collective security alliances formed during the Peloponnesian War. Quite obviously, what changes is the *form* that multilateralism takes, that is, the collective meaning institutionalized among various actors. John Ruggie highlights this difference as between nominal and qualitative multilateralism; the latter includes the collective understanding among actors regarding "the principles of ordering."[3]

How do increased levels of interaction, such as through the Internet, shape patterns of global governance?[4] What are the implications of these emerging patterns of governance for security? This chapter answers these questions at three levels. First, to understand the constitution of new meanings among global actors, it introduces the concept of *meta-power*. Meta-power refers to how interactions reconfigure, constitute, or reconstitute the identities of the issues and actors. By contrast, *instrumental power*, in a material sense, merely denotes what $X$ does to $Y$, once we know the identities of $X$ and $Y$ and the meaning of the issue over which they interact. Similarly, *structural power* is habituation of this activity over a period of time, in a way that constrains or encourages an unchanging notion of interests. If, for example, a group of great powers concurs that a perpetual peace will exist among them if there is no war, then by this definition the principles of ordering include peace, understood as the cessation of war, and the salience given to the nation-states as central actors. An alternative principle would be the cessation of the underlying causes that lead to war, which might include the efforts of multiple actors, including civil society. Meta-power, then, is the ability of human interactions, especially as regulated by flows of ideas and representations, to change the collective meanings or the worldviews of actors, which includes their own identities. It is the epistemic and social dimension of power.[5]

The second claim of this chapter is that the contested nature of global governance, the underlying theme of this volume, manifests in the case of the Internet as a battle of collective epistemes, one in which commerce seeks the help of states (especially hegemonic states) to preserve a particular "order," and the other in which global civil society struggles to define an alternative conception of multilateral relations, with or without the help of nation-states. I call the former "statist multilateralism," and the latter "networked multilateralism." The third point regards differences in the meanings of security between statist and networked multilateralism.

The chapter provides answers from two major case studies: first, the World Summit on the Information Society (WSIS) (2001–present), which has sought to challenge the U.S.-backed hegemony of the Internet Corporation for Assigned Names and Numbers (ICANN); and second, the U.S. government's insistence since 2002 that commercial airlines turn over passenger data before landing on U.S. soil. In the former case, this study shows that the episteme favored by commerce, and backed by a hegemonic state, remains intact. In the latter case, commerce has reluctantly gone along with the hegemonic state's conception of security. In both cases, a rival episteme that favors individual- or societal-level notions of security is being proposed, but it has not gained currency beyond multilateral conference diplomacy. ICANN and data privacy issues are considered currently to be the most important issues for global electronic commerce, and thus their possible links to global security issues are significant: the ungoverned spaces, if any, over which states and other global actors are trying to legitimize their shared values might lie in the interstices of global commerce and security. The following section offers alternative conceptualizations of security and links them to the concepts of meta-power and multilateralism. It is followed by a discussion of the two empirical cases and how they embody the security-commerce nexus.

## Cultures of Security

Information networks propose new social epistemes that overlap prior social constructs and can be the basis of an intergenerational cultural conflict within the same society or multicultural conflicts among societies.[6] Ronald Deibert proposes that the kinds of collective images that information networks or hypermedia privilege differ from the authoritative, nation-state–oriented images of the past.[7] Ideas of security centered on nations or states are unlikely to endure in interconnected information networks. He notes the rise of "network security," in which the "primary object of security is *the network*," but he also recognizes that the collective images of national, state, private, and network security all overlap each other.[8] Deibert's essay, written before the terrorist attacks of September 11, 2001, did not highlight the political circumstances that would impel some states to fervently replicate the state security image. If anything, the ideas of state security favored by states, and of network security favored by a host of interests ranging from commercial to insurgent, define the cultural conflict of the information age.

In a cultural sense, both the material and information-based dimensions of power are important. Information networks, at the material level, can be seen only to enhance or diminish the capabilities of actors. Most of the literature in security studies dealing with cyber-threats, information operations, electronic warfare, and the "revolution in military affairs" (RMA) fits into this line of reasoning.[9] In a meta-power sense, however, information networks change the social context—understood here as identities of issues and actors—within which interactions take place. Thus, meta-power is antecedent to instrumental power and supplements our understanding of the context within which instrumental power works. This dynamic is best described as a process wherein information networks transform—by changing the base of information or episteme—the capabilities of actors and thus shape their instrumental power, which in turn affects international outcomes.

It is no coincidence that issues of culture have come to the fore in thinking about security.[10] Security in a cultural sense means countering threats to identity, a way of life, and the territorial or extraterritorial boundaries that contain this identity.[11] Meta-power calculations can inform us here of the relevant collective notions of identity, boundaries, and the actors involved. For example, the threats that realist international-relations scholars have most readily recognized are those to national identity. In networked environments, such threats may not be reducible to national contexts.

Samuel Huntington wrote the most well-known realist thesis linking national culture and security.[12] But his analysis mentions no networks and does not understand identity in an anthropological, micro sense, at the level of everyday life. Instead, Huntington conceives identity in the context of the "broader reaches of human history," at the "civilizational" level of Christianity versus Islam and Confucianism. Nation-states arbitrate this conflict: "Nation-states will remain the most powerful actors in world affairs, but the principal conflicts will occur between nations and groups of different civilizations."[13] For many, the 9/11 attacks and events thereafter lent credence to Huntington's prognosis.

Dominant analyses, at least in the United States, continue to examine information networks in an instrumental, material sense. Joseph Nye's states use persuasion or soft power to enhance their objectives.[14] Richard Rosecrance's "virtual states" can realize their interests only by networking with other states.[15] Jack Goldsmith and Tim Wu note that disputes regarding the Internet privilege the territorial laws of the nation-state where they take place.[16] These analyses stipulate the continuation of particular patterns, but they do not ask how these patterns came into being in the first place or how they may be changing. Actor identities and interests are held to be constant. Realists get around the problem of constructing national interests by deducing them from systemic or structural-level influences. Thus, they assume that a nation-state derives its interests from its position in the hierarchy of power, or by the power posturing of other states in the system.[17] What is missing here is the idea of a transformation of interests through successive interactions, or that security interests might change as a result of changes in other issue areas. Johann Eriksson and Giampiero Giacomello even note that most realists might consider that security threats related to information technology are "largely an economic issue."[18]

An understanding of meta-power and information networks supplements rather than replaces such traditional notions of security. The relevant questions are: What is security? Whose security is at stake? Who provides it? The answers must be contingent upon an idea of security as historically understood by a community, and as it might conflict with emergent notions such as networked security. Ole Waever, detailing various constructs of security in Europe, writes, "While not wanting any power external to themselves to dominate, Europeans increasingly accept the idea that Europe should be organized in some mixed form combining independent states and a center."[19] Later he notes: "A concept and vision of Europe has become critical to each nation's 'vision of itself' and therefore it is very hard notably in Germany and France to construct convincing narratives of 'where we are heading' without presenting or drawing upon a project of European integration."[20]

Table 12.1 contrasts the major differences between state-centric and networked security scenarios, both within the multilateral context.

An example drawn from the U.S. context may be illustrative. In national security terms, the "war on terror," as George W. Bush's administration termed it, was an abstraction unlimited in space or time and called for transforming the use of terrorism into a national-level category and then waging a war on a nation-state. A Pew Research Center survey, fourth in a series since 1987, found that Americans who favor threats of military action to deal with terrorism outnumber those who believe such threats only create more insecurity.[21] Such thinking does not reduce the security threat, but it does comfort those who prefer to meet such threats with military force. It is in this context of two contrasting worldviews that one can understand the resigna-

**TABLE 12.1**  State-centric versus networked multilateralism

| Multilateral dimensions | State-centric security | Networked security |
| --- | --- | --- |
| Actors | Nation-states | Nation-states and non-state actors |
| Authority structures | Hierarchical | Networked |
| Security threats | Understood territorially in terms of national identity | Understood territorially and extraterritorially |
| Absence of security threats | Balance of power | Secure identities; democratic and deliberative politics locally and globally |
| Containing threats | Arms races, military alliances | Effective networking |
| Linkages with other issues | Military threats dominate over others | Issue structures contain complex linkages among issues |

SOURCE: Adapted from J. P. Singh, "Meta-power, Networks, Security and Commerce," in *Power and Security in the Information Age: Investigating the Role of the State in Cyberspace*, ed. Myriam Dunn Cavelty, Victor Mauer, and Sai Felicia Krishna-Hensel (Aldershoot, UK: Ashgate, 2007), 56.

tion statement offered by John Brady Kiesling, a career foreign service officer, to former Secretary of State Colin Powell: "We have begun to dismantle the largest and most effective web of international relationships the world has ever known. Our current course will bring instability and danger, not security."[22] It is also this context that helps us understand the emphasis of the administration of Barack Obama on diplomacy and the deliberate eschewal of the term "war on terror."

Meta-power issues in security, in turn brought to the fore by the proliferation of information networks, highlight the varied cultural contexts in which security must be understood. Here the meaning of the issue area, namely security, or the identity of the actors involved (the enemy, for example) must be reunderstood. Security comprehended as a function of territory, and the enemy as a particular nation-state, takes the world "as-was," not how it has been transformed by technology. As a result, we not only misunderstand the world theoretically, but more importantly, we prescribe ineffective policies.

The cultural context of security means that information networks cannot be understood in territorial terms alone. Security is rooted in the epistemic level at which people experience the world, through their identities. Two recent cases involving information networks and the circulation of images highlight this point: photographs taken by U.S. soldiers of inmates at the Abu Ghraib prison outside of Baghdad and circulated over global media channels, starting in April 2004; and the publication of cartoons caricaturing the Prophet Mohammed by the Danish newspaper *Jyllands-Posten* on 30 September 2005. In instrumental terms, the effect of both of these sets of images can be examined within the context of nation-states (the U.S.-Iraq war; protests against Denmark). In meta-power terms, the very definition of security and the actors involved must be questioned. Why were the images so important? How did they speak to identity issues? How do these images fit our understanding of the meaning of security?[23] Our answers to these questions will bring to the fore the issues listed in the third column of Table 12.1: relations between nation-states and other actors, networked interactions, territoriality and extraterritoriality, identity of actors and issues, and complex linkages among issue areas.

## Internet Governance

Economic interdependence has always featured interstitial issues related to security. With high-tech globalization, security questions often involve threats to identity or echo the frustrations of those who feel excluded from globalization's benefits. The two "economic" issues discussed below are interesting both for broadening our conception of security and for situating such conceptions in the infrastructures of the information age.[24] In both cases, global commerce and great powers are able to define outcomes in their favor, but not without opposition from the weaker actors or recourse to some coercion. That a great power can "win" under many circumstances should not be much of a surprise. That a great power is unable, however, either to understand the cultural divide in the multilateral contests or to do anything to diffuse the underlying conflict remains worrisome.

### The World Summit on the Information Society

Internet governance is the domain mostly of the California-based ICANN and the dispute settlement functions of the Uniform Dispute Resolution Policy (UDRP) of the World Intellectual Property Organization. ICANN itself arose from a contest between an international coalition that favored mostly a civil society–led international governance mechanism and U.S.-backed private industry interests that feared, perhaps rightly so, that they would suffer from the loss of U.S. oversight. Nevertheless, when ICANN and UDRP came into being, they were hailed as success stories in international governance that prudently balanced various stakeholders' interests. The WSIS, however, undid this U.S.-supported consensus over Internet governance. The WSIS processes, therefore, exhibit the tensions between a state-centric versus a networked multiple-stakeholder governance of the Internet.

The WSIS began in 1998 as an ITU initiative to examine issues of the "digital divide" between those with access to global digital communications and those without.[25] Quite soon, it became the forum for addressing the grievances of developing countries that were left out of domain name governance and a host of other issues, many of which—spam, child pornography, data privacy, freedom of speech—went far beyond the ICANN mandate. The main demand of the international coalition, to which the European Union (EU) lent support in mid-2005, was to bring ICANN under the auspices of the United Nations (U.N.). The U.S. government and ICANN, supported by business groups worldwide, resisted this move and it eventually failed.

The WSIS covered a host of issues that went beyond the Internet to address the notion of information societies as a whole and raised to an international level the issue of information rights. At its broadest, the WSIS also implemented a 2001 U.N. General Assembly resolution to create a global vision of an information society, including governance, information security and civil liberties, and the digital divide.[26] But the main success of the WSIS initiative was to question state-level control over the agenda of Internet governance and reflect the concerns of the plurality of its stakeholders and their frustrations with U.S. dominance of ICANN.

When the WSIS process began in 1998, Internet governance was not on the agenda. It emerged in the planning for the Preparatory Committee meetings for the first WSIS, to be held in Geneva in December 2003. Influential developing countries such as China, Brazil, India, and South Africa led the move.[27] Although Internet governance soon became the most important issue at the WSIS, developing countries continued to consider a host of other issues. Senegal led the African countries in asking for a special investment scheme for Internet diffusion in poor countries, but donor countries remained reluctant and preferred existing mechanisms.[28] On the issue of Internet governance itself, at this time the EU continued to support the United States and oppose any alternatives to ICANN.

The Geneva WSIS diffused the issue of Internet governance with the appointment of a U.N. Secretary General's Working Group on Internet Governance (WGIG), led by Nitin Desai, special advisor to the secretary general on the WSIS.[29] From its inception, however, WGIG faced fierce opposition from ICANN, international business, the United States, and the EU. Paul Twomey, president and chief executive of ICANN, dismissed most concerns as a misunderstanding of his organization's role: "We are not the government of the internet. We're responsible for the plumbing, that's all."[30]

The fact that the WSIS brought together multiple stakeholders in an international forum was both its strength and, ultimately, in terms of reaching any kind of focus and consensus, its weakness. Derrick Cogburn identifies five types of stakeholders in Internet governance: international businesses, governments of developed countries, governments of developing countries, international organizations, and nongovernmental organizations.[31] The forty members of WGIG reflected the multiplicity of interests and diversity, with nineteen governmental representatives and twenty-one nongovernmental representatives; eighteen of the forty members were from developing countries. WGIG presented its report in July 2005, and even though the document reflected many areas of divergence, it called for recognition of the multiple stakeholders and a forum for all stakeholders to decide Internet governance. The terms "multiple stakeholders," "collaboration," and "cooperation" occur throughout the report and were quickly picked up by the developing world and the media as key frames for characterizing equitable Internet governance.[32]

The frame of "multiple stakeholders" also represented a move away from the U.S.-led private governance arrangement represented by ICANN. The first defection came at meetings in Geneva in late September 2005 to prepare for the second WSIS, to be held in Tunis in November 2005. In Geneva, the EU threw its support behind the developing world, calling for a "new cooperation model" while denying that this marked an abrupt change in its position. David Hendon, spokesman for the EU delegation, said simply, "We want Icann [sic] to operate under international law and be responsible to all governments."[33] ITU Secretary General Yoshio Utsumi supported Europe's change of heart, characterizing the EU's announcement at a news conference as "a radical shift of position."[34] The ITU, marginalized by the World Trade Organization on governance issues since 1997, had directed the WSIS process and would benefit from the move toward a U.N.-led governance arrangement.[35] Utsumi also noted: "As the Internet has become an infrastructure for all people, all nations want to have a sense of ownership. And if the headquarters is dominated by one company or one country, then you do not have this sense of ownership."[36] The critique from ICANN was swift. President Twomey, in colorful language that was becoming his trademark, noted that those who sought to fold ICANN into the U.N. were "living in a political fantasy land."[37] The Geneva meetings closed without any consensus being reached, and the issue was referred to the WSIS in Tunis.

Analysts examining the WSIS failure to move authority away from ICANN note that a host of issues and a multiplicity of actors—governmental, intergovernmental, nongovernmental, and business—and the difficulty they found in reaching any kind of consensus, overburdened the WSIS process.[38] Going into the Tunis summit, nevertheless, there was a consensus within the WSIS coalition on internationalizing Internet governance. Furthermore, among the many issues discussed, the authority to allocate Internet domain names stood out. As such, the failure at Geneva may not lie with the intent or nature of the WSIS or ITU, but with the incumbent power of ICANN, the United States, and international businesses. Google, for example, was worried that any loss of ICANN's authority would result in the fragmentation of domain names and reduce the Internet's interoperability. Twomey's assessment of WSIS members' political naiveté thus may not be that far off the mark.[39]

The Tunis summit ended in mid-November 2005, with the issue of Internet governance getting shelved for further international discussions. While ICANN kept its mandate, the WSIS process succeeded in calling attention to U.S. dominance of Internet domain name allocation and the lack of international consultations in the process. The difficulties developing countries face through ICANN, such as slow allocation of multilingual domain names, stood out. In the short run, the Governmental Advisory Committee, which itself came into being as a result of EU pressures in 1998, is likely to increase its influence within ICANN. In the long run, the slow evolution of ICANN is typical of the privatization of international rules, with ebbs and flows of governmental influence within these emergent rules.[40]

With respect to what it called "U.S. unilateralism," one report noted, "It is inconsistent for the U.S. to warn of 'governmental intervention' in the Internet while reserving to its own national government special and exclusive powers."[41] The report warned of alternative root server systems, such as in Europe. For example, right now there are thirteen root servers for the Internet, most of which appear to be located in the United States. Root servers recognize the generic and country code top-level domain names, such as ".com" and ".us," and redirect the traffic accordingly to other servers responsible for that domain name. Thus, root servers can be described as the database for all top-level domain names. In 2002, the Europeans began designing an alternative root server called the European Open Root Server Network, currently available for the German Internet area. The fact that all domain name addresses are ostensibly resolved predominantly through U.S.-based root servers could provide an enormous material advantage to the U.S. government. However, most top-level domain name addresses are not actually resolved though the top thirteen root servers. Existing below these thirteen root servers are layers of other servers that generally resolve the Internet protocol (IP) addresses. Even if the thirteen U.S.-based root servers wanted to block any addresses from getting resolved, they would be quickly side-stepped by servers at other levels, and also probably create a huge negative political fallout for the United States.[42] More importantly, at the level of meta-power, however, the flows of ideas and representations over the Internet, or the ability of the U.S. government to curtail these flows, are moot points.

A U.N.-led arrangement for ICANN would seek to change the market-driven character of the current regime and its support, materially and legally, in the United States. In "defeating" the international coalition at the WSIS for such an arrangement, the larger issues within which ICANN is embedded—information rights, the digital divide, and, at a less tangible level, alienation from processes of global governance—also remain unaddressed. The Tunis meetings led to the constitution of the Internet Governance Forum (IGF), through U.N. auspices with a five-year mandate, and it has brought together states and actors in business and civil society to discuss Internet governance. However, beyond posing an alternative vision of governance, the IGF lacks clout. This suits U.S. intentions.[43] However, multilateral pressures are indirectly effective. In October 2009, the U.S. Department of Commerce's National Telecommunications and Information Administration let go of its direct oversight control of ICANN that had been instituted through a series of Joint Project Agreements since 1998.[44] Thus, while the contest between U.S.-led statist-multilateralism and the multiple stakeholder–led networked multilateralism has, for now, settled in favor of the former, the contest remains open at the level of meta-power.

The WSIS process shows how the consensus around ICANN came undone when another international coalition demanded changes to Internet governance. Despite international efforts, the United States did not compromise. The fallout was the resulting loss of legitimacy for the ICANN arrangement and a heightened sense among civil society actors, especially from the developing world, that their voices are generally unheard in international forums.[45]

## The Passenger Name Record Dispute

The passenger name record (PNR) dispute, arising from a U.S. requirement to collect the passenger data that airlines store on their computer reservation systems, highlights the shaky foundation on which a prior accord between the United States and the EU on data flows, called the Safe Harbor accord, was negotiated. The Safe Harbor agreement, concluded in 2000, allowed the U.S. Federal Trade Commission to step in if U.S. firms did not follow adequate data safety precautions in their European operations. The accord also reflected the institutional and cultural differences in data regulation between the two continents. In the United States, private authorities—rather than individuals—control data collection and transmission. EU members have instituted data protection directorates, on the assumption that data about individuals belong to the individual and should not be relayed to third parties easily without adequate precautions. Safe Harbor was negotiated with considerable difficulty, but also with creative problem-solving, though at one time it threatened to interrupt more than $134 billion of transatlantic electronic commerce.[46] The European Parliament challenged the European Commission's authority to negotiate Safe Harbor, but its opposition was not binding.

The cultural, institutional, and legal obstacles underlying data transfers surfaced again with the PNR dispute. In particular, this applied to concerns about safeguards for data in the United States and, at the European end, the testy relationship between the commission and the member states on this issue. The specific dispute arose from the U.S. Aviation and Transportation Security Act passed by Congress on 19 November 2001, shortly after the September terrorist attacks. It authorized the U.S. Customs and Border Protection agency to ask airlines to turn over data on thirty-nine pieces of information contained in passports, but also other pieces of a passenger's travel and credit card information, and certain dietary information. Airlines failing to comply would be fined five thousand dollars for each passenger; nearly all airlines complied.

The dispute between the EU and the United States arose over the issue of transferring data collected for commercial reasons to use for security purposes.[47] The 1995 EU data privacy directive, which was the context for the Safe Harbor settlement, does not allow such transfers and thus puts European airlines' compliance with Safe Harbor on a shaky legal footing. The Safe

Harbor agreement stipulated that data transfers would take place on a case-by-case basis for law enforcement purposes, whereas the U.S. government requested all PNRs. In the Safe Harbor case, the EU was the agenda-setter and enforced compliance; the roles are reversed in the PNR case. The U.S. government set the agenda on this issue and possessed enormous regulatory capacity and clout to force compliance.[48] Furthermore, it had a market advantage in that many airlines depend on the large U.S. market. These two factors taken together would make the U.S. threat of levying fines on airlines credible, even though polling data and other evidence continue to find that individuals do not like their data being used for security reasons.[49] While the European Commission sought a negotiated solution, the European Parliament and the data directorates challenged its moves, as discussed below.

As noted, the United States was the agenda-setter and incumbent market power in the PNR negotiations. In the case of Safe Harbor, pressures from the Transatlantic Business Dialogue spanned the divide between the EU and the United States and prompted them to keep negotiating. In the PNR case, airline compliance and U.S. regulatory authority weakened the alternatives for the EU. Even after a European Court of Justice (ECJ) judgment in May 2006 annulled the commission's authority to sign an agreement in this regard, the airlines have continued to comply, and the commission has continued to seek a legal compromise that would lead to a negotiated solution.

Formal negotiations began in December 2001 with a U.S.-EU bilateral treaty, following the November passage of the U.S. Aviation Act.[50] For a year, Washington failed even to take European objections to data problems seriously but, nevertheless, held off applying any penalties to the airlines until March 2003, in the hope of finding a negotiated solution. The Article 29 Data Protection Working Party—so named to implement the EU's data privacy directive, Article 29 of 1995, and consisting of members from the data protectorates and the European Commission—gave its opinion three times in the negotiations: in October 2002, June 2003, and January 2004. The first opinion pointed to the basic underlying legal conflict between the U.S. and EU positions; the second opinion noted that a negotiated solution might not be possible; and the third opinion reiterated the Working Party's earlier position. Meanwhile the commission's negotiator, Fritz Bolkenstein, mindful of the difficulties of getting the earlier Safe Harbor agreement passed in the EU, noted to the European Parliament in March 2003 that U.S. "unilateral action and threats of penalties [are] unacceptable."[51] But he also sought to regularize the status quo (by October 2003, most airlines were complying with the U.S. data transfer requirements). Bolkenstein tried to buffer his position by noting that even the Article 29 Working Party had accepted that "political judgments" would be necessary to reach any agreement. The draft agreement was ready in December 2003, and was signed and brought into effect by the Council of Europe in May 2004. The agreement found that the U.S. request did indeed meet the 1995 privacy directive stipulation of "adequacy" that would prevent the misuse of PNR data beyond the purposes, in this case law enforcement, for which it was being requested.

The reaction from the European Parliament was swift. It had found the commission's stance to be too "accommodationist" toward the United States. In March 2004, the Parliament voted 229 to 202 against the PNR agreement. In the Safe Harbor case, the commission had let Safe Harbor stand against the parliament's vote. In April 2004, the parliament, supported by data protection directorates and civil society groups, voted 276 to 260 to take the commission to the ECJ for overstepping its authority. In July 2004, the ECJ stepped in, but the agreement continued in effect until 30 May 2006, when the ECJ issued its finding that "neither the Commission decision finding that the data are adequately protected by the United States nor the Council decision approving the conclusion of an agreement on their transfer to that country are founded on an appropriate legal basis."[52] As two European legal analysts pointed out about the ECJ judgment: "It is disappointing that in this judgment, the ECJ on the one hand concluded that the collection of PNR data by the airlines falls within the scope of the Community law and on the other hand seemed to accept that if the same data are to be transferred for public security reasons they no longer need the protection of the EC data protection directive."[53] For its part, the commission began to look for a new legal basis for a negotiated agreement with the United States. Meanwhile, in July 2006 another scandal erupted when the New York Times reported that the U.S. government had obtained data on international financial transactions by subpoenaing the Society for Worldwide Interbank Financial Transactions (SWIFT). SWIFT stood accused by European data privacy advocates of breaking European law in particular.[54]

The dispute is unlikely to go away soon, even though a new EU-U.S. agreement on PNR data was signed on 28 June 2007.[55] It made PNR transfers permissible for law enforcement reasons, and the negotiating parties also agreed to keep the details of the negotiations secret for ten years. Soon after the agreement was signed, however, the George W. Bush administration announced it would not comply with requests (from the EU, in this case) for data held by the U.S. Department of Homeland Security. Meanwhile, the Article 29 Data Protection Working Party forwarded an opinion on 17 August 2007 that was skeptical of the agreement, especially its emergency provisions.

The PNR dispute, SWIFT, and, in the United States, the National Security Agency's surveillance moves, have exposed rifts in the U.S.-EU alliance. First, diverting data collected for commercial purposes to security use is even more controversial in the EU than it is in the United States. Second, in the EU itself there is a rift between those who at least nominally support the U.S. position and those who remain opposed to it. The United Kingdom was one of the first countries in the EU to pass legislation that allows data retention for security purposes.[56]

As with the WSIS and ICANN, the PNR dispute undid a prior international accommodation, in this case the Safe Harbor agreement. Just as the WSIS must be understood within the larger context of stakeholders and international governance mechanisms, the same applies to the PNR dispute. Most airlines are complying with the U.S. requirements to transfer data; this outcome reflects U.S. market and regulatory coercion and is counterintuitive in light of the fact that EU data privacy guidelines are becoming the de facto international guidelines.[57] Despite United Kingdom–led moves for data retention, there was and continues to be stiff opposition, at both civil and governmental levels, to the way the Bush administration conducted its surveillance and anti-terror activities. Forced compliance on PNR must be understood in that context.

## Analysis

Multilateralism is neither dead nor transformed, but it is being redefined at the level of the *problematique*, which Ernst Haas defined as "the problem of all the problems."[58] The *problematique* here concerns the constitutive dimensions of multilateralism and the role that the various actors will play in it. This chapter advances three conclusions.

First, multilateralism remains the appropriate arena for building legitimacy for international rules and norms, in the case of both state-centric and networked multilateralism. In the ICANN case, the U.S. vision of Internet governance is embedded in multilateral processes, and in the PNR case, the United States is challenging another multilateral vision backed by the Europeans.

Second, to understand how the interactions among actors and issues reconstitute and reconfigure their identities in the process of negotiation, we need an understanding of power that can account for such transformations. The concept of meta-power is important in this context. At the level of meta-power, the contested nature of multilateral processes distinguishes what John Ruggie called "the principled meaning of multilateralism from actual historical practices, by showing how and why those principled meanings have come to be institutionalized throughout history."[59]

Third, this chapter has postulated some links between economic and security issues as they affect and are affected by Internet governance. At this point a cautionary conclusion may be advanced: explicitly linking security to economic multilateralism is impractical, and, to the extent that compromises may be made for security purposes, this option is available to everyone. Both WSIS advocates of information security and opponents of the PNR system cited U.S.-backed "unilateralism" as a threat to global security and included the commercial enterprises that the United States backs as part of this threat. Opposition by civil society in economic matters also does not bode well for claims regarding state sovereignty over security issues. Andrew Hurrell summarizes the case well in noting that "globalization has created the conditions for an ever more intense and activist transnational civil society that challenges the state as the dominant locus of identity and as the primary site of political mobilization; and the extent to which states have become far more enmeshed in a web of international institutions."[60]

The cases discussed here show that even though the economic implications of the cases are clear, the security implications, especially in terms of the underlying cultural concerns, may be unclear or less well understood (see Table 12.2). Norms or fundamental values regarding the desired type of multilateralism are in conflict despite the short-term gains in rules that favor the United States. Emblematic of these conflicts are the movement to internationalize Internet governance and the uses of commercial data for security purposes. More importantly, nowhere in the two cases above did Washington seem to be aware of the cultural dimension of the conflicts that underlie the framing of Internet governance rules or norms.

Acknowledging the cultural dimension of these mainly commercial conflicts neither legitimizes nor diffuses them. However, such an acknowledgment can at least foster U.S. empathy with networked multilateralism and help fine-tune its state-centric approach. Until the Obama administration,

**TABLE 12.2** Case summaries

|  |  | WSIS | PNR dispute |
|---|---|---|---|
| Type of power | Instrumental | Coalition-building for WSIS versus ICANN and U.S. responses | U.S. forces airlines into compliance |
|  | Meta-power | Identity framing in terms of information rights and information have-nots | U.S. identity ("unilateralism") in security seriously questioned in EU and elsewhere |
| Context | U.S.-centric multilateralism | North-south divide, ICANN backed by U.S. | U.S. versus EU mostly in PNR dispute |
|  | Network multilateralism | Multi-stakeholderism with civil society groups at an international summit | International processes expressly left out by stakeholders |
| Outcomes | Rules | Status-quo continues | U.S. gets airline compliance |
|  | Norms | Market driven norm in conflict with information society norm | Security versus antisurveillance |
| Implications | Economic interdependence | Electronic commerce secure with ICANN and U.S. government oversight | Airlines function normally |
|  | Security | Information have-nots disenfranchised unless markets deliver on their wants | Heightened surveillance of passengers may lead to further conflict |

NOTE: WSIS indicates World Summit on the Information Society; PNR, passenger name record; ICANN, Internet Corporation for Assigned Names and Numbers; EU, European Union.

multilateralism was a term rarely invoked in U.S. politics, but when it was used, U.S. officials overlooked their own preference for a particular type of multilateralism: a statist multilateralism that helped them maximize their own interests. In the view of this author, this does not mean that the United States needs to compromise on its market competitiveness, but it does mean that U.S. officials need to be careful about scorning multilateral diplomacy if they want to reach an international accommodation or get other players to go along with their agenda.

The case for multilateral diplomacy was often made as a general critique of the George W. Bush administration, without detailing what needed to be done. This chapter makes the case in the micro-terms of particular issue areas, where the opportunities for multilateral diplomacy are varied and unlikely to impose an excessive burden on the U.S. economy. It is also less than obvious that this failure of diplomacy is the fault of the Bush administration alone. The roots of the cases discussed here lie in accommodations reached during the years of the administration of Bill Clinton. More recently, moves by a protectionist Congress to scuttle multilateral trade processes, just as trading partners in the developing world are coming around to accepting them, also do not bode well for multilateralism.

The situation is not hopeless and should not be exaggerated. Despite the stance taken by U.S. governmental or other actors, global economic interdependence is not going away. This means there will be increasing, not diminishing, opportunities for U.S. commercial diplomacy in the future, which can speak effectively to security issues as well. The United States can strengthen its commitment to multilateralism in significant ways. This could mean everything from participation in multilateral forums to persuasion and bridge-building with other actors. In the cases outlined above, many of the parties started out opposed to the U.S. position, but the United States made the situation worse by not even trying to build an international coalition for its position, or by openly scoffing at such moves. This also discredits the work of private U.S. firms, which need international support for effective engagement abroad.

The Obama administration has moved recently to restore multilateral diplomacy and networks to the realization of U.S. interests and foreign policy. Nevertheless, the U.S. government is epistemically constrained in understanding security threats and responses in national terms. In a speech on cybersecurity, President Obama noted, "it's now clear this cyber threat is one of the most serious economic and national security challenges we face as a nation."[61] However, the speech did detail the threats and responses in networked terms by outlining the links between economics and security, and in suggesting possible partnerships among government, business, and civil society. The speech also outlined the case for appointing a Cybersecurity Coordinator—as opposed to the often-used term "czar"—who would also be a member of the national security staff and the National Economic Council.

Nation-states in general act according to instrumental power relations, but in the cases analyzed above, a host of actors feel delegitimized or disenfranchised by the rules as they are being negotiated. At the global level, there are two contending norms, one that favors market-driven processes and another that favors the disenfranchised, but it is not exactly certain how the latter's voices can be addressed in the international system. Networked interactions are complex and may have clear security implications. The solution is not to securitize economic interdependence. The solution lies in returning to the arena of multilateral global governance negotiations, where networks are best understood and shaped. It is at the multilateral level that conflicting norms can legitimately be reconciled.

## Notes

1. John Perry Barlow, "A Declaration of the Independence of Cyberspace," 8 February 1996, Davos, Switzerland, http://homes.eff.org/~barlow/Declaration-Final.html.

2. For an example of the former position, see Jack Goldsmith and Tim Wu, *Who Controls the Internet? Illusions of a Borderless World* (New York: Oxford University Press, 2006). For examples of several authors who posit long-term trends, see James N. Rosenau and J. P. Singh, eds., *Information Technologies and Global Politics: The Changing Scope of Power and Governance* (Albany: State University of New York Press, 2002). Recent examples emphasize transnational activism. See, for example, M. I. Franklin, "NGOs and 'The Information Society': Grassroots Advocacy at the UN—A Cautionary Tale," *Review of Policy Research* 24:4 (July 2007): 309–29; and Milton Mueller, Brendan N. Kuerbis, and Christiane Page, "Democratizing Global Communication? Global Civil Society and the Campaign for Communication Rights in the Information Society," *International Journal of Communication* 1 (2007): 1–31.

3. John Gerard Ruggie, ed., *Multilateralism Matters: The Theory and Praxis of an Institutional Form* (New York: Columbia University Press, 1993), 6. In somewhat similar veins, Ernst Haas had distinguished between mechanical and organic worldviews, and more recently, Andrew Hurrell has distinguished between international orders analyzed as facts versus socially constructed values. Ernst B. Haas, "Words Can Hurt You; or, Who Said What to Whom about Regimes," *International Organization* 36:2 (Spring 1982): 207–43; and Andrew Hurrell, *On Global Order: Power, Values, and the Constitution of International Society* (Oxford: Oxford University Press, 2007).

4. This chapter includes issues of Internet domain names and data flows, both collectively referred to here as Internet governance.

5. For earlier iterations of this concept, see J. P. Singh, *Negotiation and the Global Information Economy* (Cambridge: Cambridge University Press, 2008); and J. P. Singh, "Introduction: Information Technologies and the Changing Scope of Power and Governance," in Rosenau and Singh, *Information Technologies and Global Politics*.

6. This section is adapted from J. P. Singh, "Meta-power, Networks, Security and Commerce," in *Power and Security in the Information Age: Investigating the Role of the State in Cyberspace*, ed. Myriam Dunn Cavelty, Victor Mauer, and Sai Felicia Krishna-Hensel (Aldershoot, UK: Ashgate, 2007).

7. Ronald Deibert, *Parchment, Printing, and Hypermedia: Communication and World Order Transformation* (New York: Columbia University Press, 1997).

8. Ronald Deibert, "Black Code: Censorship, Surveillance, and the Militarization of Cyberspace," *Millennium* 30:3 (2003): 501–30.

9. For an overview of how security studies ignore the deeper and constitutive implications of information networks, see Johann Eriksson and Giampiero Giacomello, eds., *International Relations and Security in the Digital Age* (London: Routledge, 2007).

10. Early work included Yosef Lapid and Friedrich Kratochwil, eds., *The Return of Culture and Identity in IR Theory* (Boulder, CO: Lynne Reinner, 1996); and Peter J. Katzenstein, ed., *The Culture of National Security: Norms and Identity in World Politics* (Ithaca, NY: Cornell University Press, 1996).

11. Understood in a networked sense, this definition tries not to reduce security threats to a particular actor or the act that it finds threatening. Nevertheless, it tries to build upon the idea of "securitization" offered by Barry Buzan: "When something is constituted as a security issue (i.e., securitized), it means that somebody (a securitizing actor) argues that this (the threat) poses an existential threat to something (the referent object) that has to survive (e.g., the state, the nation, or the environment)." Ole Waever, "The Constellations of Security in Europe," in *Globalization, Security, and the Nation-State: Paradigms in Transition*, ed. Ersel Aydinli and James N. Rosenau (Albany: State University of New York Press, 2005), 153.

12. Samuel Huntington, "The Clash of Civilizations?" *Foreign Affairs* 73 (1993): 22–49.

13. Ibid., 22.

14. Joseph Nye, *The Paradox of American Power: Why the World's One Superpower Can't Go It Alone* (Oxford: Oxford University Press, 2002); and Joseph Nye, *Bound to Lead: The Changing Nature of American Power* (New York: Basic Books, 1990).

15. Richard Rosecrance, "The Rise of the Virtual State," *Foreign Affairs* 75 (Fall 1996): 45–61.

16. Goldsmith and Wu, *Who Controls the Internet?*

17. Kenneth Waltz, *Theories of International Politics* (New York: McGraw Hill, 1979).

18. Eriksson and Giacomello, *International Relations*, 12.

19. Ole Waever, "The Constellation of Securities in Europe," in Aydinli and Rosenau, *Paradigms in Transition*," 161. Also see, Ole Waever, "Securitization and Desecuritization," in *On Security*, ed. Ronnie D. Lipshutz (New York: Columbia University Press, 1995), 46–86.

20. Waever, "Constellation of Securities," 161–62.

21. Edward Alden, "Foreign Policy Wins Votes for Republicans," *Financial Times*, 13 May 2005: 1.

22. The statement was sent on 27 February 2003 (copy available at http://www.commondreams.org/views03/0227-13.htm, accessed 5 November 2009). See also John Brady Kiesling, *Diplomacy Lessons: Realism for an Unloved Superpower* (Washington, DC: Potomac Books, 2007).

23. I have deliberately avoided trying to answer these questions in this chapter. The concept of meta-power only calls these issues into question; ontologies such as constructivism must be used to answer them.

24. The case studies described here are adapted from and discussed more fully in Singh, *Negotiation and the Global Information Economy.*

25. See the WSIS Website, "Basic Information-Frequently Asked Questions (FAQs)," available at http://www.itu.int/wsis/basic/faqs.asp.

26. Franklin, "NGOs and 'The Information Society.'"

27. Frances Williams, "Geneva Summit Aims to Bridge 'Digital Divide,'" *Financial Times,* 15–16 November 2003: 9.

28. *Financial Times,* 8 December 2003: 4.

29. For more information on WGIG, see its Website, http://www.wgig.org/.

30. Frances Williams, "Internet Address System Defended ICANN Response," *Financial Times,* 9 December 2003: 7.

31. Derrick L. Cogburn, "Global Internet Governance: Who's Winning, Who's Losing, and Who Cares?" paper presented at the American Political Science Association, Washington, D.C., August 2005.

32. The multi-stakeholder governance process is sometimes called MuSH. See Mueller et al., "Democratizing Global Communication," for an interesting analysis of the strengths and weaknesses of MuSH.

33. Frances Williams, "US Holds Firm on Control of Web Address System," *Financial Times,* 1–2 October 2005: 3.

34. "Give Up Web Domination, US Told," Agence France-Presse, 30 September 2005.

35. J. P. Singh, "Negotiating Regime Change: The Weak, the Strong, and the WTO Telecom Accord," in Rosenau and Singh, *Information Technologies and Global Politics,* 239–72; and J. P. Singh, *Leapfrogging Development? The Political Economy of Telecommunications Restructuring* (Albany: State University of New York Press, 1999).

36. Jim Ashling, "The Future of Internet Governance Remains Unresolved," *Information Today* 22:8 (September 2005): 24.

37. Ibid.

38. See the Website of the Internet Governance Project for various reports and papers on this topic: http://www.internetgovernance.org.

39. The WSIS coalition also hoped for support from protesters in the United States who disputed the right of a private corporation, ICANN, to rule on private issues. In mid-2005, U.S. Assistant Secretary for Commerce Michael Gallagher received almost six thousand letters from conservative groups asking him to intervene and stop ICANN from approving triple X–rated pornographic domain names. Although President Twomey had earlier insisted that ICANN ruled only on technical matters and not moral ones, ICANN complied with the request from the Department of Commerce, which led to protests from those in favor of freedom of speech. Keith Regan, "ICANN Delays Final Decision on '.xxx' Domain," *E-Commerce Times,* 15 November 2005, accessed at http://www.ecommercetimes.com/story/45546.html;

and Keith Regan, "ICANN Reverses Course on '.XXX' Domain," *E-Commerce Times*, 2 December 2005, accessed at http://www.ecommercetimes.com/story/47649.html.

40. Milton Mueller and Dale Thompson, "ICANN and Intelsat: Global Communication Technologies and Their Incorporation into International Regimes," in *The Emergent Global Information Policy Regime*, ed. Sandra Braman (Houndsmill, UK: Palgrave Macmillan, 2004); Ralf Bendrath and Jeanette Hofman, "The Return of the State in Cyberspace: Regulation and Legitimacy on the Internet—The Domain Name System and Privacy," paper prepared for the CISS/ETH conference, The Internet and the Changing Face of International Relations and Security, Lucerne, Switzerland, 23–25 May 2005. Another issue area of interest to scholars and journalists is the increasing regulation of Internet content by national governments, such as France's restrictions on Yahoo! and an Australian court's decision to hold Dow Jones responsible for libelous comments published on the Internet. Patti Waldmeir, "Material Published on the Internet and Thus Accessible Anywhere in the World Is Increasingly Being Challenged under the Laws of Individual Nation States," *Financial Times*, 16 December 2002: 13.

41. "Political Oversight of ICANN: A Briefing for the WSIS Summit," Internet Governance Project, 1 November 2005: 6.

42. My thanks to Michael Nelson for clarifying this point for me.

43. Interestingly, China opposes the IGF, especially the involvement of civil society actors at the level of a U.N. forum. Despite China's opposition, however, the mandate for the IGF is likely to be renewed for another five years at its annual meeting in November 2009 in Sharm al-Sheikh, Egypt.

44. See ICANN, "The Affirmation of Commitments: What It Means," 30 September 2009, accessed 18 November 2009 at http://www.icann.net/en/announcements /announcement-30sep09-en.htm#announcement.

45. This final point is made in ethnographic detail by Franklin, "NGOs and 'The Information Society.'"

46. Dorothee Heisenberg, *Negotiating Privacy: The European Union, the United States, and Personal Data Protection* (Boulder, CO: Lynne Reinner, 2005).

47. "Data-mining" commercial data or requisitioning its use for security purposes has been a controversial practice in the United States, especially since 9/11, and raises many constitutional and privacy concerns. Surveillance technologies such as biometric identification and radio-frequency identification chips are sure to raise these concerns further.

48. Bach and Newman note that PNR compliance was a function of U.S. regulatory capacity. David Bach and Abraham Newman, "The European Regulatory State and Global Public Policy: Micro-Institutions and Macro-Influence" *Journal of European Public Policy* 16:4 (2007): 827–46. See also Peter Cowhey and Joseph Richards, "Building Global Service Markets: Economic Structure and State Capacity," in *The State after Statism: New State Activities in the Age of Liberalization*, ed. Jonah D. Levy (Cambridge, MA: Harvard University Press, 2006).

49. Miriam Metzger, "Consumer Privacy Management in Electronic Commerce," *Journal of Computer Mediated Communication* 12 (2007): 335–61. Heisenberg cites a

CBS/*New York Times* poll from November 2002 in which nearly two-thirds, or 62 percent, of the respondents were "not willing" to allow government to monitor their telephones or e-mails for security reasons. Heisenberg, *Negotiating Privacy*, 140–41.

50. This paragraph relies heavily on Heisenberg, *Negotiating Privacy*, chapter 7.

51. Quoted in ibid., 143.

52. Judgment of the Court of Justice in Joined Cases C-317/04 and C-318/04, "The Court annuls the Council decision concerning the conclusion of an agreement between the European Community and the United States of America on the processing and transfer of personal data and the commission decision on the adequate protection of those data," press release 46/06, 30 May 2006, accessed at http://europa.eu/rapid/pressReleasesAction.do?reference=CJE/06/46&format=PDF&aged=1&language=EN&guiLanguage=en.

53. Elspeth Guild and Evelein Brouwer, "The Political Life of Data: The ECJ Decision on the PNR Agreement between the EU and the US," CEPS Policy Brief, Centre for European Policy Studies, 109 (26 July 2006): 4. Available from http://www.ceps.be.

54. Henry Farrell, "Privacy in Europe Is a Casualty of America's Terror War," *Financial Times*, 2 July 2006. In the United States, a few Republican politicians wanted the *New York Times* to be charged with espionage.

55. "Agreement between the European Union and the United States of America on the processing and transfer of Passenger Name Record (PNR) data by air carriers to the United States Department of Homeland Security (DHS) (2007 PNR Agreement)," *EU News and Press Release* 22 (7 August 2007): 21, available at http://www.dhs.gov/xlibrary/assets/pnr-2007agreement-usversion.pdf (accessed 30 November 2009).

56. Ian Hosein and Johann Eriksson, "International Policy Dynamics and the Regulation of Dataflows: Bypassing Domestic Restrictions," in Johann Eriksson and Giacomello, *International Relations*.

57. More than thirty countries on five continents now have EU-type rules for data privacy. See Bach and Newman, "The European Regulatory State."

58. Haas, "Words Can Hurt You," 223.

59. Ruggie, *Multilateralism Matters*, 7.

60. Hurrell, *On Global Order*, 198.

61. The White House, "Remarks by the President on Securing Our Nation's Cyber Infrastructure," Office of the Press Secretary, Washington, D.C., 29 May 2009, available at http://www.whitehouse.gov/the_press_office/Remarks-by-the-President-on-Securing-Our-Nations-Cyber-Infrastructure/ (accessed 28 July 2009).

# 13 Under Cover of the Net

*The Hidden Governance Mechanisms of Cyberspace*

Ronald J. Deibert and Rafal Rohozinski

Throughout its history, common perceptions of the Internet have been characterized by two prominent and closely related myths. The first, and arguably the founding myth, is that the Internet is an ungoverned, anarchic space that no state, corporation, or other modern institution of governance can control. From this perspective, the Internet is a unique medium of communication whose decentralized, networked architecture makes it resistant to traditional governance.[1] This resilience, it is argued, can be traced back to its constitutive design principles as a U.S. military communications system meant to withstand a nuclear attack.[2] As John Gilmore, member of the board of the Electronic Freedom Foundation, said, "The internet interprets censorship as damage and routes around it."[3] It is a space of constant innovation and change, according to the myth, too swift for slow, cumbersome bureaucracies to capture and regulate.

Among other things, many believe this ungoverned character of the Internet allows for a kind of safe harbor or escape—a characteristic captured by the infamous phrase, "On the Internet, no one knows you are a dog." Whether dogs have ever actually disguised their persona on the Internet is an open question, but there are those who assume a more sinister set of actors have and do. Law enforcement, intelligence personnel, and many security analysts argue that the Internet has provided a safe haven and an operating and recruiting environment for terrorists, militants, pornographers, and racists precisely because (like the tribal regions of Pakistan) it is a space that cannot be controlled.[4]

The other founding myth of the Internet, closely related to the first, is that the space of the Internet—cyberspace—constitutes a distinct realm of interaction separate from reality: a *virtual reality*.[5] Although the concept of virtual reality can be traced back to at least the time of Plato, it has dominated the culture of the Internet, computers, and digital technologies since their inception. From the first text-based multiuser dimensions to the vast expanses of the online interactive world Second Life, the Internet has offered intensely consuming worlds of users' own making.[6] By emphasizing the disconnect from material reality—or "metaspace" as it is sometimes referred to—this type of virtual "world creationism" feeds into and complements the other founding myth of the Internet.

The main argument of this chapter is that although parts of these myths have a basis in reality, they have obscured much that is important, yet not widely known, about the governance of the Internet. The thesis of this chapter is that, contrary to the myths above, the Internet is very much a *governed space*. At the most basic level, it is governed by rules of physics as well as code, which give it predictability and finite characteristics. It is governed by consensual practices among the network's providers and operators that have their basis in norms without which the Internet could not function. And most importantly, it is increasingly governed by actors—states and corporations primarily, but increasingly civic networks as well—who understand how leveraging and exploiting key nodes within the physical infrastructure of the Internet can give them strategic political and economic advantages.[7] Each of these nodes— from routers to Internet exchange points to autonomous systems—presents opportunities for authorities to impose order on Internet traffic through some mechanism of filtering and surveillance and/or to seek out and eliminate sources of information deemed strategically threatening. Some of this control takes place for reasons of efficiency (for example, eliminating spam); some of it takes place for cultural, political, economic, or national security reasons. Moreover, these actors have, in some cases, deliberately shrouded their governance in secrecy and indeed benefit from the promulgation of the myths above to keep their activities under cover. The mechanisms of governance we describe below, therefore, are largely informal, insofar as they are uncodified and shielded from public view, but they are no less consequential as a result.

In this chapter, we describe some of the ways states and corporate entities exercise governance and what the consequences of these interventions mean for the character and constitution of the Internet. We highlight the way that, contrary to the founding myths of the Internet outlined above, the material constitution of the Internet matters and how its physical characteristics create opportunities for control. The picture we paint here of the Internet is of a real physical network of networks that has become an object of geopolitical contestation, rather than an ethereal "virtual" space that no one can control.

## Probing the Internet's Infrastructure

When most people think of the Internet, they do not think much beyond the computer screens in front of them. They send an e-mail and it is gone. But the Internet comprises a rich and complex logical and physical network of interconnected systems through which information travels. Such a complex globally distributed network could not function were it not for at least several layers of formal and informal governance. These include, at a most basic level, the laws of physics, which govern the speed, character, and transmission of information flows. Furthermore, the many services that constitute and maintain the network as a whole entail a very dense regime of norms, rules, and principles that span the private and public sectors and hundreds of sovereign territorial jurisdictions involving thousands of actors and organizations.[8]

The myth of ungovernability derives in large part from the decentralized and distributed architecture that purportedly characterizes the Internet. It is important to understand, however, in the context of discussions about the hidden governance mechanisms of the Internet, that the Internet is both a distributed *and* a hierarchical network insofar as some nodes are more important than others. It is not a pure *network* per se.[9] The hierarchical elements of the Internet matter, not only for redundancy and vulnerability, but also in terms of points of intervention. Key nodes in the Internet infrastructure offer critical chokepoints where filtering and surveillance mechanisms can be imposed. For example, although the Internet operates on the basis of a protocol (TCP/IP) common to all network-capable devices, the routing of requests for information is organized in a hierarchical manner, with a cluster of thirteen top-level domain name servers responsible for steering traffic in the proper direction. At one point, these thirteen servers were physically located in the United States, but today they are dispersed in multiple international locations.

Hierarchy is also present with respect to the providers of the Internet's backbone—the so-called "Tier 1" telecommunications providers: AT&T, Verizon, NTT, and others. Tier 1 networks connect to the entire Internet, while other tiers connect to only portions of it or lease their connectivity from other providers. Today, there are ten Tier 1 providers, of which seven are headquartered in the United States and thus are subject to U.S. law. Traffic routing among the various telecommunications providers that make up the network is, in turn, handled through a system of peering and transit arrangements that find their physical manifestation in about 150 Internet exchange points worldwide.[10]

Although there is still enormous complexity and distributedness to the Internet, the hierarchical elements of the infrastructure are important for both security and governance. The physical vulnerability of the network was vividly illustrated by the collapse in 2008 of Internet services in large parts of the Middle East, South Asia, and the Persian Gulf following the failure of four undersea fiber-optic trunk lines, apparently by coincidence, as a result of either wayward ships' anchors or undersea tectonic activity.[11] Egypt lost 70 percent of its connection to the outside Internet, and between 50 and 60 percent of India's net outbound connectivity was similarly lost on the westbound route critical to that country's outsourcing industry. Although other parts of the global Internet tend to have more redundancy in case of failure, many parts of the developing world do not.

## Surveillance of the Internet at Key Chokepoints

For many decades, states have developed an extensive set of practices around the interception and analysis of electronic communications for purposes of intelligence. As long ago as the U.S. Civil War (1861–1865), U.S. Army signals intelligence officers intercepted and decoded messages sent over the new medium of the telegraph. Cryptographic systems were, in turn, deployed in order to secure communications traffic. From the beginning, state militaries recognized the importance of controlling major nodes in information networks, often relying on the collusion of private actors to do so. During the Spanish American War (1898–1899), for example, a U.S. military officer recruited a source in the Western Union telegraph office in Havana to intercept communications between Madrid and Spanish commanders in Cuba.[12]

Signals intelligence matured following World War II and particularly during the height of the Cold War.[13] The United States led a coalition of states in the so-called Atlantic Alliance that included the United Kingdom, New Zealand, Australia, and Canada.[14] The technological infrastructure for this signals intelligence capacity involved a network of sea-, land-, air-, and space-based planetary observation and interception systems. The ease with which electronic communications can be intercepted and understood depends on a number of factors, including the method of transmission, the frequencies employed, and the level of security surrounding the communications system. As a consequence, the United States and its allies (and adversary states operating in competition) have continuously sought technologies and other means of access to provide the most efficient interception capabilities, including everything from tapping undersea cables to placing specially designed electronic collection satellites in geosynchronous orbit to ground stations placed in the path of microwave towers.

These electronic signals intelligence activities have been among the most secretive of all state intelligence practices, in an area that is already deeply shrouded in secrecy.[15] Because of its closely guarded nature, empirical evidence is lacking. A number of inferences can nevertheless be made from circumstantial evidence and revelations from the occasional whistleblower. For example, the 1994 U.S. Communications Assistance for Law Enforcement Act (CALEA) attempts to preserve the ability of law enforcement agencies to conduct electronic surveillance by requiring that telecommunications carriers and manufacturers of telecommunications equipment modify and design their equipment, facilities, and services to ensure that they have the necessary surveillance capabilities. Although it is domestic legislation, CALEA in effect internationalizes U.S. capabilities by virtue of the fact that seven of the ten Tier 1 telecommunication companies are U.S.-based. A more direct example comes from an AT&T employee who revealed in 2005 that for years the National Security Agency (NSA) had been operating surveillance systems in collusion with the company at key Internet peering points in the United States. Documents viewed by the whistleblower revealed that special technologies had been set up to "split" the light from fiber-optic cables connecting domestic and international networks to special, closely guarded collection systems.

Apart from the contentious issues of illegality and accountability surrounding the surveillance practices,[16] the case is instructive for the extent to which it revealed, as one article noted, that the "NSA is capable of conducting what amounts to vacuum-cleaner surveillance of all the data crossing the internet—whether that be people's e-mail, web surfing or any other data."[17] In this case, the strategic location of surveillance at physical peering points for international traffic based on U.S. soil is very important. The move away from

microwave and wireless means of transmission (which are more readily intercepted by space-based satellites) toward undersea fiber optic has hampered
the collection efforts of the NSA. Obtaining the cooperation of U.S.-based
companies and intercepting traffic at U.S.-based peering and exchange points
is much easier (however much they may have to be cajoled to cooperate outside the strict rule of law) than sending submarines to split cable hundreds of
feet under the ocean in international waters.[18] It is also more practical, considering the concentration of global information traffic crossing within U.S. jurisdiction, a function of both historical legacy and pricing patterns and tariffs
on telecommunications traffic. For the past several decades, the vast majority
of Internet and telephone traffic, even that which is extraregionally based,
has passed through key chokepoints in the United States because of these institutional and economic factors. Perhaps not surprisingly in light of these
circumstances, the George W. Bush administration responded to the NSA
surveillance controversy not by backing off, but by pushing for a validation of
such measures through new legislation.[19] Likewise, one of the more surprising
areas of policy convergence between the outgoing Bush and incoming Barack
Obama administration has been support for enhanced electronic surveillance
and warrantless wiretapping measures.

Although it is rare for electronic intelligence activities to see the light of
day, one can presume that states around the world, to varying degrees, employ as a matter of practice a similar set of network interrogation techniques
to intercept and monitor communications traffic at key Internet chokepoints
within and beyond their territorial boundaries. Such practices are part of a
systematic leveraging of the subterranean realm of the global information
infrastructure for intelligence purposes. The shroud of secrecy around such
practices works in conjunction with the myths of the ungoverned space of the
Internet to keep such practices hidden from public view and thus to maintain
democratic accountability. Yet they are one illustration, however foggy, of the
potent methods long available to states to shape and govern Internet traffic for
strategic military purposes.

## Content Filtering and Packet Shaping

One of the other ways in which intervention in the Internet's material infrastructure is leveraged for governance occurs in the areas of content filtering
and packet shaping. Internet content filtering is the practice of restricting ac-

cess to information by blocking requests for information from being successfully completed. Filtering can take place in a variety of ways, although the most common is to insert into the software that routes information along the Internet's pathways a list of banned domains, keywords, IP addresses, or URLs. This means that any critical chokepoint described above, from the computer connecting to the Internet all the way to the international gateway through which information passes out of one national jurisdiction to another, is a potential site for controlling information flows. While filtering traditionally occurs either by blocking requests for information from reaching their destination or by preventing the return of the requested information, other nonfiltering mechanisms can be used to achieve the same ends.[20] After all, the aim of filtering is simply denial of access to information. As we show below, new forms of blocking are emerging based on the use of distributed denial of service attacks. Such information warfare attacks bring Web servers down by overwhelming them with requests for information, thus blocking information at its source and denying access to all users equally.

Although state-level content filtering practices are widespread and growing, knowledge of them has tended to be limited. In part, this is a function of a lack of accountability and transparency about these practices. In part, it is a function of the lack of empirical evidence. Until recently, most reports of Internet content filtering tended to emerge from users, news reports, or advocacy organizations. Not surprisingly, they have tended to be unsystematic, sometimes unreliable, and contradicted by the states themselves. Moreover, because of the complex and varied ways in which filtering can be implemented, reports have occasionally been made in error or have contained contradictory information.

Overcoming this problem has been one of the main goals of the OpenNet Initiative (ONI), a collaborative project among researchers at the universities of Toronto, Harvard, Cambridge, and Oxford, plus partner organizations worldwide.[21] The aim of the ONI has been to develop a systematic way to investigate empirically Internet filtering practices from behind national firewalls over an extended period of time, to give an accurate picture of state content filtering practices. The ONI employs a unique methodology that combines in-field investigations undertaken by researchers in the countries concerned with a suite of technical interrogation tools that probe the Internet directly for forensic evidence of content filtering and filtering technologies. The aim of the ONI is to provide a comprehensive picture of Internet content filtering in a particular country by probing all aspects of the national information infrastructure (Internet cafes, ISPs, wireless networks, backbone gateways) over the long term, testing accessibility in both English and local languages.

Since 2002, the ONI has produced eleven country reports (Belarus, Yemen, Tunisia, Burma, Singapore, Iran, China, Bahrain, United Arab Emirates, Vietnam, and Saudi Arabia) and various bulletins and advisories. In 2006, it conducted the first global survey of Internet censorship, running field tests in more than forty countries worldwide. The ONI is presently testing for evidence of Internet content filtering in seventy-one countries. As the research makes clear, the scope, scale, and sophistication of Internet content filtering practices are on the rise worldwide. Furthermore, these practices are spreading in a largely unaccountable and nontransparent fashion.

## Increasing Scope

At the start of the ONI project in 2002, only a handful of countries were known to actively engage in Internet content filtering practices, including China, Iran, and Saudi Arabia. Over the past four years, however, that number has grown rapidly. In response, the ONI has expanded its global testing regime from eleven to seventy-one countries worldwide based on reports of Internet filtering. Its 2006 reports found evidence of filtering in twenty-six of forty-four countries tested. Tests conducted in early 2009 show the numbers rising to more than thirty. The types of countries engaged in filtering range from advanced industrialized democracies such as Norway, the United Kingdom, Germany, France, Australia, the United States, and Canada, to nondemocratic or authoritarian regimes such as Tunisia, Iran, China, and Uzbekistan. There are many reasons for this increasing scope: growing securitization of information and communication policies since the terrorist attacks of September 11, 2001; the spread of "best practices" and imitation among states that censor; the increased sophistication of commercially available filtering technologies marketed to countries as "solutions" to economic, social, political, and security problems; and concerns over access to material involving the sexual exploitation of children or "extremist" websites.[22] Whatever the specific reasons in each case, Internet content filtering is on the rise worldwide.

## Increasing Scale

The actual content and services that authorities are targeting for filtering are increasing as well, suggesting that states are reaching further down into the information and communications matrix to which their citizens have access. Typically, most states justify their content filtering practices in terms of blocking "culturally offensive" information, such as pornography. Pornography remains the single most common category of content that is blocked on the Internet, compared with the full spectrum of categories tested by the ONI. Once content filtering mechanisms are put in, however, authorities are tempted to further encroach upon access to information by blocking other types of content. In Pakistan, for example, the government started by filtering access to websites containing imagery offensive to Islam, but it now targets content relating to the Baluchistan independence movement and a variety of extremist sites. In Thailand, what started out as the filtering of pornography has now expanded to include political opposition websites and streaming media services, like YouTube.[23] Among the countries that the ONI examined, at least nine states were found to be pervasive filterers of news, human rights information, opposition movements, and local dissident groups; websites providing access to translation; and anonymizer, privacy, and security-enhancing tools, such as encryption systems and circumvention tools. Many other states block access to selective content categories, such as regional security issues (South Korea, India) or religious conversion websites (Saudi Arabia, United Arab Emirates) or blogging services (Ethiopia).

## Increasing Sophistication

Not surprisingly, the methods used to filter Internet content have become more sophisticated, as states and the firms that sell censorship technologies continually refine them. There are several examples of increasing sophistication. First, authorities are becoming increasingly adept at targeting newly developed modes of communication, such as blogs, text messaging or SMS (short message service), Internet relay chat (IRC), instant messaging protocols, and voice over IP (VOIP) services. In the past, such newly devised methods of information sharing could be used as a means to circumvent Internet censorship, to mobilize political opposition, or both. Today, authorities are becoming more skilled at targeting new media and developing filtering methods particular to such services.

Second, although content filtering is prone to overblocking and error, there are examples where authorities have been able to use such technologies with precision—such as China's targeting of the specific string of codes embedded in the URL of the Google cache function. This is a service provided by Google whereby users can connect to archived information from websites stored on Google's servers, rather than on the servers of the original websites.

The service was designed to provide a way for users to access information through redundancy, but it is also a very effective way to get around content filtering. Since users connect to Google servers, rather than to the blacklisted servers, they bypass the content filters. Upon learning of this technique, China implemented a blocked string on its backbone/gateway routers that prevented any use of the Google cache function from within China.[24]

Although there is no prima facie reason why states should withhold information about content filtering, the area is shrouded in secrecy and unaccountability. In some states, the methods and targets of content filtering are not disclosed because of the connections to intelligence gathering, both domestic and international. Filtering technologies can and often are placed "beneath the surface" of a country's national information infrastructure, for all intents and purposes "hidden" from public scrutiny and not acknowledged even to exist. Second, many, though not all, of the states that engage in Internet content filtering are not democratic states and so base decisions about what information to release to citizens on regime power and national security interests, imposing uneven and largely arbitrarily defined levels of oversight and feedback. The result is a mixed range of openness and transparency among states that filter. Saudi Arabia, on one hand, is relatively open about the fact that it engages in Internet filtering, going so far as to provide extensive documentation for public consumption about its Internet content filtering regime. It even makes some gestures toward public accountability by offering an online avenue for public complaints and feedback. When users try to visit a banned site in Saudi Arabia, a standard blockpage message is returned to their browser with an option to register complaints or suggest further sites for filtering.[25]

China, on the other hand, has at least once officially admitted to its Internet filtering practices, while at other times denying that it does so. Moreover, its filtering practices are deliberately deceptive. When users try to visit a site that triggers the filtering mechanisms at China's backbone, the connection times out and the user's machine is effectively penalized from making further requests to the same server for a variable period of time. Likewise, although Tunisia employs a commercial filtering product called SmartFilter, which includes a standard transparent blockpage function, Tunisian ISPs have replaced the blockpage message with a page that delivers to the user an "error message," to give the impression of connectivity problems rather than of deliberate filtering.[26] One might hypothesize that the more filtering practices are withheld from public scrutiny and accountability, the more tempting it is for state authorities to employ these tools for illegitimate reasons, such as to secretly stifle opposition and civil society networks.

The proprietary nature of commercial filtering technologies, used by many regimes that filter access to information, also contributes to secrecy and a lack of accountability. For example, ONI research has documented the use of SmartFilter, made by the U.S. company Secure Computing Corporation (purchased by McAfee in 2008), in the filtering systems of Kuwait, Oman, Saudi Arabia, Tunisia, and the United Arab Emirates, and in the past, of some in Iran. The company does not advertise its sales of filtering technologies to regimes that restrict access to information. ONI research was able to ascertain the use of SmartFilter in these cases by a series of "forensic fingerprints": categorization errors unique to the SmartFilter program, and a detailed analysis of http header information. In addition to the use of SmartFilter, ONI research documented the use of several other U.S.-made commercial products for information suppression: NetCache, often used in conjunction with filtering products like SmartFilter, is employed in Iran;[27] Websense was used in Iran and is now used by Yemen;[28] Fortinet is used in Burma;[29] specially configured Cisco routers filter at the backbone level in China;[30] and Singapore uses a product called SurfControl.[31]

The ONI's research indicates that state filtering is evolving toward a next generation of more refined filtering practices. First-generation filtering relied on passive means, in which lists of banned websites were loaded into routers so that requests to the servers hosting those websites were denied. These methods, used by countries such as China, Iran, and Saudi Arabia, are relatively unsophisticated and easy to defeat. Moreover, they are difficult to hide. As ONI testing revealed, it is not too difficult to determine what content is being filtered, and by whom. As a result, countries engaging in first-generation–type filtering have been quickly targeted by advocacy groups and labeled as "pariahs." It is therefore hardly surprising that first-generation methods are being supplanted by *next-generation* strategies designed to be more stealthy, dynamic, and sophisticated.

Evidence gathered by ONI points to several emerging trends that characterize next-generation filtering strategies. First, the value of information is fixed in time, and therefore filtering does not have to be permanent, but present only when a particular kind of information has greatest value (or potential for disruption). This is particularly true during elections, when interest in media reporting and political communications is heightened, and where the consequences of an electoral loss may have major repercussions. In two cases, the February 2005 election in Kyrgyzstan (which led to the toppling of President Askar Akayev in the "Tulip Revolution") and the 2006 presidential elections in Belarus, ONI documented "just in time" filtering against key opposition media and political sites. This filtering differed from first-generation strategies in two ways: first, its temporary application, in these cases during the election period; and second, in the method used to apply it. In the Kyrgyzstan and Belarus cases, access to sites was prevented through offensive means, by attacks on those Web servers hosting information services using denial-of-service attacks, which flooded the servers with requests and rendered them unable to respond. In the Kyrgyzstan case, these attacks were accompanied by an ultimatum to the ISP hosting the websites demanding that the sites be removed.[32] In the case of Belarus, denial-of-service attacks were accompanied by other tactics, such as introducing deliberate errors in domain name servers (which are necessary for finding servers on the Internet), and once temporarily shutting down all Internet access in the capital city of Minsk.[33] There are indications that these second-generation techniques are not restricted to technologically sophisticated states. During 2007, Ethiopia, Uganda, and Cambodia shut down access to SMS services during politically sensitive times, presumably in recognition that these technologies offer a means for opposition movements to mobilize.[34] Following the June 2009 Iranian elections, authorities slowed connections to the Internet, blocked social networking platforms such as Twitter and Facebook, and tampered with SMS services.

Another trend of next-generation filtering emerging from ONI research is the specific targeting of critical resources, rather than broad-brush censorship of whole categories of content. This form of filtering is also closely linked to surveillance. In several countries, notably Egypt, a combination of surveillance and selective prosecution effectively curtails bloggers and specific minority groups (especially the gay and lesbian community). The message being sent by the state is that you cannot hide in cyberspace. It is a clear warning to anyone seeking the anonymity of cyberspace to voice political criticism or express alternative lifestyles: you can be found, and you can be prosecuted.

A third emerging, but yet unverified, means of information suppression is for countries to buy "prefiltered" Internet access from countries that apply these practices on their national segments. In 2004, ONI research revealed that an ISP in Uzbekistan demonstrated the same patterns of filtered content as that used by China Telecom. Further investigation revealed that the ISP purchased its connectivity from China Telecom. Similar patterns, albeit on a lesser scale, were highlighted by the 2007 ONI survey, which found that several Commonwealth of Independent States members that buy their access through a Russian-based ISP shared similar filtering patterns.[35] Evidence is preliminary, but the idea of outsourcing national filtering to a third country has appeal in that it provides the purchaser with a plausible pretext for denying culpability in censorship, or at least the ability to deflect criticism by blaming a third party. It is also perhaps indicative of a broader trend in the Internet as regional powers such as Russia, China, and potentially India increasingly control larger parts of the "core" global Internet infrastructure.

While national governments are the primary drivers of filtering practices, corporate actors—in particular ISPs—are becoming the main implementers of filtering and packet shaping practices, either as a consequence of the legal requirements of the states in which they are based or of their own accord and reflecting monetary or proprietary concerns. ISPs in a number of countries either have been mandated by their governments or have entered into voluntary arrangements to implement filtering, typically to prevent accidental access to child sexual abuse material on the Internet.[36] In other cases, ISPs are being asked to retain data for law enforcement purposes or to filter traffic for copyright violations. In one notable instance, a major ISP in the United States, Comcast, was found to be inspecting and shaping traffic to limit and contain the use of BitTorrent traffic—a protocol associated with the illegal sharing of copyrighted material. The case drew notoriety for the way in which it potentially violates an important legal and normative principle of Internet governance called "network neutrality," defined by Tim Wu as a network design principle whereby "a maximally useful public information network aspires to treat all content, sites, and platforms equally."[37] It is a sign of the times, and a powerful illustration of the argument of this chapter, that many perceive the network neutrality principle to be under threat, not only in the United States, but around the world. Whereas once ISPs were mere technical-functional nodes in a seamless global network, today they are increasingly taking on governance responsibilities at the behest of states or of their own accord.[38]

In authoritarian and democratically challenged countries, corporations find themselves facing difficult choices in order to do business, as authorities seek to control their services to make sure they are consistent with government filtering policy or even seek to enlist their help to maintain and extend such policy. Compliance with local government policies can generate intense public criticism at home, shareholder activism, lawsuits, and fines. Choosing not to comply can mean the withholding of market opportunities, contracts, and licenses; frivolous lawsuits and harassment; filtering and network tampering; and even public safety concerns for employees. These choices have been most apparent in the Chinese Internet market, where Internet service companies such as Microsoft, Google, and Yahoo! have all tailored their services and cooperated with authorities while facing intense public scrutiny in the United States.[39] For both commercial and political reasons, then, corporate actors are becoming more involved as active "shapers" of the Internet's constitutive architecture.

## Implications

The main thesis of this chapter is that the structures and opportunities of global Internet communications are the product of often hidden and under-recognized mechanisms of governance.[40] Some of this governance has been with the Internet since its inception and is the product of the epistemic/technical communities that keep it functioning through peering and transit arrangements. These practices have been largely obscured as a result of specialization. Others forms of Internet governance, however, have been obscured deliberately as a function of national security. Moreover, these latter practices are growing in scope, scale, and sophistication and have important policy, normative, and theoretical implications.

Among those who study Internet governance, this discussion should strongly suggest that more concerted attention be given to the mechanisms of governance that exist "beneath the surface" of the Internet. As J. P. Singh notes in Chapter 12, at two recent policy forums concerning Internet governance, the World Summit of the Information Society and its follow-on, the Internet Governance Forum, the vast majority of policy debate has focused on those elements of Internet governance that do engender public discussion, such as addressing and top-level domain name allocation.[41] However, very little corresponding attention—in part, no doubt, because of secrecy—has been given to the issues of surveillance and filtering outlined here, which may arguably have a much greater effect on the overall constitution and character of the Internet.[42]

The preceding discussion frames in a new light the importance of debates concerning network neutrality, ISP data retention, lawful access, digital rights management, and others in a variety of disparate arenas, by embedding them in a deeper theoretical framework concerning the material constitution of the Internet as a whole. It also highlights the importance of the grassroots projects among civil society networks to build software tools that support censorship circumvention, privacy, and anonymity online. To date, these engineering projects have been dispersed among limited networks of groups and individuals and supported by small grants from a few concerned foundations. They are nevertheless critical insofar as they aim directly at the code itself, so to speak: the material infrastructure of the Internet.[43]

Lastly, this discussion underscores the importance of probing and understanding the material elements of power, particularly the technological environment that surrounds us all. Contemporary studies of global governance by international relations theorists tend to be dominated by social constructivist approaches that treat material factors as malleable and largely ineffectual apart from the ideas that give them shape. Although it is true that social forces and ideas construct technological systems, these in turn can shape and constrain social forces and ideas, often in unintended ways. The analysis above suggests that a new geopolitics of the Internet's deep material infrastructure is under way. Theorists of global governance would do well to excavate the dynamics of this largely hidden realm.

## Notes

1. Manuel Castells, *The Rise of the Network Society*, 2nd ed., vol. 1. (Malden, MA: Blackwell, 2000).

2. Katie Hafner and Matthew Lyon, *Where Wizards Stay Up Late: The Origins of the Internet* (New York: Simon & Schuster, 1996); Paul Baran, *On Distributed Communications* (Santa Monica, CA: Rand Corporation, 1964).

3. Quoted in Philip Elmer-Dewitt, "First Nation in Cyberspace," *Time* (6 December 1993), http://www.time.com/time/magazine/article/0,9171,979768-3,00.html.

4. Timothy L. Thomas, "Cyber Mobilization: A Growing Counterinsurgency Campaign," Foreign Military Studies Office (2006): 7, http://www.dtic.mil/cgi-bin/Get TRDoc?AD=ADA465348&Location=U2&doc=GetTRDoc.pdf; Michael Y. Dartnell, *Insurgency Online: Web Activism and Global Conflict* (Toronto: University of Toronto Press, 2006); Gary Wolf, "Weapons of Mass Mobilization," *Wired* 12:9 (September 2004), http://www.wired.com/wired/archive/12.09/moveon.html.

5. Paul C. Adams, "Cyberspace and Virtual Places," *Geographical Review* 87 (1997): 155–71; William Gibson, *Neuromancer* (New York: Ace Books, 1984); Michael Heim, *The Metaphysics of Virtual Reality* (New York: Oxford University Press, 1993).

6. Jack M. Balkin, "Virtual Liberty: Freedom to Design and Freedom to Play in

Virtual Worlds," *Virginia Law Review* 90:8 (2004): 2043–98; Sherry Turkle, *Life on the Screen: Identity in the Age of the Internet* (Toronto: Simon & Schuster, 1995).

7.  See Ronald J. Deibert, "Black Code: Censorship, Surveillance and Militarization of Cyberspace," *Millennium: Journal of International Studies* 32:3 (2003): 501–30. In this chapter, we focus on governance by states and corporations, while setting aside the activities of civil society networks, which are covered extensively in the previous article as well as in Ronald J. Deibert, "Hacking Back: Civic Networks and the Fight to Protect the Net," in *Access Controlled*, ed. Ronald Deibert, John Palfrey, Rafal Rohozinski, and Jonathan Zittrain (forthcoming).

8.  Ernest J. Wilson, "What Is Internet Governance and Where Does It Come From?" *Journal of Public Policy* 25:1 (2005): 29–50.

9.  Ronald J. Deibert and Janice Gross Stein, "Social and Electronic Networks in the War on Terror," in *Bombs and Bandwidth: The Emerging Relationship between Information Technology and Security*, ed. Robert Latham (New York: Free Press, 2004).

10.  "Peering" is the voluntary and free exchange of information among separately administered networks. A "transit arrangement" is where a network pays money to another network for Internet access.

11.  John Borland, "Analyzing the Internet Collapse," *Technology Review* (5 February 2008), http://www.technologyreview.com/Infotech/20152/?nlid=854.

12.  "An Overview of American Intelligence until World War II," Central Intelligence Agency (6 December 2007), https://www.cia.gov/news-information/featured -story-archive/2007-featured-story-archive/overview-of-american-intelligence.html.

13.  James Bamford, *Body of Secrets: Anatomy of the Ultra-Secret National Security Agency* (New York: Anchor Books, 2002).

14.  Jeffrey Richelson and Desmond Ball, *The Ties that Bind: Intelligence Cooperation between the UKUSA Countries, the United Kingdom, the United States of America, Canada, Australia, and New Zealand* (Boston: Allen & Unwin, 1985).

15.  Jeffrey Richelson, *The U.S. Intelligence Community* (Cambridge, MA: Ballinger, 1985).

16.  Elizabeth B. Bazan and Jennifer K. Elsea, "Presidential Authority to Conduct Warrantless Electronic Surveillance to Gather Foreign Intelligence Information," Congressional Research Service Memorandum (5 January 2006), http://epic.org/privacy /terrorism/fisa/crs_analysis.pdf.

17.  Mark Klein, "Wiretap Whistle-Blower's Account," *Wired* (7 April 2006), http://www.wired.com/science/discoveries/news/2006/04/70621.

18.  Though challenging, it is not impossible. See Neil Jr., "Spy Agency Taps into Undersea Cable," ZDNet Technology News (23 May 2001), http://news.zdnet.com /2100-9595_22-529826.html.

19.  Matt Bedan, "Echelon's Effect: The Obsolescence of the U.S. Foreign Intelligence Legal Regime," *Federal Communications Law Journal* 59:2 (2007): 425–44.

20.  Nart Villeneuve, "The Filtering Matrix: Integrated Mechanisms of Information Control and the Demarcation of Borders in Cyberspace," *First Monday* 11:1 (2006), http://www.uic.edu/htbin/cgiwrap/bin/ojs/index.php/fm/article/view/1307/1227.

21. For more information on ONI, see its website at http://opennet.net/.

22. Ronald Deibert, John Palfrey, Rafal Rohozinski, and Jonathan Zittrain, eds., *Access Denied: The Practice and Policy of Global Internet Filtering* (Cambridge, MA: MIT Press, 2008).

23. Ronald J. Deibert, "The Geopolitics of Asian Cyberspace," *Far Eastern Economic Review* 169:10 (2006): 22–25.

24. ONI, *Internet Filtering in China in 2004–2005, A Country Study* (April 2005), http://opennet.net/studies/china.

25. ONI, *Internet Filtering in Saudi Arabia in 2004* (2005), http://opennet.net/studies/saudi.

26. ONI, *Internet Filtering in Tunisia in 2005: A Country Study* (November 2005), http://opennet.net/studies/tunisia.

27. ONI, *Internet Filtering in Iran in 2004–2005: A Country Study* (2005), http://opennet.net/studies/iran.

28. ONI, *Internet Filtering in Yemen in 2004–2005: A Country Study* (2005), http://opennet.net/studies/yemen.

29. ONI, *Internet Filtering in Burma in 2005: A Country Study* (October 2005), http://opennet.net/studies/burma.

30. ONI, *Internet Filtering in China in 2004–2005*.

31. ONI, *Internet Filtering in Singapore in 2004–2005: A Country Study* (2005), http://opennet.net/studies/singapore.

32. See Deibert et al., *Access Denied;* ONI, "Commonwealth of Independent States," http://opennet.net/research/regions/cis; and ONI, "Special Report: Kyrgyzstan," http://opennet.net/special/kg/.

33. ONI, *The Internet and Elections: The 2006 Presidential Election in Belarus (and Its Implications)*, Internet Watch (April 2006), http://opennet.net/sites/opennet.net/files/ONI_Belarus_Country_Study.pdf.

34. Ethan Zuckerman, "Mobile Phones and Social Activism," Mobileactive.org (9 May 2007), available at http://mobileactive.org/mobile-phones-and-social-activism-ethan-zuckerman-white-paper.

35. See ONI, "Commonwealth of Independent States."

36. "ISP 'Voluntary'/Mandatory Filtering" (updated 28 February 2008), Libertus.net, http://libertus.net/censor/ispfiltering-gl.html.

37. Tim Wu, "Network Neutrality FAQ," http://timwu.org/network_neutrality.html on 20 October 2008.

38. Paul Ganley and Ben Allgrove, "Net Neutrality: A User's Guide," *Computer Law and Security Report* 22:6 (2006): 454–63; Milton L. Mueller, "IP Addressing: The Next Frontier of Internet Governance Debate," *Info* 8:5 (2006): 3–12.

39. Jonathan Zittrain and John Palfrey, "Reluctant Gatekeepers: Corporate Ethics on a Filtered Internet," in Deibert et al., *Access Denied,* 103–22. Recently, these companies have entered into an self-governance arrangement, called the "Global Network Initiative," that outlines principles according to which their services would be offered in jurisdictions where filtering occurs.

40. Rafal Rohozinski, "Bullets to Bytes: Reflections on ICTs and 'Local' Conflict," in Latham, *Bombs and Bandwidth*.

41. Kenneth Neil Cukier, "Who Will Control the Internet?" *Foreign Affairs* 84:6 (2005): 7–12.

42. Lisa McLaughlin and Victor Pickard, "What Is Bottom-Up about Global Internet Governance?" *Global Media and Communication* 1:3 (2005): 357–73; Wilson, "What Is Internet Governance?"; Zoe Baird, "Governing the Internet," *Foreign Affairs* 81:6 (2002): 15–20.

43. Deibert, "Black Code."

# CONCLUSIONS:
## UNGOVERNED SPACES
## AND SECURITY

# 14 Alternative Governance and Security

Anne L. Clunan and Harold A. Trinkunas

If one thing should be clear at the end of this volume, it is that ungoverned spaces are both more widespread than is popularly imagined, and at the same time less ungoverned than some might expect. Ungoverned spaces are not merely areas lacking in governance; rather, they are spaces where territorial state control has been voluntarily or involuntarily ceded to or shared with actors other than legally recognized sovereign authorities. Almost all spaces inhabited by human beings exhibit governance, in some sense, even though the dominance of the Westphalian state in governance provision has steadily eroded since the end of the Cold War. The emergence of new ungoverned spaces and the increased attention we now pay to more traditional alternative authority structures in places such as Waziristan are testaments to both the theoretical challenge these phenomena present and the ongoing concern of policymakers as to precisely what kind of threat these spaces pose. This concluding chapter takes stock of the human, national, and global security implications of such alternative forms of governance and what is new about the global and local conditions that generate them.

The increasing salience of ungoverned spaces among policymakers' security concerns is well documented in this volume. As we find in multiple instances, this attention is often not well focused, driven more by fear of the unknown and the "other" than by hard facts on the ground. It may actually be quite difficult for armed non-state actors to operate in putatively ungoverned areas, as Chapter 4 documents in the case of Somalia. In other instances, emergent local alternatives are the only governance structure that is feasible, as Chapter 7 shows in the highly fragmented West Bank.

What is required of policymakers and analysts is a nuanced understanding of the conditions under which ungoverned spaces become threats and what sorts of security they threaten. Alternative forms of authoritative governance may promote some types of security, such as human security, while having a neutral or negative effect on national or global security, or vice versa. Therefore, policymakers need to expand their understanding of security beyond the state-centric conception of national security to the security of people in order to fully grasp the impact of ungoverned spaces. We also argue that the limits of the standard interventionist templates used by the international community for remedying ungoverned spaces should be acknowledged. Instead, creative and tailored approaches that may not put the "state" at the center of response should be devised.

From a theoretical perspective, this volume establishes that in the current historical epoch, the state is increasingly competing in a significant way for authority, legitimacy, and sovereignty with traditional and emergent alternative modes of governance. In contrast to the literature on "new" modes of governance, this volume emphasizes that these alternative forms of governance are not necessarily new.[1] What is new is their linkages with other authoritative governance structures under conditions of softened sovereignty. These alternative modes of governance are sometimes more effective at providing for human security and development than the nominal territorial sovereign, but they are also frequently better positioned to compete for the loyalty of populations they serve or control. Since state sovereignty can be expected to soften further in the face of globalization, technological innovation, and transnational and subnational challengers, state-centric theories in the social sciences may be hard pressed to explain such emergent phenomena. Discussions since the terrorist attacks of September 11, 2001, over the possibility of deterring terrorists are only one example of how nonstate actors operating from ungoverned spaces pose challenges to the conventional paradigm of state-centric responses. Other theories that focus on state-building, state legitimacy, and state capacity will also need to take these emergent alternative forms of governance, and the global and local conditions that generate them, into account.

## New Constants and Variables in the Production of Alternative Governance

While geography, demography, and remoteness may be relatively constant sources of "ungovernability," this volume suggests that the uneven effect of globalization on societies and states is by far the biggest driver of new ungoverned spaces. Globalization accentuates asymmetries in wealth and rates of development, accelerates demographic shifts and urbanization, empowers individuals and non-state actors through access to emerging technologies and the dissemination of norms and ideas, and shrinks time and distance. When traditional structural variables, such as geography and demographic density, and new variables, such as relative exposure to globalization, coincide, the likelihood of ungoverned spaces increases. However, it is also the response or non-response of state bureaucracies, political and economic elites, non-state actors, and populations that shapes the opportunity structure available for the emergence of alternative governance structures. It is both the exceedingly complex challenges to governance posed by coincident factors and the withdrawal of the state (or its historical absence) from addressing that challenge that leads human beings to develop or support governance alternatives to the state.

What produces new ungoverned spaces in the contemporary era? At the root, this volume suggests, are the global spread and institutionalization of Western ideas regarding the locus and organization of political and economic authority and Western ideas in their technological form. The evolution of globalization has yielded changing expectations of whether and how states should govern, while providing opportunities and incentives for creating governance with, without, alongside, and beyond the state.[2] These forces combine with geography, demography, population flows, local cultural institutions, and rates of development to produce alternatives to state governance not just in the territorial reaches of space, but also in the virtual realms of cyberspace and international finance.

Ungoverned spaces could not exist without a conception of governance rooted in both territoriality and a normative preference for rule by sovereign states. As noted in Chapter 1, this conception of governance arises out of several waves of globalization emanating in the West over three centuries that created the current state-centric paradigm. The dominance of this paradigm of sovereign statehood can be explained by an extraordinarily successful diffusion of a liberal ideology enshrining the notion of popular sovereignty. In the twentieth century, this included the freedom of colonies and territories to choose their own forms of government and protect themselves from harm through the legal norm of sovereign equality. In the wake of decolonization, it was expected that newly sovereign territories would follow in the paths of the West to develop "effective sovereignty," meaning the ability to control the use of force and enforce political decisions within sovereign territory and repel attacks on it. Yet as Robert Jackson and, more recently, Thomas Risse have emphasized, this paradigm has never accurately described two-thirds of the planet, which includes only "quasi-states" or "areas of limited sovereignty."[3] The disconnect between legal and effective sovereignty over great expanses of the globe is fertile ground for the emergence of alternative governance structures.

Economically, the global extension of market capitalism led colonial areas—places that today are often included in the list of "fragile states"—to be incorporated into the world trading system, creating economic interdependencies between these regions and their markets. Colonial powers and transnational corporations entrenched a system of governance that relied on patrimonial and neopatrimonial forms of rule within often arbitrarily drawn territorial borders that did not provide governance goods to all groups equally. These patterns of rule did not necessarily disappear after decolonization.[4] Inclusion in the global economy has complicated the ability of developing countries to organize political authority and effectively exercise control within their own borders to achieve what Stephen Krasner terms "domestic sovereignty."[5] The authority structures that were empowered by global market capitalism frequently do not coincide with those that hold legal sovereignty in given territories, again creating a space for and providing resources conducive to the emergence of alternative governance structures.

The next global diffusion of liberalism—neoclassical economic liberalism—began in the 1960s in the West, and in Thomas Biersteker's words, wrought the "sudden and dramatic transformation of economic policy throughout the developing world between the 1970s and 1980s."[6] It also led to demands from Western and international donors that economic aid and development assistance be conditioned on increasing private control of the market and decreasing state regulation. This wave of neoliberal globalization led to the deregulation of trade and financial markets, the increased porousness of national borders to economic actors, and changes in national-level institutions throughout the world. This in turn significantly compromised the ability of all states to regulate cross-border flows of goods, services, information, technology, people, and environmental harm, or what Krasner calls "interdependence sovereignty."[7] Indeed, the rise of global financial markets led to calls that the state was in retreat and that the ability to set the rules of the game lay in the hands of powerful international economic actors.[8] Neoliberal economics frequently achieved its greatest purchase in those "quasi-states" most vulnerable to exogenous economic shocks, and the consequent shrinking of the legally sovereign state opened new spaces for alternative modes of governance to emerge and gain legitimacy.

The global financial crisis of 2007–2009 that originated in the ungoverned space of the unregulated markets for complex financial derivatives and other financial instruments dramatically illustrates the relationship among globalization, softened sovereignty, and the production of alternative authority. The diffusion of neoliberalism globally has severely compromised the ability and legitimacy of state efforts to exert government control over financial markets and ultimately to provide the governance goods that create favorable conditions for domestic and global economic prosperity. Efforts by governments to control the crisis led to massive expenditures exceeding 50 percent of the advanced economies' combined 2008 gross domestic product and much criticism of "socialist" measures, with little certainty on anyone's part that such actions would be effective.[9] Such lack of what Krasner terms "interdependence sovereignty" in such cases has direct consequences for the ability of states to exercise effective control within their borders, as state coffers are spent and credit and tax bases dry up.[10] The ideological dominance of neoliberalism has made efforts to exert such control through state intervention illegitimate and slowed the response of many governments to the crisis. This recent example suggests that even the most powerful states in the international system face significant barriers to remedying ungoverned spaces in their midst, especially ones where transnational economic actors, such as the international financial markets, wield significant power.

The global diffusion of neoliberal economic ideology met up with the spread of liberal ideas about democracy and human rights to generate new standards of statehood and governance, ones equating governance with the rule of law, government accountability to its citizens and Western donors, and humane treatment of and provision for the population. States failing to provide these goods were subject to outside intervention, whether in the form of humanitarian nongovernmental organizations providing emergency service delivery or international financial institutions and Western governments conditioning assistance on improvements in transparency, human rights, and environmental protection. These most recent waves of ideological liberalism decrease the normative relevance of international legal sovereignty—based on formal recognition—and Westphalian sovereignty—based on the notion that external actors should not exert political authority within a state's borders. The decreased legitimacy of formal sovereignty in instances where internal state actions violate international norms, such as in Darfur, provides an opportunity for non-state actors to limit the effective sovereignty of states and empower alternative governance structures.

The globalization of technology, particularly in the areas of transportation and information and communication, has accelerated and deepened the effect of the global spread of liberal ideas. The liberal conception of statehood has defined sovereign legal jurisdictions, and in doing so, it has also created their negatives in the form of illicit and sovereign-free spaces. The asymmetry in governance among these spaces opens opportunities for economic or other kinds of gain, as Chapters 9 and 11 highlight. They show how the existence and the profitability of illicit economies (ranging from small arms to drugs to sex slavery) and unregulated financial markets depend on the establishment of legal jurisdictions. The incentives for flows between these spaces is created with the establishment of sovereign jurisdiction; as discussed below, these incentives grow when other factors, such as economic development, infrastructure, and demography, make exchange across them more profitable, economically and politically.

The spread of a global communication and transportation infrastructure premised on high-speed exchange has radically improved connections between historically distant spaces and reduced the costs associated with exchange for regulated, unregulated, and illicit markets. James Russell has shown how lightly regulated free trade zones and export processing platforms made the United Arab Emirates a convenient hub for traffickers of weapons of mass destruction.[11] The globalization of the Internet and real-time movement of capital globally has massively complicated the efforts of states to control markets, but it has also enabled the spread of anti-statist ideas that threaten the entire notion of a state-centric system, whether those ideas are supportive of an Islamic caliphate or human rights. Technological globalization has undoubtedly challenged the ability of states to control the flow of information within their borders.[12]

Information technology, however, is not in and of itself preventing state control and regulation, but it has created political and economic bases of opposition to the state-centric system of Westphalian sovereignty. Chapter 13 demonstrates that technology does not necessarily always cut against state control, though it does require additional expenditure of state resources to retain it. The authors argue that, contrary to the big myth of a decentralized Internet, the physical architecture of the Internet gives states the upper hand with respect to the cross-border flow of information, an important facet of interdependence sovereignty.[13] Powerful states such as the United States, and the powerful companies whose interests they protect, continue to set the rules for governance of the Internet in ways that favor themselves rather than other actors (Chapter 12). The creation of these technologies and the spaces of flows they enable also create conflicts between states and non-state actors and give rise to political demands, not just economic incentives, for these spaces to not be controlled by states (Chapters 11, 12, and 13).

In addition to significantly burdening the state with new concerns regarding financial stability, cybersecurity, and controlling the "information battlespace," these virtual spaces complicate states' ability to exercise interdependence sovereignty—control over cross-border flows.[14] These flows challenge the ability of states to raise tax revenues necessary to provide governance goods and to exercise sovereignty independent of wealthy individuals and corporations (Chapter 11). They also threaten the normative status of state sovereignty itself by facilitating the mobilization of anti-statist forces. Globalization of a particular set of liberal ideas has thus created the possibility for a normative benchmark for statehood, one that defines some jurisdictions as well-governed, low-risk, and stable and one that marks others as ungoverned spaces. It has also ideologically and technologically enabled non-state actors to acquire more power and authority, leading to today's world of softened sovereignty.

This is not to suggest that the traditional structural factors that favor "ungovernability"—remoteness, geographically difficult terrain, demography, linguistic differences, etc.—no longer matter. After all, Afghanistan, Waziristan, and Somalia are all examples in this volume of how these factors remain relevant to any discussion of alternative governance structures. However, this volume makes it clear that globalization is driving the linkages between traditional and new alternative governance structures and national, international, and human security. After all, the reason that outsiders care about remote ungoverned spaces such as Waziristan and Somalia is that globalization has connected these spaces to the governed parts of the world ever more intimately.

## The Security Implications of Ungoverned Spaces

When do alternatively governed spaces threaten security? The answer largely hangs on whether one is interested in human, national, or international security, as threats to one may not entail threats to the others. To understand when ungoverned spaces are dangerous, we first must define whom they threaten. The discipline of security studies traditionally has concerned itself with the paradigm of a state-centric system. National security in this sense is the effort state officials take to protect their national interests, usually understood to be physical survival, territorial integrity, and continuation of the political regime and economic system. It also includes actions taken to ensure that the state retains the means to secure the national interest, through what Kenneth Waltz terms "internal and external balancing."[15] Such balancing is said to require in particular the human, economic, and natural resources necessary to raise and fund armed forces capable of defense, or to attract the allegiance of other states capable of doing so. National security, particularly in developing countries, also entails not only such efforts to defend against foreign attackers, but also internal forces seeking to change the domestic regime violently or even peacefully.[16]

Since the establishment of the United Nations system after the Second World War, international security is traditionally viewed through the state-centric paradigm and is based on the premise that states are the legitimate actors in the system whose sovereignty is a system-wide good to be upheld. In this view, states are the best means of ensuring that internal disturbances do not harm other states and that one state cannot conquer others and establish a hierarchically, rather than horizontally, organized system of world politics. Traditional threats to international security are therefore the outbreak of interstate and intrastate wars that might spread geographically or involve additional states, and the harboring of non-state actors—ranging from pirates to terrorists—who attack states.

In contrast, human security is people-oriented. Although there is no consensus on what the term "human security" encompasses, it takes the individual human being as the core interest. Beyond this, debate rages over whether human security incorporates some or all of the following: freedom from physical violence, disease, drug use, starvation, poverty, and environmental degradation; freedom from political, sectarian, cultural, and ethnic oppression; and freedom to enact civil, political, and cultural rights.[17] On the broader side, Gary King and Christopher Murray's definition concentrates on "only *those domains of well-being that have been important enough for human beings to fight over or to put their lives or property at great risk*," which include "income, health, education, political freedom, and democracy" (emphasis in original).[18] The Human Security Report Project focuses somewhat more narrowly on "violent threats to individuals, while recognizing that these threats are strongly associated with poverty, lack of state capacity and various forms of socio-economic and political inequity."[19]

These conceptions focus on the link between social, political, and economic development and violence to individuals. We take that link as the crucial factor distinguishing human security from the traditional development, state-building, and human rights agendas. We also highlight that, as with traditional notions of security, there is an inherent bias in the concept toward Western standards of political, economic, and social development and governance and the paradigm of the Western Westphalian state.[20] The deaths resulting from interstate wars and from the actions of governments against their own populations have far outstripped those due to non-state actors, according to the *Human Security Report*, so whether state or non-state governance is a greater threat to humans is not an easy question.[21] Whether alternative governance structures are seen as a threat depends on the reader's core values. Humanitarians will applaud governance structures that provide human security and well-being; neoconservatives will applaud only democratic government and reject other modes of governance; and neoliberals will favor private over state governance in many areas. Those viewing the state as the best actor capable of protecting against arbitrary violence and widespread conflict will support a state-building agenda focused on strengthening state military and policing capacity.

## Security Threats from Alternative Forms of Control over Violence, Resources, and Rulemaking

In light of these conceptions of security, when are alternatively governed spaces threats? The answer depends on the consequences, whether direct or indirect, of non-state control over violence, resources, and rulemaking for security at the human, national, and global levels, and on the reader's values.

While all of the causal linkages between control of violence, resources, rule-making, and security apply in principle to both states and non-state actors, we focus here only on the implications of alternative governance involving non-state actors. In doing so, we again note the unfortunate irony that despite the growing concern since the end of the Cold War with ungoverned spaces and efforts at state building, much of the harm done to humans in the course of the rise of modern states has occurred at the hands of state actors and their proxies, as the genocides in Darfur and Cambodia and the world wars of the twentieth century all too tragically illustrate.[22]

*Control of Violence*    Control of violence is clearly the variable most directly linked to security. When non-state actors control violence and are predatory, physically harming humans and their livelihoods and preventing the exercise of their rights, alternative governance directly threatens human security. Control of violence by non-state actors also can harm the environment, affect human health and economic development, and in turn threaten human and national security. The Human Security Report Project estimates that combat deaths account for only 3 to 30 percent of deaths related to war; the rest stem from war-related famine, disease, and economic dislocation.[23]

When non-state actors control violence in ways that are popularly legitimate, a shift in the loci of political authority away from governments can also be produced. As Chapter 9 notes with respect to the Peruvian terrorist organization Sendero Luminoso, Chapter 7 with regard to Hizbullah and militias in the Middle East, and Chapter 5 with respect to the Pashtun tribes and Al-Qa'ida, such a shift produces potential internal threats to national and international security. Non-state control of violence has the potential to threaten human, national, and international security when it generates cross-border skirmishes, flows of refugees, and constraints on economic exchange and provides sanctuary for foreign or domestic violent actors with transnational agendas, as in the case of the Pashtun tribal regions and Al-Qa'ida.

*Control of Resources*    Control over the production of wealth also has an important effect on security, and it has increasingly passed beyond the ability of states to effectively regulate. Neoliberals assume that when the control of financial resources and means of wealth production are in the hands of individuals, human, national, and global well-being are improved. However, mercantilists and economic nationalists have long viewed control over resources and the private entities that own them as a necessary component of national security and a source of interstate conflict. When non-state actors decrease a state's ability to raise revenues and control the nation's money supply, currency value, and trade balance, as noted in Chapter 11, the state's ability to provide domestic order and welfare, as well as to fund national defense, is constrained. As the current global financial crisis highlights, this can lead to shifts in the global balance of power, which realists associate with war and others with a changing role for the United States and all states in world politics.[24] At the level of human security, non-state control of resources is a threat when it reduces human welfare and human rights. Chapter 3 shows how warlords' control over natural resources in Africa can lead to both predation on and protection of communities. The key variable determining whether control over resources produces predation or protection of human security is not economic incentive or opportunity, but the nature of the warlords' social networks. Licit non-state economic actors can also threaten human security through control of local wealth when they ally with armed state actors to prevent its local investment, as in the cases of Royal Dutch Shell in the Niger Delta region and Union Oil Company of California (UNOCAL) and Total in Myanmar.[25] As Chapters 2, 6, 9, and 10 suggest, control over the production of wealth affects all three types of security when wealth creation involves the proliferation of drugs, weapons of mass destruction, and small arms.

*Control over Rulemaking*    Those who control the making of rules, whether they are state or non-state actors, get to determine to whom the rules apply. State actors who create rules that exclude populations or spaces open them up for non-state rulemaking, as the chapters in Parts III and IV emphasize. Those excluded from the rules are likely to face arbitrary violence and discrimination (Chapter 8). When non-state actors create rules that exclude the majority of people living in the area where the rules are applied, to the benefit of the few, human security is threatened (Chapter 3). Human security is also threatened when the rules created by non-state actors violate contemporary conceptions of human rights, such as the Taliban and the treatment of women, or the treatment of migrants in South Africa (Chapter 8).

In today's globalized financial markets, when illicit non-state actors are in charge of rules governing economic activity, capital flight can be stimulated, as investors seek more predictable environments. Access to foreign capital, particularly foreign direct investment, is critical to economic development and state revenue collection; lack of access to it negatively affects national and human security. Conversely, when licit non-state actors, as illustrated in

Chapter 11 on tax havens, set the rules of the economic game, they can punish governments for actions they do not like through rapid divestment, particularly in cases in which states are highly dependent on foreign capital for development. It was the equity market that punished the Russian government in 2008 with a 40 percent drop in its stock market, both for Russia's moves toward nationalization of private assets and for the invasion of Georgia.

Non-state actors who reject existing international laws regarding state sovereignty and seek the creation of new political entities are a familiar threat to national and international security, whether they take the form of traditional secessionist movements or what is now sometimes referred to as the global jihadist insurgency.[26] Finally, efforts by non-state actors to set the international rules that govern how governments treat human beings may increase human security by improving human rights and welfare, but they may also threaten international and national security by undermining the norm of sovereignty and establishing rationales for intervention.

## Differentiating between Threatening and Nonthreatening Ungoverned Spaces

Not all ungoverned spaces are dangerous, at least not simultaneously threatening to human, national, and global security. Lack of state governance is not in and of itself necessarily threatening at these levels of security.[27] When control in geographic or virtual spaces over violence, resources, and rulemaking produces negative consequences for human welfare and state capacity and continuity, then these spaces are dangerous for human or national security. When such control yields cross-border effects either regional or global in nature, then we can speak of ungoverned spaces that threaten international security. What matters from the perspective of security is whether alternative modes of governance interact with their environment, the human population, states, and the international community in such a way as to produce negative outcomes. The outline of dangerous spaces in Chapter 2 gives us a first cut at pinpointing potential problems, but the determination of threat must be premised first on the analyst's normative concern (human welfare, national security, or international security) and second on a detailed analysis of how the existing modes of governance in such areas do and do not produce harm. As demonstrated in Chapter 4, Al-Qa'ida's efforts to create a new normative basis for governance based on a variant of Wahabbi Islamism failed to supplant local norms; as a result, this ungoverned space was not as threatening to national and international security as is commonly expected. The opposite held in Waziristan where, Chapter 5 suggests, Al-Qa'ida's ability to work within the tribal customs of Pashtunwali has threatened both the national security of the Afghan government and international security.

In attempting to predict where such threats will emerge, we might expect that the most threatening ungoverned spaces will be those where multiple dangerous spaces overlap. As documented in Chapter 10, from a national and international security perspective, the dark networks that support the proliferation of weapons of mass destruction in the former Soviet republics are so worrisome because of the combination of weak states with capacity gaps and spaces that facilitate illicit flows, and strong states with governance gaps and plentiful nuclear and radiological material. On the other hand, some dangerous spaces primarily reduce the human security of their inhabitants, as was the case in Somalia during the 1990s; yet the same spaces may be actually quite resistant to attempts by terrorists to weld them into a broader network that threatens national or global security.

Finally, we need to keep the temporal dimension in mind as we examine the emergence of ungoverned spaces. Even as these spaces emerge in particular configurations that initially pose little or no threat, they may evolve and become more dangerous over time as new actors begin to wield economic and technological power once reserved to states. As noted in Chapter 11, during times of crisis, such as the 2008 global collapse of credit and liquidity, states may find that they are unable to control and limit damage to national economies, to international financial stability, and ultimately to human security in the form of higher food prices and lost income. Non-state control of resources and rulemaking in global financial markets has much longer term consequences for security, when such control limits the ability of states to afford the measures that are required to provide for their populations' welfare, and the state's own security.

## Policy Responses to Emerging Ungoverned Spaces

This volume is not conceived as an effort to develop policy responses to ungoverned spaces, but rather as an effort to understand the phenomenon of alternative modes of governance. Based on the findings in these chapters, however, we can suggest a few alternatives to existing policy responses that are grounded in a more nuanced understanding of ungoverned spaces and of the world of softened sovereignty in which states operate.

Fundamentally, alternatively governed spaces, dangerous or otherwise, are characterized by blended spheres of authority. Juridical sovereignty resides with only one of many actors within a space: the state. But as this volume demonstrates, the state is at best one of many competitors for authority in ungoverned spaces, and in the most extreme cases, it is the weakest and least effective of the contenders. This presents a challenge for policymakers and scholars on two levels. First, the blending of spheres of authority suggests that traditional ways of thinking about policy responses that used to fall into separate disciplines such as international relations (deterrence, foreign intervention, and war) and comparative government (development assistance, democracy assistance, and civil society building) need rethinking and merging to produce new ways of managing ungoverned spaces. The threats posed by non-state actors in ungoverned spaces and the remedies that might counter them cross disciplinary boundaries. Second, many of the tools that policymakers reach for today tend to focus on state-to-state, top-down mechanisms and models because the international system and legal framework privilege the status of states, even in cases where they are weak and ineffective actors. To highlight this dilemma, consider that in any other type of contest, backing the weakest player would generally not be the surest path to success (although it might be the moral or ethical one).

Traditional responses to ungoverned spaces generally center on some sort of intervention, usually conducted by states or a group of states, aimed at restoring the effective sovereignty and capacity of a weakened or failing state. Since 1991, external interventions, including those in Cambodia, Somalia, Liberia, and Sierra Leone (to name but a few), have all followed such a model. Across such cases, we can discern a continuum of interventionist practices that have come to have an almost template-like quality. Frequently, the remedies begin with development and foreign assistance programs and diplomatic protests, followed by economic sanctions and nonmilitary coercion, and when these do not work, multilateral or unilateral military coercion and occupation.

Undoubtedly, some traditional interventions have worked, in the best of cases, to end wholesale slaughter, starvation, and human rights abuses. However, the trend since the end of the Cold War shows that the enthusiasm for solving difficult ungoverned or dangerous spaces wanes relatively quickly, and "donor fatigue," characterized by declining economic assistance to troubled states or reluctance to provide troop contingents for peacekeeping or coalition operations, has become the norm. This has led to a growing preference for "quick" humanitarian assistance operations rather than state-building and development projects.

In the worst of cases, such as Somalia in 1990, failure of state-led intervention may justify years of nonintervention in other very difficult but important cases, such as the 1994 Rwandan genocide. In more recent cases, such as the genocide in the Darfur region of Sudan, the threat to the human security of populations and the national security of neighbors is as great as any we have seen since 1991, yet the appetite for effective intervention is almost nil. This, of course, showcases the limits of state-led, top-down interventionist models for cases in which the interests of great powers are not at stake. On one hand, the state-led model for remediating dangerous spaces justifies an interventionist approach to foreign policy, sometimes with significant negative consequences on all sides of an intervention. On the other hand, it falls short when addressing the cases in which the very high levels of threat to human security are not perceived as immediate or dire by important external actors.

Alternative approaches to addressing the threats identified in this volume begin with greater knowledge of the characteristics of existing spaces and improved detection mechanisms for identifying emerging or potential ungoverned spaces. States are either not very good at or have become less capable of "seeing" inside ungoverned spaces. In part, this is a side effect of a state-centric mentality among the main diplomatic and international security actors. As documented in Chapters 3 and 4, ungoverned spaces can also be quite dangerous, particularly to outsiders, which has led to a focus on force protection among interventionist powers. However, the primacy of force protection increases the potential for blindness (or blinders) among the very agents who are trying to determine the level of threat posed by a given space. Without knowledge of what is happening in ungoverned spaces, all appear threatening. This blindness can lead to unwarranted paranoia and a misallocation of state resources by policymakers, or at worst, a proliferation of poorly targeted interventions that precipitate blowback by the actors and inhabitants of ungoverned spaces that might have never been a threat in the first place. Contemporary policymakers might consider what Frederick the Great once observed: He who defends everything, defends nothing.

What alternatives exist to traditional interventionist templates? First, we would argue that states should consider accommodating alternatives to governance that pose no threat to their security. In essence, this means adopting a neomedieval approach to international (or interspatial) politics in which juridical state sovereignty is acknowledged (even if only de facto) as not the only approach to structuring authority in a space. Policymakers would have to acknowledge that there are numerous spaces in which authority is best shared. Even in such cases where that is not a state's preferred outcome, the costs of turning juridical sovereignty into effective state governance may simply be too high.

Policymakers would also find it easier to address truly dangerous spaces if they were to recognize that they are part of a network that includes actors in the very spaces they fear. A wide range of non-state actors operates in the international system to address threats to human and global security, and many of these share networks with both state and non-state actors in ungoverned spaces. These networks may provide an avenue for developing consensual international understandings of what the actual level of threat is in various ungoverned spaces. They may also provide an arena or a space to foster bottom-up approaches for remediating threats or containing bad actors within ungoverned spaces. Such an approach would juxtapose the top-down responses that are available on a state-to-state level (both intervention and international development assistance) with bottom-up or midrange responses that focus on interconnections among multiple spheres of authority and the creation of networks to influence the situation on the ground and leverage scarce resources. This is not a rejection of a state role in achieving positive outcomes, but a suggestion for a new and different pathway for state and non-state actors to achieve shared goals of lessening threats to human, national, and global security.

In those cases in which there is either a security concern or a potential for one to emerge, drawing alternative governance structures into a broader network that includes nongovernmental organizations, international agencies, and states may provide a mechanism for establishing norms that contribute to security. The networks can also serve as conduits for diffusing norms that are particularly important to states, such as "avoid providing refuge to terrorists" or "do not facilitate the proliferation of weapons of mass destruction." This does not mean that force should be eliminated as an instrument for deterring, containing, or eliminating bad actors. What it does mean is that more knowledgeable state actors, armed with more accurate assessments of what constitutes a dangerous space or actor and new tools for threat reduction, will be less likely to use force, less likely to resort to overt and costly direct intervention, and less likely to generate blowback when they do intervene.

Our recommendation is for policymakers to rely on tailored approaches to ungoverned spaces that recognize the fact of softened sovereignty. These responses should not ignore the nominal sovereign state, but should be developed with a more nuanced understanding of de facto governance structures already in place. State policymakers need to establish means to work with the multiple networks of non-state actors that share overlapping concerns about security and also to interact (maybe at a distance or through other channels) with the threatening non-state actors about which they are most concerned. Through such a networked approach, it may be possible to focus attention on violent non-state actors so as to change their incentive structures and develop new norms of acceptable behavior compatible with security in a broad sense. In addition, we may be able to strengthen existing local and international structures that are hostile to violent non-state actors, such as the clan social norms in Somalia that led to a rejection of Al-Qa'ida. Such networks can strengthen international norms against targeting civilians and establish a broad consensus against the use of weapons of mass destruction. This does not mean that all violent non-state actors will suddenly abandon their traditional tactics or foreswear threats to human, national, and global security. It does mean that policymakers will have a more accurate view of what kind of threat they pose under what circumstances. They will also find themselves integrated into a broader web of like-minded state and non-state actors that are supportive of their shared security objectives.

## Notes

1. James Rosenau and Ernst-Otto Czempiel, eds., *Governance without Government: Order and Change in World Politics* (Cambridge: Cambridge University Press, 1992), 95–109; Wolfgang Reinecke, *Global Public Policy: Governing without Governance?* (Washington, DC: Brookings Institution, 1998); Anne-Marie Slaughter, "The Real New World Order," *Foreign Affairs* 67, no. 5 (1997): 183–97; Martha Finnemore and Kathryn Sikkink, "International Norm Dynamics and Political Change," *International Organization* 52, no. 4 (1998): 887–917; A. Claire Cutler, *Private Power and Global Authority: Transnational Merchant Law in the Global Political Economy*, Cambridge Studies in International Relations, no. 90 (Cambridge: Cambridge University Press, 2003); Pauline Vaillancourt Rosenau, ed., *Public-Private Policy Partnerships* (Cambridge, MA: MIT Press, 2000); Thomas Risse, "Governance in Areas of Limited Statehood: How Far Do Concepts Travel?" paper presented at the International Studies Association Annual Convention, San Francisco, 26–30 March 2008.

2. Philipp Genschel and Bernhard Zangl, "Transformations of the State—From Monopolist to Manager of Political Authority," paper presented at the International Studies Association Annual Convention, San Francisco, 26–30 March 2008; Rosenau

and Czempiel, *Governance without Government;* Andrew Hurrell, *On Global Order: Power, Values, and the Constitution of International Society* (Oxford: Oxford University Press, 2007), 95–109; Reinecke, *Global Public Policy;* Slaughter, "Real New World Order"; Finnemore and Sikkink, "International Norm Dynamics"; Cutler, *Private Power and Global Authority;* Michael Zürn and Stephan Leibfried, "Reconfiguring the National Constellation," in *Transformations of the State?* ed. Stephan Leibfried and Michal Zürn (Cambridge: Cambridge University Press, 2005); Anne-Marie Slaughter, *A New World Order* (Princeton, NJ: Princeton University Press, 2004).

3. Robert H. Jackson, "Quasi-States, Dual Regimes, and Neoclassical Theory: International Jurisprudence and the Third World," *International Organization* 41, no. 4 (1987): 519–49; Risse, "Governance," 3.

4. Jana Hönke, "Governing Security in Enclaves of Extraction: Private Self-Help, Partnership Policing or Shadow Networks of Public-Private Rule," paper presented at the American Political Science Association Annual Meeting, Boston, 28–31 August 2008; Thomas Risse and Ursula Lehmkuhl, *Governance in Areas of Limited Statehood—New Modes of Governance?* Sfb-Governance Working Paper Series (Berlin: Freie Universität SFB 700, 2006).

5. Stephen D. Krasner, *Sovereignty: Organized Hypocrisy* (Princeton, NJ: Princeton University Press, 1999), 4.

6. John Gerard Ruggie, "International Regimes, Transactions, and Change: Embedded Liberalism in the Postwar Economic Order," *International Organization* 36, no. 2 (1982): 413; Thomas Biersteker, "The Triumph of Neoclassical Economics in the Developing World: Policy Convergence and Bases of Governance in the International Economic Order," in *Governance without Government: Order and Change in World Politics,* ed. James Rosenau and Ernst-Otto Czempiel (Cambridge: Cambridge University Press, 1992), 105.

7. Krasner, *Sovereignty,* 4.

8. Susan Strange, *Retreat of the State: The Diffusion of Power in the World Economy* (Cambridge: Cambridge University Press, 1996).

9. International Monetary Fund, "Fiscal Implications of the Global Economic and Financial Crisis," *IMF Staff Position Note* SPN/09/13, 9 June 2009, accessed 20 August 2009 at http://www.imf.org/external/pubs/ft/spn/2009/spn0913.pdf.

10. Krasner, *Sovereignty,* 4.

11. James A. Russell, "Non-State Actors on the 'Ungoverned Frontier' of Proliferation," paper presented at the Naval Postgraduate School Conference on Ungoverned Spaces, 2–3 August 2007; see also James A. Russell, "Non-State Actors and the 2016 Proliferation Environment: Peering into the Abyss," *Nonproliferation Review* 13, no. 3 (November 2006): 645–57.

12. Jeff Gerth, "Military's Information War Is Vast and Often Secretive," *New York Times,* 11 December 2005; and Eric Schmitt and David McCloud, "Senate Summons Pentagon to Explain Effort to Plant News Stories in Iraqi Media," *New York Times,* 2 December 2005.

13. Krasner, *Sovereignty,* 4.

14. Ibid.

15. Kenneth Waltz, *Theory of International Politics* (Reading, MA: Addison-Wesley, 1979).

16. Steven David, *Choosing Sides: Alignment and Realignment in the Third World* (Baltimore, MD: Johns Hopkins University Press, 1991).

17. See United Nations Development Programme, *Human Development Report, 1994* (New York: Oxford University Press, 1994); Roland Paris, "Human Security: Paradigm Shift or Hot Air?" *International Security* 26, no. 2 (2001): 87–102; Gary King and Christopher J. L. Murray, "Rethinking Human Security," *Political Science Quarterly* 116, no. 4 (2001–2002): 585–610; Sabina Alkire, "A Conceptual Framework for Human Security," Centre for Research on Inequality, Human Security, and Ethnicity (CRISE), University of Oxford (UK), 2003, http://www.crise.ox.ac.uk/pubs/working paper2.pdf; Sharbanou Tadjbakhsh and Anuradha Chenoy, *Human Security, Concepts and Implications* (London: Routledge, 2006).

18. King and Murray, "Rethinking Human Security," 593.

19. Human Security Centre, "What Is Human Security?" *Human Security Report 2005*, http://www.humansecurityreport.org/index.php?option=content&task=view &id=24&Itemid=59.

20. UNESCO, "Human Security: Approaches and Challenges," 2008, http:/unesdoc .unesco.org/images/0015/001593/159307e.pdf.

21. Human Security Centre, *Human Security Report 2005*, http://www.human securityreport.info/.

22. For just one of many studies documenting this, see Heather Rae, *State Identities and the Homogenisation of Peoples* (Cambridge: Cambridge University Press, 2002).

23. Human Security Centre, *Human Security Report 2005*.

24. Robert Gilpin, *War and Change in World Politics* (Cambridge: Cambridge University Press, 1981); Robert Gilpin, *Global Political Economy* (Princeton, NJ: Princeton University Press, 2001); and Joseph Nye, "American Power after the Financial Crisis," *Foresight*, accessed 11 August 2009 at http://www.foresightproject.net/publications /articles/article.asp?p=3533.

25. Deborah D. Avant, "Ungoverned Spaces and Private Responses to Security," paper presented at the Ungoverned Spaces Conference, Naval Postgraduate School, Monterey, CA, 2–3 August 2007; Anthony J. Sebok, "Unocal Announces It Will Settle a Human Rights Suit: What Is the Real Story behind Its Decision?" *FindLaw*, 10 January 2005, accessed 11 August 2009 at http://writ.lp.findlaw.com/sebok/20050110.html.

26. Andrew Phillips, *War, Empire, and the Transformation of International Orders* (Cambridge: Cambridge University Press, forthcoming), chapter 9.

27. Here we disagree somewhat with Risse when he suggests that some element of normality must be included in the concept of governance. Instead, we suggest that the *reality* of various modes of governance should be measured against normative criteria, such as human, national, and international security, and then responses should be tailored taking reality into account. Risse, "Governance," 12.

# Contributors

ENRIQUE DESMOND ARIAS is Associate Professor of Government at John Jay College and a member of the Doctoral Faculty in Criminal Justice at the CUNY Graduate Center. His research focuses on security and politics in developing societies. In 2006, the University of North Carolina Press published his book *Drugs and Democracy in Rio de Janeiro: Trafficking, Social Networks, and Public Security*. He is the coeditor of *Violent Democracies in Latin America*, to be published by Duke University Press in 2010. He has published articles on the politics of crime, NGOs, social mobilization, and human rights in *Latin American Politics and Society*, *Qualitative Sociology*, *Comparative Politics*, and *The Journal of Latin American Studies*. He received his Ph.D. from the University of Wisconsin at Madison.

ANNE MARIE BAYLOUNY is Assistant Professor of National Security Affairs at the Naval Postgraduate School, specializing in Middle East politics, social organizing, and Islamism. She received her Ph.D. in Political Science from the University of California, Berkeley. Her book *Privatizing Welfare in the Middle East: Kin Mutual Aid Associations in Jordan and Lebanon* (Indiana University Press, 2010) analyzes social and political organizing resulting from new economic policies. She has traveled extensively in the Arab East, living in Syria, Lebanon, and Jordan for long periods. Baylouny's current research focuses on Hizbullah, particularly its use of the media and the influence of constituencies on the organization.

ANNE L. CLUNAN is Associate Professor of National Security Affairs at the Naval Postgraduate School in Monterey, California. Her research and teaching interests focus on how states define and respond to new security threats and on the implications of globalization for state sovereignty and governance. Her most recent book is *The Social Construction of Russia's Resurgence: Aspirations, Identity and Security Interests* (Johns Hopkins University Press, 2009). She is coeditor with Peter R. Lavoy and Susan B. Martin of *Terrorism, War or Disease? Unraveling the Use of Biological Weapons* (Stanford University Press, 2008). She earned her Ph.D. in political science at the University of California, Berkeley.

RONALD J. DEIBERT is Associate Professor of Political Science and Director of the Citizen Lab at the Munk Centre for International Studies, University of Toronto. He is a cofounder and principal investigator of the OpenNet Initiative, a research and advocacy project that examines Internet censorship and surveillance worldwide, and the InfoWar Monitor, which tracks the emergence of cyberspace as a domain of geopolitical contestation. He is Vice President of Psiphon Inc. and a principal of SecDev.Cyber. Deibert has been a consultant to numerous agencies and governments on issues relating to Internet censorship, surveillance and circumvention, space technology, and arms control.

VANDA FELBAB-BROWN is a Fellow in Foreign Policy Studies at the Brookings Institution. Her book *Shooting Up: Counterinsurgency and the War on Drugs* (Brookings Institution, 2009) analyzes the relationship between military conflict and illicit economies, such as the production and trafficking of narcotics. A frequent commentator in the media and consultant to the U.S. government, she has testified on these issues in the U.S. Congress. Felbab-Brown is the author of numerous publications, including "The Violent Drug Market in Mexico and Lessons from Colombia" (Foreign Policy at Brookings, Policy Paper No. 12, March 2009), "Peacekeepers among Poppy" (*International Peacekeeping* 16 [1], February 2009), and "From Sanctuaries to Protostates" (in *Denial of Sanctuary: Understanding Terrorist Safehavens*, ed. Michael Innes [Westport: Praeger, 2007]). She received her Ph.D. in political science from the Massachusetts Institute of Technology.

TY L. GROH is a Lieutenant Colonel in the U.S. Air Force studying international relations in the Ph.D. program at Georgetown University. His dissertation focuses on assessing the costs and benefits of using proxies in the pursuit of national interests. He received his commission from the U.S. Air

Force Academy in 1993. After completing a B.S. in aeronautical engineering, Groh trained in and flew the F-16C in a number of assignments before he attended the Naval Postgraduate School in Monterey, California, and earned an M.A. in security studies. He wrote an award-winning thesis on the Pashtun tribal regions of Afghanistan and Pakistan while at the Naval Postgraduate School and then attended the U.S. Air Force's School of Advanced Air and Space Power Studies and earned an M.A. in air and space power science, writing a thesis on the use of proxy armies to support U.S. airpower.

LOREN B. LANDAU is Director of the Forced Migration Studies Programme at the University of the Witwatersrand in Johannesburg, South Africa. His research explores human mobility, sovereignty, and citizenship in east and southern Africa. He is currently codirecting a four-country study on migration and urban transformation. Author of *The Humanitarian Hangover: Displacement, Aid, and Transformation in Western Tanzania*, he has published articles in *Millennium, African Affairs, Government and Opposition, The Journal of Ethnic and Migration Studies*, the *Journal of Refugee Studies*, and *Third World Quarterly*. He received his Ph.D. in political science from the University of California, Berkeley.

BILL MAURER is Professor and Chair of the Department of Anthropology at the University of California, Irvine. His research spans the anthropology of law, finance, and money, and he has published widely on offshore finance in the Caribbean, alternatives to financial globalization, and Islamic banking and mortgage financing. He is the author and editor of several books, including *Recharting the Caribbean: Land, Law and Citizenship in the British Virgin Islands, Pious Property: Islamic Mortgages in the United States*, and *Mutual Life, Limited: Islamic Banking, Alternative Currencies, Lateral Reason*. The latter received the Victor Turner Prize in 2005.

KEN MENKHAUS is Professor of Political Science at Davidson College, where he has taught since 1991. His research focuses on the Horn of Africa and development, conflict analysis, peace building, and political Islam. In 2002 he was recipient of a U.S. Institute of Peace grant to study protracted conflict in the Horn of Africa. Menkhaus is author of more than fifty articles, book chapters, and monographs, including *Somalia: State Collapse and the Threat of Terrorism* (2004) and "Governance without Government in Somalia," in *International Security* (Winter 2006/07). He received his Ph.D. in international studies in 1989 from the University of South Carolina.

TAMLYN MONSON is a researcher within the Migrant Rights Monitoring Project at the Forced Migration Studies Programme, University of the Witwatersrand, Johannesburg. She has an interdisciplinary background including contemporary literature and applied linguistics and is currently working on a research degree examining non-state authorities, subnational borders, and territorial control in areas of South Africa affected by xenophobic attacks.

WILLIAM RENO is Associate Professor and Director of Graduate Studies at Northwestern University. He is a specialist in African politics and the politics of "collapsing states." His current work examines violent commercial organizations in Africa, the former Soviet Union, and the Balkans and their relationships to state power and global economic actors. Reno's research takes him to places such as Sierra Leone, Congo, and Central Asia where he talks to insurgents (including so-called warlords), government officials, and foreigners involved in these conflicts. His books include *Corruption and State Politics in Sierra Leone* (Cambridge, 1995) and *Warlord Politics and African States* (Lynne Rienner, 1998). He is completing the forthcoming volume *The Evolution of Warfare in Independent Africa*. He received his Ph.D. from the University of Wisconsin at Madison.

RAFAL ROHOZINSKI a Principal with the SecDev Group and possesses more than seventeen years of field experience with the United Nations and other agencies in thirty-seven countries of the Commonwealth of Independent States (CIS), the Middle East, and Africa. He has worked in an operational, advisory, and "troubleshooting" capacity on issues of security, governance, development, negotiations, strategic national programs, and communications and information technology, with a specialization in cultural intelligence, deep field research, and the "telegeography" of ungoverned spaces. Between 2001 and 2007 Rohozinski was a Social Science Research Council (SSRC) Ford Foundation Fellow and the Director of the Advanced Network Research Group, Security Programme, Cambridge University. He is the founder and Principal Investigator of the OpenNet Initiative (ONI), where he directs the work of researchers in the CIS and Middle East, and is coeditor of the ONI's global comparative study of network surveillance and censorship in forty-five countries.

JACOB N. SHAPIRO is Assistant Professor of Politics and International Affairs at Princeton University. His primary research interests are the organizational aspects of terrorism, insurgency, and security policy. Shapiro's ongoing projects study the causes of support for militancy in Islamic countries and the relationship between aid and political violence. His research has been published in *International Security, International Studies Quarterly, Security Studies, Foreign Policy, Military Operations Research*, and a number of edited volumes. Shapiro codirects the Empirical Studies of Conflict Project. He is a member of the editorial board of *World Politics*, is a former Harmony Fellow at the Combating Terrorism Center at the United States Military Academy, and served in the U.S. Navy and Naval Reserve. He received a Ph.D. in Political Science and M.A. in Economics at Stanford University, and a B.A. in Political Science at the University of Michigan.

J. P. SINGH is Associate Professor at the graduate program in Communication, Culture, and Technology at Georgetown University. He is the author of *Negotiation and the Global Information Economy* (Cambridge 2008) and *Leapfrogging Development? The Political Economy of Telecommunications Restructuring* (1999), and coeditor (with James N. Rosenau) of *Information Technologies and Global Politics* (2002). His current book projects are *The Arts of Globalization* (Columbia, 2010), *United Nations Educational, Scientific and Cultural Organization: Creating Norms in a Complex World* (Routledge, 2010), and *International Cultural Policies and Power* (Palgrave Macmillan, 2010).

HAROLD A. TRINKUNAS is Associate Professor and Chair of the Department of National Security Affairs at the Naval Postgraduate School in Monterey, California. His recent publications include "Attention Deficits: Why Politicians Ignore Defense Policy in Latin America," with David Pion-Berlin, in *Latin American Research Review* 42:3 (2008), and *Crafting Civilian Control of the Military in Venezuela* (University of North Carolina Press, 2005). He is also coeditor with Jeanne Giraldo of *Terrorism Financing and State Responses: A Comparative Perspective* (Stanford University Press, 2007) and with Thomas Bruneau of *Global Politics and Defense Reform* (Palgrave MacMillan, 2008). Trinkunas earned a Ph.D. in political science from Stanford University in 1999.

PHIL WILLIAMS is Wesley W. Posvar Professor and Director of the Matthew B. Ridgway Center for International Security Studies at the University of Pittsburgh. He has published extensively in the field of international security. During the past sixteen years his research has focused primarily on transnational organized crime, and he has written articles on various aspects of this subject in *Survival; Washington Quarterly; Scientific American; Crime,*

*Law, and Social Change;* and *International Peacekeeping.* From 2007 to 2009 Williams was Visiting Professor at the Strategic Studies Institute, U.S. Army War College, where he published two monographs titled *From the New Middle Ages to a New Dark Age: The Decline of the State and U.S. Strategy* (2008) and *Criminals, Militias and Insurgents: Organized Crime in Iraq* (2009). In 2009 he also coauthored (with James Cockayne) a study for the International Peace Institute called *The Invisible Tide: Towards an International Strategy to Deal with Drug Trafficking through West Africa.*

LYUDMILA ZAITSEVA is an Affiliate Researcher at the Division of Physics and Biophysics, University of Salzburg (Austria), where she works on the issues of emergency response to catastrophic terrorism within the framework of an EU-funded security research project. She first engaged in the research of illicit trafficking in nuclear and other radioactive materials as Visiting Scholar at Stanford University's Institute for International Studies (1999–2003), where she developed the Database on Nuclear Smuggling, Theft, and Orphan Radiation Sources (DSTO). Zaitseva started her professional activities at the National Nuclear Center of Kazakhstan, where she participated in U.S.-Kazakh projects concerning the elimination of the remaining nuclear weapons infrastructure at the former Semipalatinsk nuclear test site (1996–1999). She is author of more than twenty publications.

# Index